Fundamentals of Healthcare Quality Management

5th Edition

Patrice L. Spath

Brown-Spath & Associates
Forest Grove, Oregon

2019

Fundamentals of Healthcare Quality Management, 5th Edition
Patrice L. Spath, MA, RHIT

© 2019 by Brown-Spath & Associates

ISBN-13: 978-1-929955-48-6
ISBN-10: 1-929955-48-0

Printed in the United States of America

Care has been taken to confirm the accuracy of the information presented and to describe generally accepted practices. However, the authors and the publisher cannot accept any responsibility for errors or omissions or for any consequences from application of the information in this book and make no warranty, express or implied, with respect to the contents of the book.

If you find an error or typo, please email the details to: sales@brownspath.com.

Brown-Spath & Associates
PO Box 721
Forest Grove, OR 97116
(503) 357-9185 Fax: (503) 357-9267
Internet site: http://www.brownspath.com

TABLE OF CONTENTS

About the Author

Patrice L. Spath, MA, RHIT, is a health information management professional with broad experience in healthcare quality and safety improvement. She is president of Brown-Spath & Associates (www.brownspath.com), a healthcare publishing and training company based in Forest Grove, Oregon. During the past 35 years, Patrice has presented more than 400 educational programs on healthcare quality management topics and has completed numerous quality and patient safety program consultations for healthcare organizations.

Patrice has authored and edited many books, book chapters, and peer-reviewed journal articles for Health Administration Press, Health Forum/AHA Press, Jossey-Bass, Brown-Spath & Associates, and other groups. Her recent books include *Fundamentals of Health Care Quality Management, 5th ed.* (Brown-Spath & Associates, 2019); *Introduction to Healthcare Quality Management, 3nd ed.* (Health Administration Press, 2018); *Applying Quality Management in Healthcare: A Systems Approach, 4th ed.* (Health Administration Press, 2017); *Strategic Management of Health Care Organizations* (Bridgepoint Education, 2014); and *Error Reduction in Health Care, 2nd ed.* (Jossey-Bass, 2011).

Since 2004 Patrice has taught undergraduate and graduate online courses on healthcare quality management and patient safety at several schools, including the University of Alabama in Birmingham, Oregon Health & Science University, Missouri Western State University in St. Joseph, Pacific University in Forest Grove, OR and Drexel University College of Medicine, Philadelphia, PA.

Patrice is currently consulting editor for *Hospital Peer Review,* on the advisory board for *Hospital Case Management,* and a past member of the advisory board for WebM&M (https://psnet.ahrq.gov/webmm), an online case-based journal and forum on patient safety and healthcare quality that is supported by the Agency for Healthcare Research and Quality. She is an active member of the American Health Information Management Association (AHIMA) and has been a member of the Council on Certification and Council on Accreditation and co-chair of the Data Governance & Analytics Practice Council.

INTRODUCTION TO HEALTHCARE QUALITY MANAGEMENT

Reader Objectives

After reading this chapter and reflecting on the contents, you will be able to:
1. Demonstrate an understanding of the varied dimensions of healthcare quality.
2. Identify major stakeholders in healthcare quality.
3. Describe the three primary quality management activities.
4. Identify groups influencing healthcare quality.
5. Describe common components of an organization's quality management system.

Key Terms

Accreditation standards: Statements of expectation set by a competent authority concerning a degree or level of requirement, excellence, or attainment in quality or performance.

Assessment: Use of performance information to determine the degree to which an acceptable level of quality has been achieved.

Continuous improvement: System in which individuals in an organization look for ways to do things better, usually based on understanding and control of performance variation.

Governing board: Individuals, group, or agency with ultimate legal authority and responsibility for overall operation of an organization; sometimes called the board of trustees.

Healthcare quality: Degree to which health services for individuals and populations increase the likelihood of desired health outcomes and are consistent with current professional knowledge.

Improvement: Planning and making changes to current practices so performance will be better in the future.

Measurement: Collection of information for the purpose of understanding current performance and seeing how performance changes over time.

Medical staff executive committee: Leadership group of a hospital's organized medical staff that exercises primary authority over activities of the medical staff and over performance of individuals with hospital clinical privileges.

Misuse: Health services misuse includes incorrect diagnoses as well as medical errors and other sources of avoidable complications.

Overuse: Overuse occurs when a health service is provided even though its risk of harm exceeds its likely benefit.

Patient safety: Actions taken to reduce the risk of patients being unintentionally harmed by effects of healthcare services.

Processes: Collections of actions following prescribed procedures for bringing about a result.

Quality management: Way of doing business which continuously improves products and services to achieve ever better levels of performance.

Quality management plan: Written description of the organizational structure, responsibilities, procedures, processes and resources supporting an organization's quality management system.

Quality management system: Organizational structure, responsibilities, procedures, processes and resources supporting the design, measurement, assessment, and improvement of key functions and key processes; sometimes referred to as the quality program or performance improvement program.

Stakeholder: Person, group, organization, or entity with a direct or indirect stake in an organization because it can affect or be affected by that organization's actions, objectives, and performance.

Triple Aim: Improving the individual experience of care; improving the health of populations; and reducing the per capita costs of care for populations.

Underuse: Underuse occurs when a health service is not provided though it would have been medically beneficial.

Healthcare Quality

Quality management is a system by which healthcare is measured, assessed and constantly improved. It is sometimes referred to as performance improvement, continuous quality improvement, total quality management, or performance management. Whatever the terminology, the goal is the same: to make sure patients receive high quality healthcare services. This goal is not new. In 1917, the American College of Surgeons developed the Hospital Standardization Program, a set of uniform, minimum standards for hospitals. By 1945 these standards included a requirement that physician practices be evaluated to make certain they complied with present day scientific medicine (Gorgas, 1948). The scope and activities of healthcare quality management have broadened considerably over the years, yet the goal – high quality patient care – remains the same.

Quality Defined

What is high quality patient care? The word quality means different things to different people. For example, a quality automobile may be one which has no defects and works exactly as the customer expects. Products or services that exceed customer expectations are likely to be judged as having high quality. Quality is an attribute that can be managed. However, first it must be defined

Describing healthcare quality is not easy because there are many customers and each has slightly expectations. Healthcare customers are individuals, groups, and organizations that have a stake in the quality of healthcare services. Customers fall into three stakeholder groups: providers, purchasers, and consumers. Described in Exhibit 1.1 are examples of customers in these groups. Customers have unique expectations that must be considered when defining healthcare quality.

Exhibit 1.1. Stakeholders in Healthcare Quality

Stakeholder Group	Customers
Providers	Any organization or individual that is licensed or trained to give healthcare. Examples: Physicians, nurses, technicians, hospitals, skilled nursing facilities, rehabilitation facilities, outpatient clinics, and home health agencies
Purchasers	Any organization or individual that pays for healthcare services either directly or indirectly. Examples: Government funded health insurance programs (e.g., Medicare, Medicaid), private health insurance companies, employers that purchase health insurance for their employees, and consumers that pay out-of-pocket
Consumers	Any recipient of healthcare services. Examples: patients, residents, clients

In 1990, the Institute of Medicine (now called the National Academy of Medicine) brought together representatives from the stakeholder groups to discuss how healthcare quality could be improved. This workgroup created a definition of healthcare quality that has stood the test of time (IOM, 1990):

> "Quality of care is the degree to which health services for individuals and populations increase the likelihood of desired health outcomes and are consistent with current professional knowledge."

Eleven years later the IOM Committee on Quality of Health Care in America, in its report *Crossing the Quality Chasm: A New Health System for the 21st Century* (IOM, 2001), identified six key dimensions of healthcare that need improving (see Exhibit 1.2). These dimensions represent the attributes of quality providers and purchasers now seek to achieve.

Exhibit 1.2. Key Dimensions of Healthcare Quality Identified by the Institute of Medicine in 2001

- ***Safe*** – unintended patient injuries should be avoided.
- ***Effective*** – based on scientific knowledge, service should be provided to all who could benefit; services should not be provided to people who are not likely to benefit.
- ***Patient-Centered*** – care provided is respectful of and responsive to individual patient preferences, needs, and values and ensures patient values guide clinical decisions.
- ***Timely*** – no unnecessary waits and sometimes harmful delays for those receiving care.
- ***Efficient*** – avoidance of waste, including waste of equipment, supplies, ideas, and energy.
- ***Equitable*** – quality does not vary because of a patient's personal characteristics such as gender, ethnicity, geographic location, and socioeconomic status.

In 2008 the Boston-based Institute for Healthcare Improvement (HI), under the direction of Dr. Donald Berwick, championed the concept of healthcare quality improvement as a "Triple Aim" (Berwick, Nolan & Whittington, 2008). Leaders in the IHI proposed that achieving high-value health care in the U.S. will require improvement initiatives focused on three linked goals:
1. Improve the patient experience of care, including quality and satisfaction;
2. Improve the health of populations; and
3. Reduce per-capita costs.

This "Triple-Aim" influenced the content of the National Quality Strategy. First published in 2011, this strategy is developed with input from more than 300 individuals, groups, organizations and other stakeholders representing all part of the public and private healthcare sector and the public. This document establishes national healthcare improvement goals that reflect the key quality dimensions. These goals influence activities at the local, state, and national levels. The 2017 National Quality Strategy focused on six priorities (AHRQ, 2017):
1. Make care safer by reducing harm caused in the delivery of care.
2. Ensure that each person and family is engaged as partners in their care.
3. Promote effective communication and coordination of care.
4. Promote the most effective prevention and treatment practices for the leading causes of mortality, starting with cardiovascular disease.
5. Work with communities to promote wide use of best practices to enable healthy living.
6. Make quality care more affordable for individuals, families, employers, and governments by developing and spreading new healthcare delivery models.

Quality Management Defined

Quality management is a broad term encompassing all activities in healthcare organizations used to direct, control, and improve quality. Quality management is the means by which high quality patient care is maintained and improved at all levels of the system – individual, departmental, and organizational. The three primary activities of quality management are: measurement, assessment, and improvement.

Exhibit 1.3. Primary Quality Management Activities

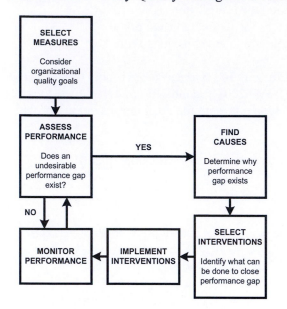

Measurement involves gathering information to determine current levels of performance. Assessment involves evaluating current levels of performance to determine if there are gaps between expected and actual quality. Improvement involves finding the cause of performance gaps and implementing interventions to correct causes of undesirable performance. The relationship between these three activities is illustrated in Exhibit 1.3.

When measurement results don't identify a performance gap, the organization continues to measure performance to make sure nothing changes. If results reveal a gap between expected and desired performance, the causes are investigated. Interventions are implemented and performance is again monitored. Quality management activities are detailed in the later chapters.

Impact of External Groups

Purchasers, regulatory agencies, and other groups have significant impact on the quality management activities of providers and health plans. Consumers and purchasers are demanding healthcare organizations be held responsible for providing high quality, safe patient care. State and federal regulations and standards of voluntary accreditation groups effecting healthcare organizations are constantly being updated and strengthened in response to accountability pressures from consumers and purchasers.

Prior to 1990 quality management activities were, for the most part, limited to hospitals. Today quality management activities are found in all healthcare delivery sites and in health insurance plans. Because federal and state regulations and accreditation standards impacting healthcare quality management are subject to change, only limited references to requirements are found in this book. Readers must contact relevant government agencies and accreditation groups to obtain current requirements.

Federal Agencies and Groups

Listed in Exhibit 1.4 are the principal federal agencies and groups influencing various aspects of quality healthcare. Some have regulations that effect quality management activities in healthcare organizations and health plans. Some are involved in performance measurement projects that furnish the public with data on the quality of patient care in various types of facilities. Some share research and best practice information with healthcare organizations for the purpose of improving quality.

Accreditation Organizations

Accreditation organizations also influence healthcare quality. These groups develop standards of acceptable quality management practices and a team of reviewers, generally called surveyors, verify compliance with the standards. Accreditation standards may be based in part on government regulations as well as input from providers and other healthcare stakeholders. There are several accrediting groups and all require some type of quality management activities. In Exhibit 1.5 is a list of common groups and the type of providers and programs they currently accredit.

Professional and Consumer Groups

There are many professional and consumer groups actively influencing healthcare quality management activities. Several high profile groups are described in Exhibit 1.6.

Exhibit 1.4. Federal Agencies and Groups Influencing Healthcare Quality

Name / Web Site	Description
Agency for Healthcare Research and Quality (www.ahrq.gov)	Lead federal agency for supporting, conducting, disseminating, and coordinating research that improves the quality and safety of healthcare services.
Baldrige National Quality Program (www.nist.gov/baldrige)	A set of performance excellence criteria and a voluntary award program designed to promote high quality in U.S. industries, including healthcare organizations.
Centers for Disease Control (www.cdc.gov)	Responsible for promoting healthy communities through health promotion, prevention of disease, injury and disability, and preparedness for new health threats.
Centers for Medicare and Medicaid Services (www.cms.gov)	Administers the Medicare program and the national portion of the Medicaid program. Providers and health insurance plans participating in these federally-funded insurance programs must comply with the CMS requirements that include several quality-related regulations.
End Stage Renal Disease Network Organizations (www.cms.gov/Medicare/End-Stage-Renal-Disease/ESRDNetworkOrganizations/)	Providers of hemodialysis and peritoneal dialysis are organized within a series of networks. Network programs include collection and analysis of quality measures to evaluate care provided to patients receiving hemodialysis and peritoneal dialysis.
Food and Drug Administration (www.fda.gov)	Regulates medical products including drugs, biologics, medical and radiation-emitting devices, and special nutritional products (e.g., infant formulas). Healthcare professionals are encouraged to report adverse events involving medical products to this agency and it disseminates product safety and recall information to the medical community and the public.
National Institutes of Health (www.nih.gov)	Seeks to improve the nation's health by conducting, supporting, and disseminating research into the causes, diagnosis, prevention, and cure of human diseases.
Quality Improvement Organizations (https://qioprogram.org)	These organizations contract with CMS to improve the effectiveness, efficiency, economy, and quality of services delivered to Medicare beneficiaries. These are private, mostly not-for-profit organizations, staffed by doctors and other healthcare professionals trained to review medical care and help beneficiaries with complaints about the quality of care

Exhibit 1.5. Accreditation Organizations Influencing Healthcare Quality

Organization / Web Site	Type of Providers Accredited
AABB (formerly named the American Association of Blood Banks) (www.aabb.org)	Blood transfusion services in any provider site
Accreditation Association for Ambulatory Healthcare, Inc. (www.aaahc.org)	Ambulatory healthcare organizations ranging from primary care clinics and medical homes to large, managed care organizations
Accreditation Commission for Healthcare (www.achc.org)	Home health agencies and specialized services such as women's post-breast surgery fitter services, sleep labs, and private duty nursing
American Association for Accreditation of Ambulatory Surgery Facilities, Inc. (www.aaaasf.org)	Free-standing ambulatory surgery facilities
Commission on Accreditation of Rehabilitation Facilities (www.carf.org)	Adult day services, assisted living centers, behavioral health, medical rehabilitation, employment and community services, vision rehabilitation and opioid treatment programs
Commission on Cancer of the American College of Surgeons (www.facs.org/cancer/)	Cancer programs in hospitals, treatment centers, and other facilities

Commission on Laboratory Accreditation of the College of American Pathologists (www.cap.org)	Free-standing and provider-based laboratories and surgical pathology labs
Community Health Accreditation Partner (www.chapinc.org)	home health agencies, hospice programs, and home medical equipment services
Diagnostic Modality Accreditation Program of the American College of Radiology (www.acr.org)	10 different imaging modalities. The ACR offers accreditation programs in CT, MRI, breast MRI, nuclear medicine and PET as mandated under the Medicare Improvements for Patients and Providers Act (MIPPA) as well as for modalities
DNV GL-Healthcare (www.dnvglhealthcare.com)	Hospitals
Healthcare Facilities Accreditation Program of the American Osteopathic Association (www.hfap.org)	Hospitals, hospital-based laboratories, ambulatory care/surgery, mental health, substance abuse, physical rehabilitation medicine facilities and stroke centers in accredited hospitals
Joint Commission (www.jointcommission.org)	General, psychiatric, children's, and rehabilitation hospital; critical access hospitals; medical equipment services, hospice services, and other home care organizations; nursing homes and other long-term care facilities; behavioral healthcare organizations and addiction services; rehabilitation centers, group practices, office-based surgeries, and other ambulatory care providers; independent or freestanding laboratories; and medical homes
National Commission on Correctional Healthcare (www.ncchc.org)	Healthcare services in jails, prisons and juvenile confinement facilities
National Committee for Quality Assurance (www.ncqa.org)	Health plans, managed behavioral healthcare facilities, disease management programs, case management services, wellness and health promotion programs and accountable care organizations
Public Health Accreditation Board (www.phaboard.org)	Tribal, state, local, and territorial public health departments

Exhibit 1.6. Professional and Consumer Groups Influencing Healthcare Quality

Name / Web Site	Description
American Society for Healthcare Risk Management (www.ashrm.org)	Professional society for healthcare risk management professionals and those responsible for the process of making and carrying out decisions that will promote quality care and a safe environment. The organization offers a certification exam for risk managers.
American Society for Quality (www.asq.org)	A leading world authority on quality. The healthcare division provides resources, training, certification and networking opportunities to healthcare quality professionals.
American Society of Health-System Pharmacists (www.ashp.org)	Publishes extensively on safe medication practices in its publications, in professional and scientific journals; offers educational programming and medication safety advocacy.
Anesthesia Patient Safety Foundation (www.apsf.org)	Sponsors several initiatives including research into the cause of anesthetic related adverse events and sharing of information and ideas about the causes and prevention of anesthetic morbidity and mortality.
Consumers Advancing Patient Safety (www.patientsafety.org)	A consumer-led organization that considers itself a collective voice for individuals, families and healers who wish to prevent harm in healthcare encounters through partnership and collaboration.
Institute for Healthcare Improvement (www.ihi.org)	A non-profit private sector institute and a recognized leader in healthcare quality improvement that hosts nationwide and regional improvement projects and provides free improvement tools and training on its website.
Institute for Safe Medication Practices (www.ismp.org)	An independent reviewer of medication errors that have been voluntarily submitted by hospitals, physicians, and other healthcare practitioners to the Medication Error Reporting and Prevention (MERP) Program of the United States Pharmacopeia. Information learned through this review is distributed by ISMP to healthcare providers and pharmaceutical companies.
Leapfrog Group (www.leapfroggroup.org)	This non-profit, private sector program focuses on making giant leaps forward in the safety, quality and affordability of healthcare.
National Academy of Medicine (formerly named the Institute of Medicine) (https://nam.edu)	An independent organization of eminent professionals from diverse fields including health and medicine. Its domestic and global initiatives strive to address critical issues in health, medicine, and related policy.

National Association for Healthcare Quality (www.nahq.org)	A professional association comprised of individual and institutional members involved in healthcare quality management. It sponsors a certification examination for healthcare quality managers.
National Patient Safety Foundation (www.npsf.org)	Since it was established in 1997, this organization has undertaken several initiatives aimed at patient safety improvement. It recently merged with the Institute for Healthcare Improvement.
National Quality Forum (www.qualityforum.org)	A not-for-profit membership organization created to develop and implement a national strategy for healthcare quality measurement and reporting.

Quality Management System

Quality is the responsibility of everyone working in healthcare. Supporting this responsibility is a quality management system that places a high priority on achieving safe, effective, patient-centered, timely, efficient, and equitable healthcare. The quality management system structure varies considerably depending on the size and complexity of an organization. In a small organization, such as a free-standing ambulatory surgery center or a home health agency, one person may be assigned all quality management duties and report directly to the governing board or a senior leader. In larger, more complex organizations the quality management system involves multiple people and departments. In a 2018 study of the costs associated with maintaining a quality and safety infrastructure in a teaching hospital, the authors found that nearly $30 million of direct costs—more than 1.1% of net patient service revenue—were incurred to maintain the quality infrastructure. Approximately 81.6% of the costs were associated with mandates by regulators, accreditors, and payers—49.8% of which supported required public reporting (Blanchfield et al., 2018). Although organizations have different structures, core elements are part of every quality management system.

- Leadership oversight and accountability
- Quality infrastructure, including routine meetings with cross-departmental representation
- Performance measurement of key clinical and service areas
- Activities aimed at improving performance in clinical and service areas
- Involvement of stakeholders and transparency of performance data

Joint Commission accreditation standards make it clear the governing board and senior leaders are responsible for ensuring quality performance in an organization, but a particular quality management structure is not required. The National Committee for Quality Assurance (NCQA) accreditation standards for managed care organizations indicate the governing board may form a subcommittee to oversee quality management activities, but such a subcommittee is not required.

Exhibit 1.7. Groups Involved in Quality Management System

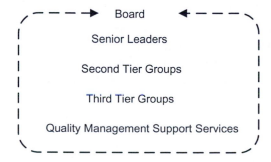

The range of groups involved in the quality management system of a healthcare organization is depicted in Exhibit 1.7. The number of people at each level varies according to the type of organization. The roles and responsibilities of groups that may be part of the quality management system in a healthcare organization are covered in the next section.

Governing Board

The governing board or board of trustees of a healthcare organization has ultimate responsibility for the quality of patient care and services provided. The board is responsible for ensuring quality of care in support of the organization's mission and strategic priorities. The board approves plans and allocates resources for quality management initiatives across the organization. For hospitals, the Medicare Conditions of Participation require the governing board make sure that quality management activities reflect the complexity of the hospital's organization and services, involve all departments and services, and include services provided under contract (Joint Commission, 2017).

In situations where a healthcare organization lacks a board of trustees (such as a limited partnership physician clinic or dental clinic), the legal business owners are ultimately responsible for quality and for supporting quality management activities. For example, the owner of a nursing home is responsible for the following (CMS, 2014):

- Ensuring that quality assurance and performance improvement (QAPI) is defined, implemented, and given high priority in the overall management of facility operations.
- Providing overall direction on QAPI goals for the organization.
- Ensuring that adequate resources are e allocated for training on QAPI and for the implementation and measurement of QAPI initiatives.

Senior Leaders

The senior leaders (president, chief operating officer, vice presidents, medical director) are responsible for ensuring continuous quality improvement and for establishing and cultivating a culture of safety. In a hospital with an organized medical staff, the senior medical staff leaders share these responsibilities. Senior leaders also provide suggestions for improving the quality management system. This includes setting performance expectations and assuring implementation of improvement actions. In small organizations, such as free-standing ambulatory clinics, the above responsibilities are often assumed by the most senior person in the facility (for example the medical director or clinic manager).

Second Tier Groups

Second tier groups are quality management oversight committees or councils. In a hospital, the medical staff executive committee is responsible for coordinating the quality management activities of the organized medical staff and for evaluating performance of physicians and licensed independent practitioners. These activities are detailed in chapter 9. To fulfill these responsibilities, the medical staff executive committee encourages physician participation in the organization's quality management initiatives, oversees credentialing and privileging actions, and maintains primary oversight of clinical activities and measures of medical staff performance.

Hospitals with a departmentalized medical staff often have a quality committee in each department. These committees are expected to assure compliance with all departmental quality management responsibilities and are accountable for the quality of patient care and services delivered in their service area. This includes involvement in credentialing, privileging, and professional practice evaluations (see chapter 9).

On the administrative side there is often a quality oversight committee comprised of senior leaders. This group is responsible for directing the quality management activities in all departments and supports development and implementation of quality management activities throughout the organization. To fulfill this responsibility, the committee meets periodically to review results of performance measurement and improvement activities occurring throughout the organization.

Third Tier Groups

Any number of third tier multi-disciplinary committees or groups may be formed to support various aspects of quality management. For example, if the facility has a cancer program approved by the American College of Surgeons' Commission on Cancer, then a cancer committee is required. Other committee requirements may be found in state and federal regulations affecting certain health service programs. For instance, institutions conducting patient research activities are required by federal regulations to have an Institutional Review Board (HHS, 2009).

Listed in Exhibit 1.8 are examples of medical staff and administrative committees with quality management duties that might be found in a hospital.

Exhibit 1.8. Common Hospital Medical staff and Administrative Committees

• Pharmacy and therapeutics committee	• Records/information management committee
• Utilization management committee	• Environmental services committee
• Infection control committee	• Radiation safety committee
• Transfusion committee	• Disaster preparedness committee
• Special care/critical care committee	• Risk management committee
• Emergency services committee	• Patient safety committee
• Surgery services committee	• Cancer committee

Most third tier groups are multi-disciplinary, interdepartmental committees charged with conducting quality management activities in a particular service or function. Periodically special project teams or task groups are created to investigate problem areas and conduct improvement projects (covered in chapter 5). These groups are disbanded upon completion of the project.

Quality Management Support Services

In years past quality management support services were done by one or just a few people in the quality department. As the scope and volume of regulatory and accreditation quality requirements increased, healthcare organizations added more staff devoted to performance measurement and improvement activities. These employees work in the quality department and in other areas.

Staff positions in quality management support services and position titles vary considerably among organizations. Positions often found in hospitals are listed in Exhibit 1.9. Similar positions are found in other types of facilities and in health plans. In small organizations responsibilities for these positions may be combined, with only one or two people supporting all organizational quality management activities. More details on some staff positions listed below are found throughout later chapters.

Exhibit 1.9. Staff Positions Supporting Quality Management Activities

Position	Common Quality Management Responsibilities
Case manager	This individual, often a nurse or social worker, helps coordinate patient services among and between caregivers and provider sites.
Compliance officer	This individual helps assure the organization adheres to external regulations and accreditation requirements related to quality management.
Health data analyst	This individual gathers, evaluates, and reports information in support of various quality management activities. Health data analysts may have clinical, health information management, or informatics expertise.
Infection control practitioner	This individual collects and analyzes health data related to patient infections and disseminates information on prevention of infections. This position is typically filled by a nurse, physician, epidemiologist, or medical technologist.
Patient representative	This individual serves as a liaison and primary customer service contact for patients and family members. Patient representatives, who come from varied backgrounds, often gather patient and family complaint data for performance measurement purposes.
Patient safety officer	This individual oversees patient safety improvement activities which may include evaluation of patient incident data, facilitation of safety improvement projects, and coordination of information flow about patient safety among relevant administrative and medical staff committees.
Physician advisor	This individual serves as a full or part-time quality management advisor. Organizations with a medical director may assign physician advisor duties to that position. The physician advisor works closely with the quality department and the medical staff president to ensure appropriate physician participation in, and communication of, quality management activities. The physician advisor may also serve as advisor for utilization management activities.
Quality director	This individual serves as the administrative head of the quality department and performs or coordinates functions assigned to that department. The quality director assists senior leadership in facilitating compliance with quality-related accreditation standards, government regulations, and purchaser requirements.
Risk manager	This individual provides guidance and assistance in support of liability control programs including reporting and analysis of patient and employee incidents and identification and control of liability risks throughout the organization.
Utilization coordinator	This individual is involved in resource management activities to prevent underuse and overuse of services. Utilization coordinators, often nurses, social workers or health information management professionals, review patient records to determine appropriateness of care. They also collect utilization-related data for quality management purposes.

Quality Management Plan

Healthcare organizations, including health plans, are often required by state or federal regulations to have a written quality management plan. This plan describes the organization's approach to management of patient safety and quality. It provides a framework for all measurement, assessment and improvement activities. A properly documented and implemented plan provides reasonable assurance the organization is in compliance with regulatory requirements and accreditation standards. The Medicare Conditions of Participation require participating providers have a written plan. The Joint Commission standards do not specify a written plan is needed, however the standards imply a quality management plan is desirable. For instance, in an accredited organization the leaders are responsible for establishing structures and processes focused on safety and quality (Joint Commission, 2018). A written plan helps demonstrate leaders are compliant with these standards.

The NCQA health plan accreditation standards (2017) require a written quality plan approved by the governing body and periodically reviewed and updated, as necessary. The standards define what must be in this plan:

- An outline of the program structure and content
- Designation of the committee responsible for overseeing the program
- Role, structure, function, and frequency of meetings of the program oversight committee and other relevant committees

In addition to an organization wide plan, department-specific quality management plans may be created. In some situations, department-specific plans are required by regulations or accreditation standards. For instance, clinical laboratories accredited by the College of American Pathologists (CAP) must have a written quality plan (CAP, 2015). In small stand-alone clinical laboratories, the quality plan usually exists on its own. In hospital-based laboratories, the laboratory quality plan may include a section specifying information to be reported to a higher-level authority, such as an organization-wide quality committee.

There is no required plan format. The quality management plan may be of the organization's own design or it may follow a template provided by an accreditation group or professional association. The plan need not be detailed but it should itemize the essential aspects of the quality management system. The plan for a small, free-standing home health agency can be as short as two typed pages in length; for a large health system, it can be several pages long.

The quality management plan can exist as a separate document or it may be a single procedure within a larger procedure manual. Some organizations maintain a separate patient safety plan while others prefer to address quality and patient safety in one combined plan. A hospital quality management plan that combines quality and patient safety activities is found in Exhibit 1.10.

Exhibit 1.10. Quality Management Plan in a 150-bed Community Hospital

Purpose
The Quality Management Plan at Valley Community Hospital describes the system used to evaluate and improve the quality, safety, and appropriateness of patient care and services.

Authority
The Board of Trustees has the ultimate responsibility and legal authority for the safety and quality of care, treatment, and services provided in the hospital. The Board collaborates with leadership from hospital management and the organized medical staff to create and maintain a culture of safety and quality throughout the hospital and to evaluate and improve performance in high-priority areas.

Organization
Quality Council
The Quality Council is chaired by the Medical Director and is comprised of:

- Medical Director (chair)
- Chief Executive Officer
- Nursing Director
- Clinical Services Director
- Vice President of the Medical Staff
- Human Resources Director
- Outpatient Services Manager
- Manager of quality and patient safety
- Board representative

The Quality Council meets monthly to review the progress of organizational quality management activities as well as any performance issues that may be identified through administrative, medical staff or alternative reporting channels. This allows early recognition of potentially problematic issues, with determination of need for action, plus integration of system improvements across the organization. The Quality Council is responsible for:

- Endorsing and recommending department or service-specific performance measures which support organizational quality objectives and the hospital strategic plan.
- Identifying improvement opportunities aligned with strategic goals.

- Incorporating national quality and safety measurement and improvement activities, such as those endorsed by CMS, The Joint Commission, and other external groups, into the hospital quality management system.
- Setting the direction and priorities for ensuring organizational quality and promoting quality and patient safety measurement and improvement activities that reflect these priorities.
- Ongoing development and oversight of the hospital quality management system.
- Supporting leadership, physicians, and staff at all levels of the hospital to advance optimal performance in quality and patient safety.
- Overseeing implementation of the annual quality plan and evaluating the effectiveness of quality management activities.
- Providing input to and approving quarterly quality and patient safety reports to the Board of Trustees.
- Identifying cross-departmental or cross-service improvement opportunities and formation of improvement teams.
- Acting on significant issues impacting quality, patient safety, liability, regulatory compliance, or performance of key organizational processes.

The Quality Council integrates input from the Board of Trustees, the Medical Staff Executive Committee and the Hospital CEO to establish organizational priorities for performance measurement and improvement. Consideration is given to:
- High volume, high risk critical procedures/processes
- Patient safety
- Compliance and legal risks
- Linkage to hospital strategic goals
- External measurement and improvement requirements

Performance measurement and improvement activities are re-evaluated and prioritized annually based on evaluation of the quality management system and in response to significant changes in the internal and external environment, including an identified significant threat to patient safety.

Departments/Medical Staff Services/Committees
Hospital departments, services of the organized medical staff, and committees with patient care responsibilities ensure that reliable, consistent data collection drives the measurement of performance and initiation of quality and safety improvement. These entities are responsible for:
- Using data-driven measurement and improvement principles and tools in daily work
- Identifying performance measures for key processes which support organizational quality objectives and the hospital strategic plan.
- Regularly evaluating performance measurement results.
- Making improvements and achieving progressively better performance.
- Reporting significant performance problems to administrative or medical staff leadership.

Medical Staff Executive Committee
The Medical Staff Executive Committee is chaired by the President of the Medical staff and membership is comprised of:
- President of the Medical Staff (chair)
- Vice President of the Medical Staff
- Immediate Past President of the Medical Staff
- Chiefs of Medicine, Surgery, Emergency, and Obstetrical Services
- Hospital CEO
- Medical Director
- Nursing Director

The Medical Staff Executive Committee meets bi-monthly and at each meeting evaluates clinical performance measurement results to promote continuous improvement in clinical quality and patient safety. The Medical Staff Executive Committee is responsible for:
- Evaluating key measures of clinical performance and promoting progressively better performance.
- Acting on proposals for clinical process improvement from medical staff services and hospital departments/committees

Measurement and Improvement Methodology
Each department, medical staff service, and committee with patient care responsibilities selects performance measures and levels of acceptable performance pertinent to their area in collaboration with leadership and in consultation with the quality and patient safety manager. Performance measures and performance expectations are evaluated and updated annually. The Plan-Do-Check-Act (PDCA) model is used to improve performance.
- **Plan** - The first step involves identifying preliminary opportunities for improvement. At this point the focus is on analyzing data to identify concerns and determine the cause of performance gaps. Interventions intended to improve performance are selected. This step requires the most time and effort. Affected staff served are identified, data compiled, and solutions proposed.

Do - This step involves pilot testing the proposed solution. If it successful as determined through measurement and assessment, the solution is implemented. If the solution does not achieve desired performance improvement, return to the Plan step.

- **Check** - At this step, data is again collected to compare the results of the new process with those of the previous one.
- **Act** - This step involves making the changes a routine part of the targeted activity. It also means "Acting" to involve others (other staff, program components or consumers) - those who will be affected by the changes, those whose cooperation is needed to implement the changes on a larger scale, and those who may benefit from what has been learned. Finally, it means documenting and reporting findings and follow-up.

Reporting

All departments, medical staff services, and committees with patient care responsibilities will do summary reports of performance measurement results at least bi-monthly. These reports will be routinely reviewed with their administrative or medical staff leadership and performance decisions made based on pre-defined performance expectations and organizational priorities. Medical staff services and committees will regularly report key clinical performance measures to the Medical Staff Executive Committee.

Quality and patient safety performance will be periodically evaluated by Directors and managers to determine achievement of performance expectations. Performance problems may be escalated to the Quality Council for awareness and potential action. The triggers for escalation include:

- Performance problem requiring inter-departmental cooperation
- Significant patient safety risk
- Significant liability legal risk
- Significant regulatory compliance risk
- Departmental efforts to improve performance unsuccessful and new strategies needed

Quality Management Plan Implementation/Support

The Quality Management Plan is executed by all levels of leadership with support from the department of quality and patient safety. The manager of this department reports to the medical director. Responsibilities include:

- Advise leadership in establishing a hospital-wide quality management structure and processes
- Provide consultation to the Quality Council and Medical Staff Executive Committee
- Serve as a resource on all implementation aspects of quality management improvement, including:
  o Selection of relevant performance measures
  o Design of data collection mechanism
  o Use of statistical techniques to display trended performance data
  o Facilitation of data analysis
  o Design of performance reports
- Advise on maintaining compliance with quality and patient safety requirements of regulatory agencies and accreditation organizations
- Provide just-in-time quality management training to individuals, units, clinics, or departments, including:
  o Training in theory, tools and techniques of continuous improvement
  o PDCA improvement methodology
  o Measurement of performance
  o Customized training for improvement teams
- Facilitate multi-disciplinary, inter-departmental improvement teams

Confidentiality

All findings and recommendations of quality management activities are confidential under state law. Information is accessible to authorized personnel only. In addition, reports are available to outside agencies such as federal and state agencies as required by law.

Summary

Quality management includes three fundamental tasks: measurement, assessment, and improvement. Measurement involves collection of data about important patient care and business processes. Assessment involves analysis of measurement results to determine if performance expectations are met and where additional improvements might be needed. Improvement involves identifying what needs changing to achieve desired goals, making the changes, and then checking to see if the changes actually accomplished the objectives.

Healthcare quality does not happen by accident. It takes an intentional organization wide effort to measure, assess, and improve performance. The organization's quality management system provides a framework for accomplishing activities supporting continual improvement. Ultimate responsibility for the quality of healthcare services lies with an organization's governing board. The board exercises this duty through oversight of quality management activities. The day-to-day activities of measurement, assessment, and improvement are delegated to senior leaders, physicians, managers, and support staff.

Student Activities

1. Contact three healthcare facilities to find out the academic and professional backgrounds of the quality director and other staff working in the quality department.
2. Interview the director of health information management (HIM) in a healthcare facility and ask what activities are done by the HIM department to support the organization's quality management/performance improvement system.
3. Describe a personal situation in which you received high quality healthcare services. Explain why you would rate the experience as high quality.
4. Describe a personal situation in which you received inferior quality healthcare services. Explain why you would rate the experience as inferior.
5. Which one of the six priorities of the current National Quality Strategy is most important for a healthcare organization to enact to ensure it is prepared for the quality challenges in the next 20 years? Explain your answer.

Website Resources

Continuous quality improvement in correctional health facilities
www.ncchc.org/filebin/Resources/Continuous-Quality-Improvement.pdf

Maine Medical Association, quality improvement plan templates and checklists
www.mainemed.com/member-services/office-based-qi-program

National Quality Strategy
www.ahrq.gov/workingforquality/

Performance improvement plan and template for long term care facilities
www.hcanj.org/files/2013/09/HCANJ_GuidelinePerformanceImprovement_4.pdf

Performance management system tools for public health departments
www.phf.org/focusareas/performancemanagement/Pages/Performance_Management.aspx

Quality Improvement Plan Toolkit: Guidance and Resources to Assist State and Territorial Health Agencies in Developing a Quality Improvement Plan
www.astho.org/qiplantoolkit.pdf

Spath, P.L. (2009). Role of HIM professionals in quality management. *Perspectives in Health Information Management.* 6(Summer): 1j
www.ncbi.nlm.nih.gov/pmc/articles/PMC2781733/

Trustee Resources of the American Hospital Association
http://trustees.aha.org

References

Agency for Healthcare Research and Quality (AHRQ). (2017, March). About the National Quality Strategy. [Online information retrieved 5/21/2018.] www.ahrq.gov/workingforquality/about/index.html.

Berwick, D., Nolan, T., & Whittington, J. (2008). The triple aim: Care, health and cost. *Health Affairs*, 27(3), 759-769.

Blanchfield, B.B., Demehin, A.A., Cummings, C.T., Ferris, T.G., & Meyer, G.S. (2018). The cost of quality: An academic health center's annual costs for its quality and patient safety infrastructure. *Joint Commission Journal on Quality and Patient Safety.* [epub]. https://doi.org/10.1016/j.jcjq.2018.03.012

Centers for Medicare and Medicaid Services. (CMS) (2014.). *Quality Assurance and Performance Improvement Workbook.* Publication No. QN-11SOW-C.2-11112014-01. [Online information retrieved 7/12/2018.] www.hsag.com/contentassets/76281297e70c41aaa3742fd00bc8eaf7/qapi-workbook_final_508.pdf

College of American Pathologists (CAP). (2015). *Laboratory Accreditation: Guide to CAP Accreditation for International Participants.* [Online document; retrieved 5/21/18.] www.cap.org/ShowProperty?nodePath=/UCMCon/Contribution%20Folders/WebContent/pdf/accreditation-guide-international-participants.pdf

Gorgas, N. (1948). Assessing the medical record's value today. In: *Medical Record Administration: A Collection of Readings Selected from the Literature in the Field* (pp. 17-23). Chicago, IL: The American Hospital Association.

Health and Human Services, Department of (HHS). (2009). Policy for protection of human research subjects. [Online document; retrieved 5/21/18.] www.hhs.gov/ohrp/humansubjects/guidance/45cfr46.html

Institute of Medicine (IOM). (2001). *Crossing the Quality Chasm: A New Health System for the 21st Century.* Washington, D.C.: National Academy Press

_____. (1990). *Medicare: A Strategy for Quality Assurance. Volume I.* Washington, DC: National Academy Press.

Joint Commission, The. (2017). Leadership standards. In *Comprehensive Accreditation Manual for Hospitals, 2018.* Oakbrook Terrace, IL: The Joint Commission.

National Association for Quality Assurance (NCQA). (2017). *2017 Health Plan Standards and Guidelines.* Washington, DC: NCQA.

Chapter

2

PERFORMANCE MEASUREMENT

Reader Objectives

After reading this chapter and reflecting on the contents, you will be able to:
1. Demonstrate an understanding of the role of measurement in quality management activities.
2. Give examples of structure, process, outcome and patient experience measures.
3. Identify factors influencing the choice of measures used in a healthcare organization.
4. Define steps for creating valid and reliable measures.
5. Recognize why and how performance goals are established.

Key Terms

Baseline: An initial level of performance at which an organization, process, or function is operating upon which future performance will be measured.

Clinical practice guidelines: Systematically developed statements to assist practitioner and patient decisions about appropriate healthcare for specific clinical circumstances.

Data: Factual information used as a basis for measuring performance; often refers to quantitative information. It is plural in form; the singular is datum.

Denominator for performance measure: Population under study; the population "at risk" of being counted in the numerator of the performance measure. A measurement results when a numerator is divided by a denominator.

Indicator: A measure of performance over time; often used synonymously with performance measure.

Measure: The criteria or metric used to evaluate performance.

Measurement: The act or process of quantitatively comparing results with performance requirements.

Numerator for performance measure: Events specified as evidence of performance. A measurement results when a numerator is divided by a denominator.

Outcome measure: Measurement used to determine whether healthcare activities have had the intended effect.

Patient experience measure: Measurement that uses feedback from patients and their families/caregivers about their experience and/or engagement in decision making around care.

Performance: The execution or accomplishment of work, activities, etc.

Performance goal: Desired condition or target performance level against which actual performance can be compared.

Performance measurement set: A set of inter-related structure, process, and outcome measures used together to evaluate performance in a unit or department or a specified patient population.

Performance result: Actual level of performance.

Process measure: Measurement used to determine acceptable completion of healthcare activities.

Reliability (statistical): Consistency of data obtained from a data collection instrument or through human judgment.

Structure measure: Measurement used to determine the adequacy of the environment in which healthcare services are delivered.

Validity: Soundness of the use and interpretation of a measurement.

Measures of Performance

Performance measures help people understand, manage, and improve healthcare activities. Sometimes called quality indicators, performance measures provide information necessary for making informed decisions about the quality of healthcare services. Measurement information helps people know:

- How various activities in the organization are performing
- If quality goals are being met
- If customers are satisfied
- If and where improvements are needed

Exhibit 2.1. Measurement: A Quality Management Activity

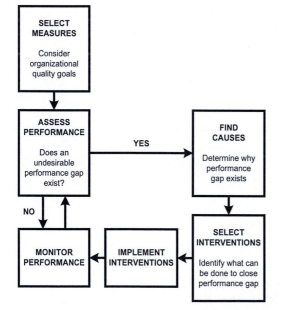

Performance measurement is a primary quality management activity. As illustrated in Exhibit 2.1, the process of quality management starts with selection of performance measures.

Measurement data are gathered, reported, and analyzed. Assessment of measurement data may lead to improvement activities. If performance is satisfactory, data will continue to be collected and analyzed.

Measuring healthcare performance is not a new phenomenon. As early as 1754 the Pennsylvania Hospital was collecting patient outcome data tabulated by diagnosis groups. Today, performance measurement is in greater demand than ever before. Purchasers want performance data to use in provider contract negotiations, for tracking patient management practices, and for judging whether care is adding value for patients. Healthcare professionals want performance data to use in designing high quality and evidence-based patient care practices and cost-efficient delivery systems. Researchers and regulatory agencies want performance data to use in developing health policies and cost-containment strategies. Consumers want performance data to use in making choices among providers. Organizations accredited by the Joint Commission are required to use data and information, which includes measures of performance, to guide decisions and to understand variation in performance of processes supporting safety and quality (Joint Commission, 2017a).

Increased demand for performance data reinforces the need for healthcare professionals to understand what patient care activities should be measured, the limitations of measurement data, and how to make data-driven performance improvement decisions. Most important, healthcare professionals must know how to develop performance measures that provide valid and reliable information about the quality and safety of patient care services.

Constructing Measures

Most performance measures are some type of number: a rate, ratio or proportion. To create these measures, two data elements are needed: a numerator and a denominator. A numerator is the upper portion of a fraction and a denominator is the lower portion of a fraction. These numbers are used to calculate a rate, proportion or ratio. The numerator is a number that provides a magnitude (how much) and the denominator gives the number meaning (what).

These elements are illustrated below in the mathematical equation used to calculate the performance measure, *Percent of hospitalized patients that develop an infection.*

$$\text{Numerator:} \quad \frac{\substack{\text{Number of patients who develop an infection} \\ \text{while in the hospital}}}{\substack{\text{Total number of patients discharged} \\ \text{from the hospital}}} \times 100 \ = \ \% \quad \text{Denominator:}$$

The denominator represents the entire population included in the measure and the numerator represents part of the entire population we are interested in. This relationship is represented by the illustration in Exhibit 2.2. The total measurement population in this example is all patients discharged from the hospital. The group of interest within this population is patients who develop an infection.

Exhibit 2.2. Total Measurement Population (Denominator) and Group of Interest (Numerator)

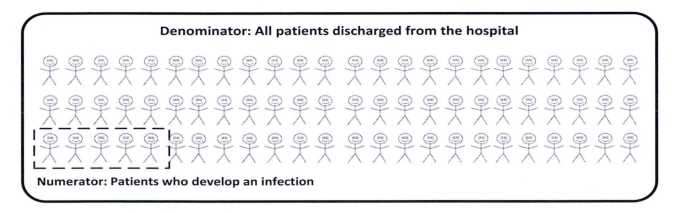

Performance measures can be used to assess how well people are performing certain tasks. For example, the number of patient records reviewed during a given time period can be compared to the number of reviewed records containing adequate physician documentation. This measure would be used to assess completeness of physician documentation. Shown below is the formula for calculating this performance measure. The measure represented by this equation is, *Percent of patient records with adequate physician documentation.*

$$\frac{\text{Number of patient records with adequate physician documentation}}{\text{Total number of patient records reviewed during the study time period}} \times 100 \ = \ \%$$

Performance measures can also be a single numeric value, for example, *Number of patient complaints.* Knowing how many complaints are received tells an organization something important about the quality of its performance. It is not always necessary to create a rate, ratio or proportion. Sometimes single numeric values tell us what we want to know about our performance.

Measurement Categories

Quality of medical care can be measured on four distinct levels: structure, process, outcome, and patient experience. Healthcare quality researcher, Dr. Avedis Donabedian (1980) first conceptualized a structure-process-outcome measurement taxonomy for healthcare in 1966. It is generally agreed that measures from each of Donabedian's measurement categories are needed to adequately evaluate all important aspects of healthcare services. With the emphasis on patient-centered care in recent years, a fourth measurement category has been added – patient experience.

Structure measures of healthcare performance are used to assess the adequacy of the environment in which healthcare takes place. Physical facilities, equipment, staffing, qualifications of physicians and staff, and organizational structure are just some of the factors taken into account. The result of a structure measure is generally binary: either the structure is acceptable or it is not acceptable. A limitation of structure measurement for the purpose of performance evaluation is that an acceptable structure by itself may not be sufficient to assure high quality healthcare.

Process measures of healthcare performance are used to assess completion of required tasks. The measure indicates whether the task was performed (or not performed) as expected. For example, the measure *Percent of clinic records containing documentation of patient allergies*, is used to evaluate completion of the task of allergy documentation. There are hundreds of tasks performed each day in a healthcare organization and completion of each one does not need to be measured. Process measures are used to evaluate important tasks – those activities with the greatest impact on healthcare quality.

Outcome measures are used to assess the end results of healthcare services. Some end results are clinical (physiologic, psychosocial, or biological). For example, the measure *Percent of nursing home residents that develop a urinary tract infection* is used to evaluate physiologic outcomes. Some end results are financial. For example, the measure *Average operating room charges for patients undergoing coronary artery bypass surgery* is used to evaluate the cost of care. A limitation of outcome measurement is that end results of health services are influenced by many factors and not all are under control of healthcare professionals. Patient outcomes are affected by the medical care they receive but also by genetic, environmental, and behavioral factors unrelated to the medical care.

Some performance results are experiential – meaning the results pertain to or are derived from experiences of health service recipients. An example of a patient experience measure is, *Percent of home care patients that report being treated with courtesy and respect*. There is growing emphasis on measuring the patient's perspective. In response to Medicare requirements, healthcare facilities are conducting patient surveys that measure many aspects of the patient experience. Patient experience measures are now viewed as a distinct fourth measurement category. These measures were formerly included in the outcome category of Donabedian's structure-process-outcome measurement taxonomy. A limitation of patient experience measures is that the results are influenced by perceptions or expectations and perhaps not what actually happened.

In Exhibit 2.3 are examples of structure, process, outcome, and patient experience measures that might be used in a hospital to evaluate performance.

Exhibit 2.3. Measures of Hospital Performance

Structure Measures	• Ratio: Registered nurses to patients
	• Number of fire drills conducted annually
	• Percent of employees who receive influenza vaccination
Process measures	• Percent of patients assessed for fall risk at time of admission
	• Percent of patients with stage III colon cancer who receive chemotherapy
	• Percent of operative reports dictated immediately following surgery
Outcome measures	• Rate: Number of patients falls per 1000 patient days
	• Rate: Number of patients that develop a hospital-acquired pressure ulcer per 1000 discharges
	• Percent of patients with the principal diagnosis code of stroke that expire in the hospital

Patient experience measures	• Percent of surgical patients who reported their surgeon definitely communicated well with them before surgery • Percent of adult patients who reported their room and bathroom were always or usually kept clean • Percentage of adult patients who reported the hospital staff was always or usually responsive to their needs

Scope of Measurement Activities

Performance measures are used to evaluate important aspects of healthcare identified in the IOM report, *Crossing the Quality Chasm* (2001). Healthcare measures often address the six key dimensions of healthcare needing improvement: effectiveness, efficiency, equity, patient centeredness, safety, and timeliness.

Departments within a healthcare organization usually have a set of measures to evaluate various key dimensions. In Exhibit 2.4 are sets of measures used to evaluate performance in an ambulatory clinic registration department and evaluate the quality of care for patients hospitalized for treatment of stroke.

Exhibit 2.4. Performance Measurement Sets

Clinic: Registration Department	• Percent of patient records containing patient demographic errors (process measure) • Percent of consent forms that are properly completed and signed (process measure) • Percent of patient record number assignments that are correct (process measure) • Percent of patients who report being 'very satisfied' with the registration process (patient experience measure) • Average time for patient registration (outcome measure)
Hospital Patient Population: Stoke	• Hospital has protocols for heparin administration (structure measure) • Average time between patient arrival at the emergency department and completion of CT/MRI scan (process measure) • Percent of patients with high cholesterol who receive lipid lowering therapy (process measure) • Percent of patients who are discharged on antiplatelet therapy (process measure) • Mortality rate for patients admitted for treatment of a stroke (outcome measure)

In healthcare facilities with an organized medical staff each medical staff department has a set of performance measurements. The measures are used to evaluate various dimensions of quality as they relate to physician practices. Listed below are examples of outcome measures that could be used to judge the quality of physician practices in the cardiac surgery service of a hospital.
• Rate of patient mortality
• Percent of patients developing postoperative acute renal failure requiring hemodialysis
• Average total length of stay reported by type of cardiac surgery
• Average cost per patient reported by type of cardiac surgery

Small healthcare organizations may not have separate performance measurement sets for departments or different patient populations. Small facilities often select an organization wide set of measures to evaluate important aspects of patient care. Listed below are examples of performance measures that might be used in a women's health clinic.
• Percent of women with an abnormal pap smear who are notified of abnormality and scheduled for reappointment within two weeks (process measure)

- Percent of pregnant patients who receive all recommended prenatal tests (process measure)
- Average time between patient sign-in with receptionist and time escorted to exam room (outcome measure)
- Average time patients must wait to schedule a complete physical appointment (outcome measure)
- Percent of patients who report being 'very satisfied' with the courtesy and helpfulness of telephone operators and receptionists (patient experience measure)

Health maintenance organizations (HMOs) and other health plans use performance measures to evaluate the quality of healthcare services provided to beneficiaries. More than 90 percent of health plans nationwide use performance measures found in the Healthcare Effectiveness Data and Information Set (HEDIS™) developed by the NCQA (2018a). The HEDIS™ data set includes more than 75 measures. Listed below are examples of HEDIS™ measures (NCQA, 2018b):

- Percent of children who receive all childhood immunizations before age two (process measure)
- Percent of members with diabetes who have annual eye exams (process measure)
- Percent of live births weighing less than 1500gms (outcome measure)
- Health plan costs per member per month (outcome measure)
- Rate of overall member satisfaction (patient experience measure)
- Number of member complaints about problems obtaining care (patient experience measure)

Joint Commission accredited organizations are expected to submit performance data to its ORYX™ accountability measure project (often called core measures). Data must be gathered for the measures in this project even if the relevant processes are not considered by an organization to be high-volume, high-risk, or problem-prone. Examples of accountability measures for hospital inpatient psychiatric services are listed below (Joint Commission, 2017b).

- Percent of patients that undergo admission screening for violence risk, substance use, psychological trauma history and patient strengths (process measure)
- Percent of patients discharged on multiple antipsychotic medications with appropriate justification (process measure)
- Number of hours of physical restraint use (outcome measure)
- Number of hours of seclusion use (outcome measure)

Developing Measures

Many performance measures used in healthcare settings today are developed by external medical professional groups, researchers, and purchasers. The National Quality Forum (NQF), a non-profit organization which includes a wide variety of healthcare stakeholders, has developed a consensus process for endorsement of healthcare quality measures that meet several criteria, including a requirement for reliability and validity testing (NQF, 2016). In addition, NQF endorsed measures are considered suitable for use based on four criteria:

- Importance to measure and report;
- Scientific acceptability of measure properties;
- Feasibility;
- Usability and use; and
- Related and measures.

Many performance measures endorsed by the NQF are incorporated into measurement reporting requirements found in federal and state regulations and accreditation standards. In addition to using measures developed by outside groups, healthcare organizations often develop their own measures. A systematic four-step process is used to develop measures:

1. Select a process to be evaluated
2. Determine what you want to know about the process
3. Translate "What you want to know" into performance measures
4. Establish performance goals

Select Process

There are many healthcare tasks and each can be measured in different ways. Because measurement is resource intensive healthcare organizations necessarily limit the number of performance measures. The following issues are taken into consideration when selecting aspects of performance to be measured in a department, medical staff service or in the organization as a whole:

- Accreditation and regulatory requirements
- Topics of national importance
- Strategic quality goals
- Customer needs and expectations

Accreditation and Regulatory Requirements

Standards of accreditation organizations contain requirements influencing selection of performance measures. These requirements change from time to time so be sure to check with the most recent standards to find current expectations. The Joint Commission accreditation standards suggest organizations measure performance in high-volume, high-risk, and problem-prone processes. In addition to this general requirement, there are standards mentioning specific processes that must be regularly evaluated. For instance, the Joint Commission (2017c) requires accredited home health agencies to measure topics such as:

- Infection prevention and control practices
- Medication management practices
- Security, integrity, and privacy of health information
- Patient perception of the safety and quality of care, treatment, or services
- Adequacy of patient access to equipment, items, services, and information

Standards of the Accreditation Association for Ambulatory Healthcare (AAAHC) contain requirements for processes that must be regularly evaluated in an ambulatory care facility. These processes include:

- Access to and availability of health services
- Diagnosis and treatment of patients
- Infection control practices
- Follow-up of abnormal findings and test results
- Continuity of care
- Clinical record documentation

State and federal regulations also influence the choice of processes to be measured. For example, the U.S. Nuclear Regulatory Commission has requirements that must be met by all healthcare facilities licensed to use radiation and radionuclides in or on humans. Departments involved in using these modalities must regularly measure performance of processes such as:

- Control of employee and visitor exposures to radiation
- Procurement of radionuclides and radiation producing devices
- Disposal of radioactive wastes
- Testing and care of radiation sources made by in-house personnel
- Administering and using sources of radiation in or on humans
- Storage radiation sources
- Calibration of radiation survey instruments

The Medicare Conditions of Participation contain requirements that should be considered when selecting healthcare processes to be measured. For example, hospitals must make certain patient records document a properly executed informed consent form for procedures and treatments that require written patient consent (42 C.F.R. § 482.24(c)(2)(v)). Hospitals will want to periodically measure compliance with this requirement.

In addition to measuring compliance with federal and state requirements, Medicare-participating providers must measure customer satisfaction. Since 1995 AHRQ has promoted the use of surveys to evaluate how consumers view the healthcare experience. Standardized consumer satisfaction surveys have been created and are required to be used by Medicare-participating provider sites and health plans offering Medicare and Medicaid coverage. Surveys developed in the AHRQ Consumer Assessment of Healthcare Providers and Systems (CAHPS) program are available online. Below are three examples of patient experience questions on the home health care CAHPS survey (AHRQ, 2018a):

- In the last 2 months of care, when you contacted this agency's office did you get the help or advice you needed?
- When you started getting home health care from this agency, did someone from the agency ask to see all the prescription and over-the-counter medicines you were taking?
- In the last 2 months of care, how often did home health providers from this agency listen carefully to you?

Topics of National Importance

The federal government periodically establishes national disease prevention and health promotion objectives. The current objectives are found in the *Healthy People 2020* document. Healthy People is a set of goals and objectives with 10-year targets designed to guide national health promotion and disease prevention efforts to improve the health of all people in the United States (HHS, 2018). These national objectives influence performance measures selected by healthcare organizations and public health entities in addition to measures required by regulations and accreditation standards.

In support of the Healthy People 2020 objectives, several agencies of the U.S. Department of Health and Human Services (HHS) are involved in promoting healthcare quality improvements through various performance measurement projects. For example, nursing homes must collect data on all residents at specified intervals during their stay. The data, known as the Minimum Data Set (MDS), are transmitted to CMS and used to evaluate various aspects of nursing home performance. Below are examples of measures for short stay (100 days or less) nursing home residents (CMS, 2017).

- Percent who improved in their ability to move around on their own
- Percent with pressure ulcers that are new or worsened
- Percent who were assessed and appropriately given the seasonal influenza vaccine

The federal government actively encourages greater use of data from electronic health records (EHRs) for performance measurement purposes. The Health Information Technology for Economic and Clinical Health (HITECH) provisions of the American Recovery and Reinvestment Act of 2009 made available an estimated $14–$27 billion in incentives over ten years for clinicians and hospitals to adopt and 'meaningfully use' health information technology (Marcotte, 2012). One requirement for receiving payments from the Medicare EHR incentive program was that providers must use an EHR system capable of capturing numerator, denominator, and/or exclusion criteria data for clinical quality measures selected by CMS. The measure results were to be calculated using this data and electronically reported to CMS. Examples of clinical quality measures selected by CMS for the EHR incentive program are listed below.

- Percent of patients aged 65 years and older who have ever received a pneumococcal vaccine
- Percent of patients aged 18 years and older and are smokers who received advice to quit smoking
- Percent of all patients aged 18 and older with a diagnosis of heart failure and paroxysmal or chronic atrial fibrillation who were prescribed warfarin therapy
- Percent of women 21-64 years of age, who received one or more Pap tests to screen for cervical cancer

In October 2017, CMS announced a new approach to quality measurement, called "Meaningful Measures." The Meaningful Measures Initiative will involve identifying the highest priorities to improve patient care through quality measurement and quality improvement efforts (CMS, 2018b). While this new approach may ultimately reduce the number of measures used by CMS to evaluate healthcare performance, the data for the measures will still need to be reported electronically to CMS as well as other external groups. Providers and health plans will need the expertise of health information management (HIM) professionals to help ensure electronic data quality and error-free transmission of measure results.

Strategic Quality Goals

Most healthcare organizations, large and small, establish strategic goals and objectives. These are set during a planning process in which the current environment and trends are considered and future business objectives defined. Strategic goals articulate the end points the organization hopes to achieve and objectives describe what will be done to achieve these goals. Goals and objectives may be focused on productivity improvements, new services, expansion of the customer base, or any number of other expectations.

One aspect of strategic planning is establishing quality goals and objectives. These are performance-oriented statements of what an organization wants to achieve over the short- and long-term. Quality goals are long-term and generally based on or derived from the organization's mission. In Exhibit 2.5 is a long-term quality goal in a hospital and some of the short-term quality objectives for this goal. Quality goals often remain the same or similar for several years. However, periodically (usually annually) the quality objectives are evaluated and may change for the upcoming year. Changes are made based on the organization's past performance, input from stakeholders, external requirements, and current topics of national and regional importance.

Exhibit 2.5. Hospital Quality Goal and Quality Objectives

Long-Term Quality Goal: Provide a consistently safe environment with integrated patient care processes resulting in outcomes equal to or better than expected.

Short-Term Quality Objectives:
1. Improve compliance with hand hygiene practices.
2. Reduce patient incidents caused by improper patient identification.
3. Reduce the number of patient falls.
4. Reduce the incidence of pressure ulcers.
5. Reduce the rate of hospital readmissions (30-day) for patients with heart failure.
6. Reduce the number of central line catheter infections in patients in critical care units.
7. Manage emergency services to improve patient experience.
8. Improve organ donor procurement.

Organization-wide quality goals and objectives are agreed upon by the governing board and senior leaders with input from internal and external stakeholders. This task is often done during an annual evaluation of the effectiveness of quality management activities. References to quality planning and the annual evaluation are commonly documented in the organization's quality management plan (see plan example in chapter 1).

An organization's quality objectives influence the processes chosen for measurement. For instance, the following performance measures could be used to evaluate achievement of the quality objectives listed in Exhibit 2.5.
1. Percent of caregivers in compliance with hand hygiene practices
2. Number of patient incidents related to improper patient identification
3. Rate of patient falls (number of patient falls per 1,000 patient days)
4. Rate of pressure ulcer prevalence (number of patients developing a pressure ulcer per 1,000 patient discharges)
5. Percent of patients with heart failure readmitted to the hospital within 30 days for same or similar condition

6. Rate of central line infections (number of infections per 1,000 central-line catheter days in critical care units)
7. Average time to treat and release patients seen in the emergency department
8. Donor conversion rate (number of donors per number of eligible donors)

Most accreditation groups have standards requiring leaders set organization-wide quality goals and objectives (sometimes called quality planning). The Joint Commission leadership standards require planning activities be focused on improving patient safety and healthcare quality. Standards of the National Integrated Accreditation for Healthcare Organizations (NHIAHO) require hospital leadership set measurable quality objectives. Leaders at NCQA-accredited health plans must establish an annual quality plan. An organization's long-term quality goals may be documented in the written quality management plan, however short-term quality objectives are frequently not included in the plan because they change more often.

The quality objectives of an organization influence the processes chosen for measurement at the department-level and within medical staff services. For instance, when an organization sets hand hygiene improvement as a quality objective all departments providing direct patient care will measure staff and physician compliance with hand hygiene. In Exhibit 2.6 are examples of HIM department performance measures related to hospital-wide quality objectives.

Exhibit 2.6. Hospital-wide Quality Objectives and Measures of Relevant HIM Department Processes

Hospital-Wide Quality Objective	HIM Department Measures
Improve patient satisfaction	Average time between patient requests for hard copies of their record and receipt of the copies
Improve transition of patient care between hospital and non-hospital providers	Percent of records transmitted to post-hospital providers within 24 hours of patient discharge
Reduce prevalence of hospital-acquired urinary tract infections	Percent of patients with documentation of a urinary tract infection at the time of admission that are correctly coded as having an infection at the time of admission

Customer Needs and Expectations

When selecting processes to be measured it is important to consider what external customers – purchasers and consumers – view as significant. All potential individual end-users of healthcare have opinions about what is important. For example, below are the four aspects of healthcare services that patients report as being most important (Deloitte Development, 2016):
*   Providers know and understand them
*   Care choices are economically manageable
*   Access is available when, where, and how it best suits them
*   Digital support is available to assist in the management of their care

There are many internal customers within an organization. The needs and expectations of these customers are also considered when selecting processes to be measured. For instance, in a hospital physicians are internal customers of the clinical laboratory. Physician customers have certain expectations of what the laboratory should provide and what level of performance is needed. For example:
*   An adequate array of testing options to meet clinical decision-making needs.
*   Information and education about which tests are appropriate for a particular clinical problem.
*   Instructions on preparing the patient prior to specimen collection and on the appropriate specimen for an assay.
*   Phlebotomy performed safely and efficiently, without discomfort to the patient.

- Analytical procedures performed without error and with appropriate analytical performance.
- Result reports clearly presented, without ambiguity; reference values, therapeutic intervals, and decision levels available as needed.
- Turnaround time, from submission of the test request to delivery of the report, within clinically acceptable limits.
- Laboratory consultation readily available when needed; appropriate interpretation of results always presented in a timely manner.

When selecting processes to measure, the laboratory must take into consideration what is important to one of their primary customers – physicians. If the performance of a process important to physicians is not already being measured for other reasons it should be added to the laboratory's performance measurement set. Departments should be familiar with their external and internal customers and be sure performance of processes important to these customers is periodically measured.

Determine What You Want to Know

There are many ways to measure performance. Structure measures are used to evaluate the environment in which the process is performed. Process measures are used to determine if the right things are being done. Outcome measures are used to judge the end results. Measures of patient experience are used to better understand how service recipients view their encounters.

To keep from being overwhelmed with data it is important to measure only critical activities and relevant outcomes. Critical activities are those tasks significantly impacting efficiency, equity, patient centeredness, safety and timeliness. Relevant outcomes are the end result of performing critical activities well. For instance, when clinic receptionists are helpful and friendly (critical activities) patient experience (an end result) will be better.

Many medical, nursing, and allied health professional groups have developed statements describing important or critical activities. These statements have various descriptive titles:

- Clinical practice guideline
- Practice guideline
- Practice standard
- Therapeutic guideline
- Position statement
- Practice advisory
- Policy statement
- Standards of practice

While different terminology is used to describe these professional statements, the recommendations all serve a similar purpose – identify critical activities that should be performed to achieve desired goals. For example, the Association for the Advancement of Wound Care (AAWC) published a guideline addressing prevention and management of skin pressure ulcers. This guideline identifies several critical activities related to skin inspection and maintenance for the purpose of preventing ulcer occurrence (AAWC, 2010):

1. Perform comprehensive visual and tactile skin inspections during patient care and regularly according to institutional guidelines.
2. Manage excess moisture at affected sites, including areas affected by incontinence or perspiration, and skin folds in bariatric patients.
3. Clean and dry skin using non-friction bathing standards with a slightly warm, non-irritating, non-sensitizing, pH-balanced no-rinse skin cleanser avoiding saline or soap regularly and after each incontinence episode.
4. Establish an individualized bowel and bladder program for patients with incontinence.
5. Reduce friction and shear.

A practice brief on release of confidential patient information published by the American Health Information Management Association (AHIMA) identifies several critical activities in this high-volume process (AHIMA, 2012):

- Record date and time the request is received
- Verify the completeness of the request
- Verify the authority of the requestor
- Verify the identity of the patient
- Verify appropriateness of information requested
- Record date and time information released

Practice briefs developed by AHIMA, as well as other associations representing professionals not directly involved in patient care, are commonly based on consensus opinions of people within the profession. The practice recommendations from groups such as the AAWC are based as much as possible on scientific research. Practice guidelines published by professional groups representing physicians, nurses, and other people who care for patients are often rigorously developed. To support a standard process for developing guidelines, the IOM (1990) created a definition of clinical practice guidelines which is still recognized today:

"Clinical practice guidelines are systematically developed statements to assist practitioner and patient decisions about appropriate healthcare for specific clinical circumstances." (p. 38)

To be considered rigorously developed, guideline recommendations must be based on the results of a systematic literature search and review of existing scientific evidence published in peer reviewed journals. Where research evidence is lacking, expert professional consensus can be used in making guideline recommendations. When the guideline is published, the developer reports how the guidelines were formulated and the source of recommendations.

In Exhibit 2.7 are excerpts from a guideline on preanesthesia evaluation developed by the American Society of Anesthesiologists (ASA) Task Force on Preanesthesia Evaluation (2012). The recommendations are based on strong scientific evidence and overwhelming consensus opinions of practitioners. These are considered critical activities – interventions that significantly impact patient outcomes. Clinicians should follow these recommendations unless there are clear and compelling reasons for an alternative action. Recommendations lacking strong evidence or professional consensus may still be implemented but would not be considered critical activities.

Exhibit 2.7. Excerpt from ASA Guidelines on Preanesthesia Evaluation

- An initial record review, patient interview, and physical examination should be performed before the day of surgery for patients with high severity of disease.
- For patients with low severity of disease and those undergoing procedures with high surgical invasiveness, the interview and physical exam should also be performed before the day of surgery.
- For patients with low severity of disease undergoing procedures with medium or low surgical invasiveness, the initial interview and physical exam may be performed on or before the day of surgery.
- *At a minimum*, a focused preanesthesia physical examination should include an assessment of the airway, lungs, and heart, with documentation of vital signs.

Guideline recommendations are a source of performance measures required to be used by regulatory agencies and accreditation standards. These measures focus on recommendations considered to be critical because of strong scientific evidence or professional consensus. For example, in 2003 the Surgical Care Improvement Project (SCIP) was initiated by 10 national organizations interested in reducing surgical complications through better adherence to evidence-based practice recommendations (Rosenberger, Politano, & Sawyer, 2011). In support of this continuing initiative the Joint Commission and CMS now require hospitals and outpatient surgery facilities gather and report performance measurement data on critical activities known to reduce the incidence of surgical wound infections. One performance measure is, *Percent of patients who receive prophylactic antibiotic within one hour prior to surgical incision*. There is strong scientific evidence that patients undergoing certain types of surgery have fewer wound infections when an antibiotic given as a preventive measure is administered close to the time of surgery.

Translate "What You Want to Know" into Performance Measures

At this point the process to be measured has been selected (step one) and the critical activities and relevant outcomes of the process have been identified (step two). Knowledge gained from completing these first two steps help people define precisely what they want to know about the critical activities and the process as a whole. Step three involves construction of performance measures for the critical activities in the process chosen for evaluation. It starts with translating what you want to know about the process into a set of performance measures. For example, what do caregivers want to know about one of the critical activities involved in the process of managing patients' post-surgical pain? This questioning process is illustrated in Exhibit 2.8.

Exhibit 2.8. Performance Questions Related to One Critical Activity of Post-Surgical Pain Management

Post-Surgical Pain Management Critical Activity	Questions That Could be Asked of This Critical Activity
A patient self-report pain assessment tool should be used and analgesia should be adjusted or other interventions considered when the patient's level of pain is not maintained below a certain level.	• Is the same self-reporting tool used for all patient assessments? • Is the patient instructed in how to use the self-reporting tool? • Is the self-reporting tool used appropriately? • Is the patient's pain medication adjusted as indicated? • Are non-medication interventions used as indicated? • Are patients reportedly satisfied with post-operative pain management?

Once people identify precisely what they want to know the measurements are constructed. At this point, people must decide how to 'say it in numbers.' The measure should provide a quantitative answer to questions in terms that relate to the question. For example, the process measure *percent of patients reportedly satisfied with postoperative pain management* would answer one of the questions about a critical activity. The mathematical formula for this measure is shown below.

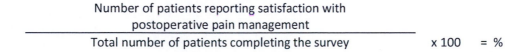

$$\frac{\text{Number of patients reporting satisfaction with postoperative pain management}}{\text{Total number of patients completing the survey}} \quad \times 100 \quad = \%$$

To avoid confusion when analyzing results for a set of measurements related to a particular process, it is best to be consistent when reporting performance. Either report all measures in the positive (how often performance meets expectations) or report all measures in the negative (how often performance does not meet expectations).

The above measurement is a patient experience measure. It will yield information about patients' perception of their healthcare experience. In some instances, outcomes measures are needed to answer questions about critical activities.

The rate of complications is an outcome measure often used to evaluate clinical practices. The mathematical formula below illustrates how complications from the use of a particular post-operative pain medication would be calculated.

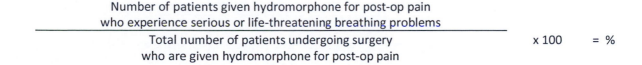

$$\frac{\text{Number of patients given hydromorphone for post-op pain who experience serious or life-threatening breathing problems}}{\text{Total number of patients undergoing surgery who are given hydromorphone for post-op pain}} \quad \times 100 \quad = \%$$

The following case illustrates how a question about a process is turned into a well-defined outcome performance measure:

> You are part of the management team in the rehabilitation department in a long-term care facility. The team has concluded that one of the fundamental questions they would like answered about the process of treating patients is, *How often do patients develop new muscle contractures while receiving regular physical therapy treatments?* Your team needs to select a performance measure to answer this question. After writing several possible performance measures on a flip chart and examining what information each measure could convey, the team decides to use, *Percent of patients receiving physical therapy each month who develop a new muscle contracture.* To ensure the team understands what information this measure will provide them, they rewrite the measure in fundamental measurement units. The outcome measure looks like this:

$$\frac{\text{Number of patients receiving physical therapy each month who develop a new muscle contracture}}{\text{Total number of patients receiving physical therapy each month}} \times 100 = \%$$

> The above formula identifies the data to be used in calculating the measurement. The team can see how the measure results will answer their question about the treatment process. Plus, it is apparent what data are needed to create the measure.

Once performance measures for a process have been selected, it is time to identify the raw data needed to generate the measures. Performance measures are seldom calculated directly in a single measurement or from a single source. They usually (but not always) consist of some combination of raw data elements as in the above physical therapy outcome measure.

The data elements used to create a performance measure must also be precisely defined. For some performance measures the meaning is quite clear, as in this example: *Percent of time the requestor's identity is validated before releasing confidential patient information.*

For other performance measures the data require further clarification. For example, the performance measure, *Percent of patients receiving physical therapy who develop a new muscle contracture,* has several ambiguous terms.

- What types of therapy and how often must patients have been receiving it to be counted in the study population?
- Are there any patients that should not be counted in the measurement population such as those with conditions placing them at high risk for contractures, e.g. patients with systemic lupus erythematous, scleroderma, gouty arthritis?
- Does this measure only include contractures caused by patient immobilization or dysfunctional positioning or does the numerator include patients who develop any type of contracture for any reason?

Ill-defined data elements can cause misunderstandings during the data collection process, not to mention confusion that occurs when people attempt to interpret measurement results. Organizations sponsoring nationwide healthcare performance measurement projects create precise definitions for measures people are expected to report. Healthcare organizations should do the same for measures developed internally.

Shown in Exhibit 2.9 are the measurement specifications for one of the Joint Commission hospital measures: *Percent of ischemic or hemorrhagic stroke patients who received venous thromboembolism (VTE) prophylaxis or have documentation why no VTE prophylaxis was given the day of or the day after hospital admission.* This is a process measure.

Exhibit 2.9. Hospital Measure Data Specifications

Performance Measure Name: Venous Thromboembolism (VTE Prophylaxis)
Numerator Statement: Ischemic or hemorrhagic stroke patients who received VTE prophylaxis or have documentation why no VTE prophylaxis was given on the day of or the day after hospital admission.
Denominator Statement: Ischemic or hemorrhagic stroke patients
Included Populations: Discharges with an ICD-10-CM Principal Diagnosis Code for ischemic or hemorrhagic stroke.
Excluded Populations:

- Patients less than 18 years of age
- Patients who have a Length of Stay less than 2 days
- Patients who have a Length of Stay greater than 120 days
- Patients with Comfort Measures Only documented on day of or day after hospital arrival
- Patients enrolled in clinical trials

Data Collection Approach: Retrospective data sources for required data elements include administrative data and medical records. Some hospitals may prefer to gather data concurrently by identifying patients in the population of interest. This approach provides opportunities for improvement at the point of care/service. However, complete documentation includes the principal or other ICD-10 diagnosis and procedure codes, which require retrospective data entry.

Source: Joint Commission. (2017). *Specifications Manual for Joint Commission National Quality Measures (v2017B2).* (https://manual.jointcommission.org/releases/TJC2017B2/MIF0126.html)

A performance measurement matrix, similar to the one illustrated below in Exhibit 2.10, can be used to document the data needed for the performance measures for a particular topic. Descriptions of the raw data should be precise so everyone understands what is being measured. A matrix is completed for each process selected for measurement.

Exhibit 2.10. Measurement Matrix for the Topic of Client Access to Outpatient Mental Health Services

Performance Measure	Numerator	Denominator
Average length of time from a new client's request for services to the first face-to-face meeting with a mental health professional	Total time between request for services and the first face-to-face contact with a mental health professional for new clinic admissions	Total number of new clients
Average length of time from an established client's request for appointment to a face-to-face meeting with a mental health professional	Total time between request for appointment and the face-to-face contact with a mental health professional for an established clinic patient	Total number of appointment requests from established clients
Percent of clients for whom the location of services is reported as convenient	Number of clients who report, 'strongly agree' or 'agree' on survey question related to convenience of the location of service (e.g. parking, public transportation, distance, etc.)	Number of clients responding to survey question

Establish Performance Goals

The purpose of performance measurement is to determine if there are gaps between expected and actual performance. To make this determination, expected performance must be defined. A performance goal – description of expected performance – is established for each measure. Performance goals are expressed in several different ways. For example, goals can be stated in finite terms: *95% of patient requests for copies of their records must be fulfilled within 72 hours of request.* Performance goals can also be expressed as improvements from baseline performance. For example: *Average patient satisfaction scores shall improve by 10% percent over the previous year scores.* Performance goals can also be expressed as investigation trigger points. For example: *If two blood specimen tubes are not properly labeled in one quarter, an in-depth investigation will be done.*

Setting an expected level of performance is an important step because people will spend time and resources trying to meet these goals. It is often best to establish realistic incremental goals – those that people have a good chance of attaining – and after reaching these goals, establish new ones.

There are various methods for setting performance goals. A common approach is to establish goals based on past performance. For example, if the length of time from a client's request for services to the first face-to-face meeting with a mental health professional has averaged 10 days over the past year, then 9 or 8 days is often set as next year's goal. Other factors are considered when establishing acceptable levels of performance. These factors include:

- Regulation and accreditation standards
- Organizational quality goals
- Guideline recommendations
- Performance in other organizations

Regulations and Accreditation Standards

When government regulations or accreditation standards state a particular activity must always be done the performance goal for that activity should be set at 100%. For example, the Medicare Hospital Conditions of Participation require that all patient records have a final diagnosis and be completed within 30 days of discharge (CMS, 2012). Performance goals for measures of compliance with these requirements are set at 100%.

Mandatory compliance requirements affecting performance goals for critical activities are also found in accreditation standards. For instance, some hospitals accredited by the Healthcare Facilities Accreditation Program (HFAP) of the American Osteopathic Association (2018) also have been designated as Primary Stroke Centers. To achieve this advanced level of certification, the following criteria must be met:

- Stroke code team arrival at bedside must be within 15 minutes
- Lab testing and advanced imaging capabilities must be available 24/7
- Must have access to neurologists 24/7
- Must have a designation stroke unit
- Staff must meet annual stroke care education requirements
- Must have neurosurgical expertise available or able to transfer patients within two hours

Organizational Quality Goals

To achieve the organization's quality objectives, departments or services may need to set high performance goals. For example, if the organization sets a goal of improving timeliness of the billing process, the HIM department may set the following goal for a performance measure related to coding: *100% of patient records will be coded for billing purposes within three days following completion of the records.*

Guideline Recommendations

Clinical practice guidelines and similar professional practice statements are sources of information on critical activities and also influence performance goals. For example, several recommendations based on strong scientific evidence are in the guidelines for infection prevention in outpatient settings developed by the infection control practices advisory committee of the Centers for Disease Control (CDC, 2016). Compliance with these recommendations should be at or close to 100% with performance goals reflecting this expectation.

Performance in Other Organizations

There are publicly available sources of healthcare performance measure results reflecting the aggregate experience of many organizations. One example is the healthcare associated infections (HAI) data available from the National Healthcare Safety Network (NHSN) of the CDC in Atlanta. Each year all types of healthcare facilities in the United States voluntarily report information about HAIs (often called nosocomial infections) to the NHSN. These data are available from several sources, including on the CMS HospitalCompare website (www.medicare.gov/hospitalcompare). On this site, the general public can see how any hospital in the U.S. performs against national and state benchmarks on a variety of measures, including nosocomial infections. Similar performance data reports for other types of facilities are available on the Medicare website (www.medicare.gov)

The NHSN nosocomial infection data are also available in published articles. An excerpt from a data table in an article on the incidence of all bloodstream infections among persons receiving outpatient dialysis is found in Exhibit 2.11. The statistics for this article came from data submitted by facilities in 2014 to the NHSN dialysis event surveillance program.

Exhibit 2.11. Percentiles of the Distribution of Rates of All Blood Stream Infections by Type of Vascular Access (2014)

Infection Type and Access	Events	Denominator	Percentile				
			10th	25th	50th	75th	90th
All blood stream infections	29,516	4,578,827	0	0.25	0.53	0.91	1.42
Fistula	7587	2,876,871	0	0	0.15	0.39	0.72
Graft	3262	827,821	0	0	0	0.55	1.33
Other	76	15,016	0	0	0	0	0
Central venous catheter	18,591	859,119	0	0.53	1.68	3.223	5.26

Denominator: total number of patient months
Source: Nguyen et al., 2017, p. 1142

At the 50th (median) percentile, 50 percent of outpatient dialysis facilities have lower infection rates than the median rate and 50 percent have higher rates. At the 75th percentile, 75 percent of facilities have lower rates and 25 percent have higher rates. At the 25th percentile, 25 percent of facilities have lower rates and 75 percent have higher rates.

This NHSN data can be used by an outpatient dialysis facility to establish internal performance goals for blood stream infection rates. At a minimum, the performance goal should be set at the median rate reported for all facilities. If this goal is continually achieved or if facility leaders choose to work on reducing blood stream infections, then the performance goal can be changed to reflect the 25th or 10th percentile results. Other sources of publicly available healthcare performance measurement data include:

- Healthcare Cost and Utilization Project sponsored by the Agency for Healthcare Research and Quality (www.ahrq.gov/data/hcup/index.html)
- Leapfrog Group (www.leapfroggroup.org)
- National Healthcare Quality and Disparities Report (www.ahrq.gov/research/findings/nhqrdr/index.html)
- NCQA report cards for health plans, health providers and other healthcare organizations (https://reportcards.ncqa.org)
- Quality Check sponsored by The Joint Commission (www.qualitycheck.org)

Healthcare organizations can also participate in performance measurement projects that provide comparative results exclusively to project participants. For instance, many cardiovascular surgeons provide performance data to the national quality and patient safety databases maintained by the Society of Thoracic Surgeons (www.sts.org). Participants can compare their patient management and outcome results with other hospitals in the areas of adult cardiac, general thoracic and congenital surgery. In addition, information from the STS databases is periodically published in professional journals and textbooks – making the aggregate outcome results publicly available.

When using comparative data to establish performance goals it is important to understand the data definitions and calculations used in creating the rates. Performance results from other organizations are only useful for setting performance goals if you are using the same data definitions and calculation methods to create your performance measure. For instance, investigation of coding error rates by AHIMA revealed considerable variation in how hospitals calculate this performance measure (Wilson, 2008). Some HIM departments calculate coding quality by dividing the total number of records reviewed by the total number of records with coding errors. Some departments calculate coding quality by dividing the total number of codes assigned by the number of inaccurate codes. Also found are variations in the definition of a coding error. A healthcare facility wanting to use coding error rate data from other facilities to set a performance target would need to thoroughly investigate the data definitions and calculation methods used by the other facilities to be sure comparisons are valid.

Summary

Performance measurement is the starting point for quality management activities. Information about performance is used by people in the organization to find out where there may be gaps between expected and actual performance. Measurement information is usually expressed as a discrete number or a statistic, e.g. percentage, average, ratio.

For a comprehensive understanding of performance, healthcare organizations measure four distinct characteristics: structure, process, outcome, and patient experience. Structure measures are used to assess the organization's capacity to provide quality care. Process measures are used to assess how well services adhere to performance expectations. Outcome measures are used to assess the end result of services. Measures of patient experience are used to evaluate consumer perspectives.

Measures are selected for use within healthcare organizations for many different reasons. Some measures are mandated by external regulatory and accreditation groups. Some measures are chosen to evaluate performance issues important to the organization and its customers. Some measures serve both purposes – the measure is required by an external group and it also provides performance information important to the organization.

To be useful for quality management purposes, performance measures must provide valid and reliable information. For this reason, measures must be carefully developed using a systematic process. Measurement construction steps can be time-consuming but are essential to creation of useful measures.

Student Activities

1. Become familiar with the performance measures endorsed by the National Quality Forum (NQF) available through NQF's Quality Positioning System, better known as QPS healthcare performance measures. This resource is available on the NQF website (www.qualityforum.org/Qps/QpsTool.aspx). Use the resources on this site to identify one structure measure, one process measure, one outcome measure, and one patient experience measure that could be used to measure performance in a women's health clinic.
2. Use resources in the NQF's Quality Positioning System to identify one performance measure for each of the six IOM key dimensions of healthcare: effectiveness, efficiency, equity, patient centeredness, safety, and timeliness.
3. When completing the student activities in chapter one, you were asked to describe a personal situation in which you received inferior quality healthcare services. Identify three measures of performance for the setting where you received less-than-satisfactory healthcare. Select measures that would evaluate the particular aspect of care or service that you found to be unsatisfactory.

Website Resources

AHRQ Quality Indicators
https://qualityindicators.ahrq.gov

CAHPS survey tools
www.ahrq.gov/cahps/index.html

Centers for Medicare and Medicaid Services Measures Inventory Tool
https://cmit.cms.gov/CMIT_public/ListMeasures

Centers for Medicare and Medicaid Services Quality of Care Center
www.cms.gov/Center/Special-Topic/Quality-of-Care-Center.html

Critical Access Hospital Measurement and Performance Assessment System
https://cahmpas.flexmonitoring.org/

HealthGrades®
www.healthgrades.com

Healthcare Effectiveness Data and Information Set (HEDIS™)
www.ncqa.org

Healthcare-Associated Infection Network, Data and Statistics, sponsored by the CDC
www.cdc.gov/hai/surveillance/index.html

Healthy People 2020
www.healthypeople.gov

Joint Commission performance measure initiatives
www.jointcommission.org/performance_measurement.aspx

The Commonwealth Fund: "Why Not the Best?"
https://whynotthebest.org

References

Agency for Healthcare Research and Quality (AHRQ). (2018). Home Health Care CAHPS Survey. [Online information; retrieved 5/28/18.] https://homehealthcahps.org
American Health Information Management Association (AHIMA). (2012). Management practices for the release of information. *Journal of AHIMA*, 83(2)
American Osteopathic Association. (2018). *Primary Stroke Center Certification*. [Online information; retrieved 5/28/18.] www.hfap.org/pdf/PSC_QualityReport.pdf.
American Society of Anesthesiologists (ASA). (2012). An updated report by the American Society of Anesthesiologists task force on preanesthesia evaluation. *Anesthesiology, 116(3)*, 522-538.
Association for the Advancement of Wound Care (AAWC). (2010). *Association for the Advancement of Wound Care Pressure Ulcer Guidelines*. Malvern, PA: AAWC.
Centers for Disease Control (CDC). (2016, September). *Guide to Infection Prevention for Outpatient Settings*. [Online information; retrieved 6/5/2018.] www.cdc.gov/infectioncontrol/pdf/outpatient/guide.pdf

Centers for Medicare and Medicaid Services (CMS) (2018a). *Home Health Care CAHPS Survey: Protocols and Guide-lines Manual*. Version 10.0. January. [Online information; retrieved 5/31/18.]
    https://homehealthcahps.org/Survey-and-Protocols/Survey-Materials

_____, (2018b). Quality Measures. June. [Online information; retrieved 6/23/2018.] www.cms.gov/Medicare/Quality-Initiatives-Patient-Assessment-Instruments/QualityMeasures/index.html

_____. (2017). Nursing Home Quality Initiative. [Online information; retrieved 6/23/2018.]
    www.cms.gov/Medicare/Quality-Initiatives-Patient-Assessment-
    Instruments/NursingHomeQualityInits/index.html

_____. (2012). §482.24(c)(2)(viii) Condition of participation: Medical record services. [Online document; retrieved 6/5/2018.] www.law.cornell.edu/cfr/text/42/482.24

Deloitte Development. (2016). *What Matters Most to the Health Care Consumer?* [Online document; retrieved 6/5/2018.] www2.deloitte.com/content/dam/Deloitte/us/Documents/life-sciences-health-care/us-lshc-cx-survey-pov-provider-paper.pdf

Donabedian, A. (1980). *Explorations In Quality Assessment And Monitoring, Vol. 1: The Definitions Of Quality And Approaches In Assessment*. Chicago, IL: Health Administration Press.

Health and Human Services, U.S. Department of (HHS). (2018). Healthy People. [Online information; retrieved 6/23/2018.] www.healthypeople.gov/2020/

Institute of Medicine. (2001). *Crossing the Quality Chasm: A New Health System for the 21st Century*. Washington, D.C.: National Academy Press.

_____. (1990). *Clinical Practice Guidelines: Directions for a New Program*, M.J. Field and K.N. Lohr (Eds.). Washington, DC: National Academy Press.

Joint Commission, The. (2017a). *2018 Comprehensive Accreditation Manual for Hospitals*. Oakbrook Terrace, IL: The Joint Commission.

_____. (2017b). Hospital-Based Inpatient Psychiatric Services. [Online information; retrieved 5/31/18.]
    https://manual.jointcommission.org/releases/TJC2017B2/HospitalBasedInpatientPsychiatricServices.html

_____. (2017c). *2018 Comprehensive Accreditation Manual for Home Care*. Oakbrook Terrace, IL: The Joint Commission.

Marcotte, L., Seidman, J., Trudel, K., Berwick, D., Blumenthal, D., Mostashari, F., & Jain, S. (2012). Achieving meaningful use of health information technology: A guide for physicians to the EHR incentive programs. *Archives of Internal Medicine, 172(*9), 731-736.

National Committee for Quality Assurance (NCQA). (2018a). HEDIS & performance measurement. [Online information; retrieved 6/23/2018.] www.ncqa.org/HEDISQualityMeasurement.aspx

_____. (2018b). *HEDIS Summary Table of Measures, Product Lines and Changes*. Washington, DC: NCQA.

National Quality Forum. (2016). *Measure Evaluation Criteria and Guidance for Evaluating Measures for Endorsement*. [Online information; retrieved 6/5/2018.]
    www.qualityforum.org/Measuring_Performance/Consensus_Development_Process/CSAC_Decision.aspx

Nguyen, D.B., Shugart, A., Lines, C., Shah, A.B., Edwards, J., Pollock, D., Sievert, D., & Patel, P.R. (2017). National Healthcare Safety Network (NHSN) Dialysis Event Surveillance Report for 2014. *CJASN*, 12(7): 1139-1146.

Rosenberger, L.H., Politano, A.D., & Sawyer, R.G. (2011). The surgical care improvement project and prevention of post-operative infection, including surgical site infection. *Surgical Infections*, 12(3): 163-168.

Wilson, D., & Dunn, R. (2008). *Benchmarking to Improve Coding Accuracy and Productivity*. Chicago: American Health Information Management Association.

OBTAINING MEASUREMENT DATA

Reader Objectives

After reading this chapter and reflecting on the contents, you will be able to:
1. Demonstrate an understanding of methods used to collect measurement data.
2. Describe advantages and drawbacks of common measurement data sources.
3. Identify issues to be considered in development of data collection plans.
4. Recognize data sources for e-measures.
5. Describe measurement sampling techniques.

Key Terms

Check sheet: Paper-based, manual data collection instrument; sometimes called a data sheet.

Data capture: Identification and extraction of data from a paper or electronic document.

Data sheet: Form designed to collect data in a simple tabular or column format; sometimes called a check sheet. Specific bits of data (numbers, words, or marks) are entered in spaces on the form.

Data source: Origin of the information you plan to collect.

Electronic clinical quality measures (eCQMS): Data for these measures are obtained exclusively from electronic health records (EHRs) and/or health information technology systems. Also called eMeasures.

Instrument: Specific tool to collect information (check sheet, data sheet, survey, observation checklist).

Sample population: The total size of the group from which measurement samples are to be drawn.

Sampling: Process of selecting a representative part of a population in order to estimate performance, without collecting data for the entire population.

Survey: Data collection tool used to gather information from individuals

Tabular check sheet: A type of check sheet that is used to tally the frequency of events

Data Collection Strategies

At this point in the performance measurement function three steps have been completed: (1) processes to be evaluated have been selected; (2) measures have been constructed to tell you what you want to know; and (3) performance expectations have been established. The next step is to design strategies for gathering the data needed to report measurement results.

Four decisions must be made for each measure:
- Where does the data reside?
- How can it be captured?
- Who is responsible for data capture?
- How often will data be captured?

Answers to these questions are used to design measurement data collection strategies. Careful planning helps ensure accurate, reliable and valid information is captured for measurement purposes.

Locate Data

Be sure all data elements necessary for creating a measure are clearly and objectively stated in the measurement specifications. This should have been done during the measure development steps (see chapter 2). If data needed to create a performance measure are still ill-defined, revisit the definition step before determining where the data reside.

In some situations, a department may already be capturing data elements necessary for every performance measure used within that department. In these situations, all that must be done is confirm the data are reliable and match measurement specifications. It is not uncommon to find that data needed for departmental and medical staff service performance measures must be obtained from more than one location. For instance, to create the hospital performance measure, *Rate of catheter-associated urinary tract infections in ICU patients per 1000 urinary catheter-days*, the following two data elements are needed: (1) Number of urinary catheter-related infections and (2) Number of urinary catheter-days.

The hospital infection control department is most likely already collecting data on the incidence of urinary catheter-related infections. This data can be retrieved from the infection control database. The number of urinary catheter-days may be a harder data element to locate. To capture this data element each day someone has to identify the number of patients in the intensive care unit (ICU) who have a urinary catheter in place. This data element is not a count of patients with catheters – it is a count of the total number of days a urinary catheter was in place for any patient. If it were merely a count of patients who had urinary catheters, the data element might be available in the hospital billing system (for example, the number of patients who were billed for a urinary catheter setup). However, if patients are not charged for urinary catheters on a per-day basis the total number of urinary catheter-days cannot be gathered from the billing database.

Automated Data Sources

A good first step in locating data for measures is to review the organization's information management plan if one is available. Because of the growing concern about information security liabilities, many facilities have a document that includes a list of existing automated systems and types of data included in these systems. Some computerized systems support enterprise-wide activities such as financial applications while others, such as a radiology management system, support department-specific functions while interfacing with network systems. The information management plan may also list non-network applications and specialized databases maintained within single departments such as a cancer registry data system.

A simplified conceptual framework of a hospital clinical information system is shown in Exhibit 3.1. Each box represents types of information that are often available electronically. Use the measure data specifications developed during the design phase to determine where information might be found in computerized systems.

Exhibit 3.1. Conceptual Framework of Hospital Clinical Information System

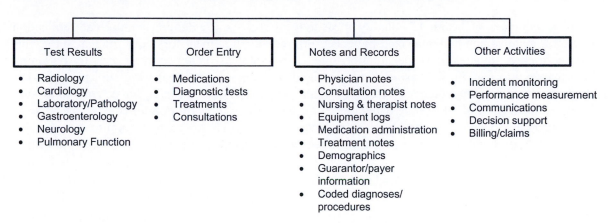

An often-overlooked electronic source of measurement data is automated patient care equipment. Many physiological monitor alarms used to alert nurses to patient problems also store information useful for measurement purposes. One rehabilitation unit regularly measures how quickly nurses respond to patients' low oxygen saturation alarms. The automated monitoring system stores data on the time an alarm sounded and when it was turned off at the bedside by a nurse checking the patient's status. It is a simple matter to capture this data and use it for reporting alarm response times.

Before using information in any electronic database talk with people who input the data to be sure the information can be used to accurately measure the factor or parameter you want to evaluate. Data validity is especially problematic when using a secondary data source. For example, the organization's billing database was not originally designed to be used as a source of information for healthcare process and outcome measures. Data definitions for information in the billing database may be somewhat different than what is needed to construct a performance measure. It is important to confirm the data definitions of electronic data elements match the performance measure data specifications. Otherwise, what appears to be a reliable electronic data source could produce inaccurate measurement results.

Using automated data sources for performance measurement purposes is of interest to national groups and federal regulators. There is an effort to transform all measurement data reported to external groups into electronic clinical quality measures (eCQMS), often simply referred to as "eMeasures." Data for these measures are obtained exclusively from electronic health records (EHRs) and/or health information technology systems (CMS, 2018). The National Quality Forum created a publicly available web-based tool for measure developers to create eMeasures. This tool, the Measure Authoring Tool (MAT), now operates under the direction of the CMS (www.emeasuretool.cms.gov). An eMeasure is found in Exhibit 3.2. All data for the numerator and denominator can very likely be captured from an automated source.

Exhibit 3.2. eMeasure and Data Sources

eMeasure: Percentage of patients with diabetes who have an adequate level of control for hyperlipidemia	
Numerator: Number of patients with LDL level <130 mg/dL	**Electronic data sources:** Laboratory results database; electronic health records
Denominator: Patients with diagnosis of diabetes active over a specified time period	**Electronic data sources:** Billing claims database; electronic health records

Efforts to identify eCQMS or eMeasures for national healthcare performance measurement activities are rapidly evolving. For current information on these efforts see the CMS Electronic Clinical Quality Improvement Resource Center (https://ecqi.healthit.gov/ecqms).

Non-Automated Data Sources

Despite continued adoption of health IT, quality measurement still requires some manual data collection from paper sources such as non-computerized patient health records, treatment logbooks, patient survey instruments, and committee minutes. In some situations only a non-automated data source is best for obtaining accurate performance information. For instance, many healthcare facilities are measuring clinical staff compliance with proper hand hygiene practices by using observers to watch people caring for patients to be sure hands are being cleaned. Some facilities are using electronic wireless systems to monitor room entry and exit of healthcare workers and their use of hand hygiene product dispensers. These systems can provide individual and unit-based data on hand hygiene compliance however there remain questions about the practicality, accuracy, and cost of such systems.

Data validity can also be problematic when non-automated data sources are used. Always check with the people documenting in the paper sources to be sure their understanding of data definitions fit with the measurement data specifications

Capture Data

If the data source is electronic, information can be captured using data transfer and query techniques. Those needing data for measurement purposes should work out how best to get electronic information by communicating with individuals responsible for managing the automated system. When an organization's electronic systems are standalone or do not integrate easily a process for capturing data from these different sources is needed. In some instances, it may be possible to 'push' or 'pull' required data elements from one system to another. Assistance from the HIM and IT departments is often needed to create interfaces and data exchanges. If all else fails, paper reports of the required data can be produced and manually shared with those needing the information.

While capturing performance measurement data from electronic systems can be less expensive than manual data gathering, it is not without cost. One Colorado measurement project involved gathering data about management of diabetic patients from automated clinic information systems. The estimated per-practice implementation cost for data collection and reporting was about $6.23 per diabetic patient per month with an additional $3.83 per diabetic patient per month required the first year for data system maintenance (West et al., 2012). A 2015 survey of quality measure data collection and reporting in medical practices found that primary care physicians spend 3.9 hours per week on these activities, followed by physicians in multispecialty practices (3.0 hours per week), cardiologists (1.7 hours per week), and orthopedists (1.1 hours per week). All the time practices spend on these activities adds up to a considerable expense, with an average cost of $40,069 per physician per year, according to the survey results (Casalino et al., 2016). In addition to the cost of collecting and reporting data from electronic systems, measuring quality using EHR data requires substantial validation to ensure data accuracy (Benin et al., 2011).

Although measurement data may often be found in electronic databases, it is likely manual data capture will also be necessary. Manual data collection frequently involves the use of checksheets, data sheets, and surveys. These can be created on paper or created as electronic forms that are basically computerized versions of the paper forms. Electronic forms can often be filled out faster and programming associated with them can automatically format, calculate, look up, and validate information for the user. The three types of forms discussed below can be created on paper or in an electronic format.

Check sheets are structured forms enabling people to systematically capture and organize data about performance of a specific process. They are constructed in whatever shape, size, and layout is appropriate for the data collection task at hand.

A tabular check sheet, also known as a tally sheet, is easy to use when people simply want to count how often something happens or record a measurement. Depending on the type of data required, the data collector simply makes a mark in a column to indicate the presence of a characteristic or enters a numeric measurement such as time (for example, seconds, minutes, hours). Simple tabular format check sheets are best to use when people are asked to capture data at the same time they are performing the work being measured. Collection forms should be simple to complete and include a minimum number of data elements because gathering data can be an added burden for staff.

In Exhibit 3.3 is a tabular check sheet used by business office staff in a primary care clinic to gather data about the causes of billing and accounts receivable (A/R) errors. Each time an error is discovered a tally mark (卅), sometimes called a hash mark, is added to the check sheet to indicate where the error occurred and why. At the end of each month the check sheet is forwarded to the office manager who tallies the results and using the information to report various measures including, *Percentage of bills rejected due to wrong account errors*.

Exhibit 3.3. Tabular Format Check Sheet

Month: *June*	
Billing and Accounts Receivable (A/R) Errors	**Tally Marks**
Billing Errors	
Wrong Account	‖‖
Wrong Amount	‖‖
A/R Errors	
Wrong Account	卅
Wrong Amount	卅‖‖

Data sheets are forms designed to manually gather data in a simple tabular or column format. Specific bits of data (numbers, words, or marks) are entered in spaces on the paper or electronic form. Some data sheets contain lots of detailed information requiring a *Yes*, *No*, or *Not Applicable* response. Sometimes the data element definitions and collection rules are included on the form to help ensure consistency among data gatherers. Data sheets can be a labor-intensive collection tool because data gatherers often must make several decisions about different aspects of patient care.

Check sheets and data sheets do not have standard formats. Instead, each tool is uniquely tailored to capture information needed for measuring a particular aspect of performance. A well-designed data collection tool makes data capture more efficient. Below are guidelines for developing easy-to-use paper-based and electronic data collection tools.

- Involve healthcare workers who will be using the data collection tool in its design.
- Organize the form so data are recorded in the same sequence as the process flows to reduce the chance data will be recorded in the wrong place or not recorded at all.
- Make sure everything on the form is well defined and easily understood by everyone capturing data.
- Include brief instructions on the back of the paper form or create 'pop-up' or 'help' instructions if the form is computerized.
- Create a form that can be completed with the least amount of effort using check marks, tally marks, numbers, letters or single keyboard or mouse clicks.
- Designate a place on the form to record the date and time data were collected as these parameters are often needed when measurement results are reported.
- Provide a place to enter the name of the individual collecting the data.
- Allow sufficient space for people to record narrative comments or additional details for unusual events.

In Exhibit 3.4 is a data sheet used to record what is being observed during patient care delivery. Health facility observers use this data sheet to document what they discover about hand hygiene as they watch physicians and frontline staff care for patients. The completed data sheets are sent to the infection control department where the results are input into a computer spreadsheet for monthly reporting of findings by discipline and unit.

Exhibit 3.4. Data Sheet for Gathering Hand Hygiene Compliance Data

Month: _____	Shift: _____
Unit: _____	Name of Observer: _____

Instructions: Circle "Yes" for compliance to hand hygiene practice or "No" for non-compliance. Denote the discipline observed in the area below the Yes/No response by using the key below.

Routine hand washing should be done for at least 15 seconds using friction, soap, and running water. The use of antiseptic alcohol hand sanitizer is acceptable in the place of hand washing as long as the hands are not visibly soiled with dirt or organic material. Per CDC guidelines artificial nails should not be worn by direct patient care staff and natural nails should be $\leq$ ¼ inch over the end of the finger.

Key

D=Doctor	RT=Respiratory Therapy	ES=Environmental Services	PT=Physical/Occupational/Therapy
N=Nursing	L=Lab	I=Imaging/Radiology	O=Other, please specify

Hands were washed or cleansed:	1	2	3	4	5
Before, between, **OR** after patient care or procedures (as required by policy) Key_____	YES / NO Key_____	YES / NO Key_____	YES / NO Key_____	YES / NO Key_____	YES / NO Key_____
Finger nail observations:	1	2	3	4	5
Are artificial nails being worn? Is nail length acceptable per policy?	YES / NO YES / NO	YES / NO YES / NO	YES / NO YES / NO	YES / NO YES / NO	YES / NO YES / NO

Surveys (also called questionnaires) are another commonly used collection instrument. Surveys can be paper-based or electronic. The purpose of the survey shapes its design and method of dissemination. To create a survey instrument it is best to involve the different stakeholders and audiences to be effected by the survey. This helps ensure greater buy-in and credibility as well as improve the survey design. A customer satisfaction survey used in a maternal and child health clinic to gather data on specific aspects of clinical performance is shown in Exhibit 3.5.

Exhibit 3.5. Maternal and Child Care Clinic Customer Satisfaction Survey

How often do the following things happen to you at Sunnyside Health Care Center?

	Always	Usually	Sometimes	Never
The health care providers listen to me	____	____	____	____
I understand what the health care providers tell me	____	____	____	____
The health care providers answer all my questions	____	____	____	____
I like talking with the social service workers	____	____	____	____
I feel comfortable and welcome at the Center	____	____	____	____
I wait more than 30 minutes for a health care provider to see me	____	____	____	____
I think the Center's services cost too much	____	____	____	____
When I call the Center, the line is busy	____	____	____	____
I can get an appointment the same day I call	____	____	____	____
I can't get an appointment when I have a day off from work	____	____	____	____
I have to wait more than one week for an appointment	____	____	____	____
I am satisfied with the medical care I receive at the Center	____	____	____	____
I tell my friends to go to Sunnyside Health Care Center	____	____	____	____

Be sure survey instruments yield actionable data. Too often survey data only provide general ratings and results cannot be acted on. For instance, it is not particularly useful to know 80% of patients feel the care provided in a clinic is very good to excellent. For the data to be useful, survey participants should respond to questions about specific aspects of service such as the questions shown in Exhibit 3.5.

Survey instruments can be used to gather patient outcome data. These surveys are completed by practitioners, institutions, or patients themselves. Keep surveys as simple as possible to maximize return rates. It is also important to use language the intended recipient will understand. For instance, most patients who have undergone a hip replacement will not be able to answer precise questions about the amount of flexion in their hip six weeks postoperatively. However, patients can usually report how far they are able to walk without experiencing hip pain. Illustrated in Exhibit 3.6 is a survey tool used by an orthopedic clinic to gather outcome data from patients who are being seen for shoulder problems. Patients are asked to complete the survey prior to the start of therapy and then again at regular intervals during the course of treatment to evaluate their progress.

Exhibit 3.6. Shoulder Pain Assessment Survey

	Yes	No
1. Is your shoulder comfortable with your arm at rest by your side?	[ ]	[ ]
2. Does your shoulder allow you to sleep comfortably?	[ ]	[ ]
3. Can you reach the small of your back to tuck in your shirt with your hand?	[ ]	[ ]
4. Can you place your hand behind your head with the elbow straight out to the side?	[ ]	[ ]
5. Can you place a coin on a shelf at the level of your shoulder without bending your elbow?	[ ]	[ ]
6. Can you lift one pound (a full pint container) to the level of your shoulder without bending your elbow?	[ ]	[ ]
7. Can you lift eight pounds (a full gallon container) to the level of your shoulder without bending your elbow?	[ ]	[ ]
8. Can you carry twenty pounds at your side with the affected extremity?	[ ]	[ ]
9. Do you think you can toss a softball under-hand twenty yards with the affected extremity?	[ ]	[ ]
10. Do you think you can toss a softball over-hand twenty yards with the affected extremity?	[ ]	[ ]
11. Can you wash the back of your opposite shoulder with the affected extremity?	[ ]	[ ]
12. Would your shoulder allow you to work full-time at your regular job?	[ ]	[ ]

Web-based technologies have greatly simplified the process of data collection and analysis. These online survey instruments (e.g., SurveyMonkey, TypeForm, Google Forms) are attractive modalities for gathering customer feedback. However, it is important to understand what tools the consumers being surveyed are most receptive to and which will produce the highest response rates and most reliable information.

Today, queries of electronic administrative and clinical databases are replacing manual data collection. However, even organizations with advanced integrated electronic information systems find it challenging to create data warehouses with flexible reporting capabilities that can keep up with ever-changing performance measurement requirements. Manual data gathering will continue to be used for some time.

Costs associated with manual data gathering are higher than collection costs associated with electronic database queries. Even when data can be captured from automated information systems, the cost of linking different data sets, cleaning the data, and doing the calculations is still quite high.

Identify Responsible People

After locating data necessary for creating performance measures, the people responsible for gathering the information are identified. If the data are in an existing electronic system, this step involves determining who will extract information from the database. Gathering electronic data may simply require the information be regularly transferred into another database. In other situations, periodic database queries will need to be done and paper reports produced and shared.

When data are not available electronically or not easily gathered from existing paper-based information sources, the data capture process must be carefully mapped out. Ideally, data can be collected at or near completion of the critical activity being evaluated. For example, suppose a home health agency wants to measure the completeness of patient authorization and consent for treatment forms. These forms are filled out during the nurse's first patient visit. After considering the steps of this process it is determined the best place to gather data for this performance measure is in the HIM department. While reviewing paperwork for new patients, the HIM clerk tallies the number of incomplete and unsigned forms. At the end of each month, the data are given to the nursing director who uses the data to report the measure, *Percent of new patients each month with incomplete or unsigned authorization and consent for treatment forms following first home visit.* The director obtains the number of new patients from the agency electronic billing database.

Determine Frequency and Population Size

There are two distinct issues to be considered when discussing how often data will be gathered: frequency of reporting and size of the measurement population. Performance results are often reported monthly or quarterly. However, some measures are used to observe real-time trends in a process with results reported daily or weekly. Often the measure specification indicates the reporting time frame. For example, this measure would be reported monthly: *Percent of new patients each month with incomplete or unsigned authorization and consent for treatment forms following first home visit.*

Another consideration regarding how often data are gathered is the size of the population to be measured. For the home health agency measure described above, all new patients are evaluated. Data are collected continuously for 100% of the measurement population.

In some situations it is not necessary to gather data continuously for 100% of the measurement population. For example, suppose you want to measure how long clinic patients wait to be seen by a health professional. Gathering wait time data on every patient would be time-consuming and probably not necessary. Wait time data could be gathered for just a sample of clinic patients.

Sampling is a process of selecting a representative part of a population to estimate performance without collecting data for the entire population. The population of interest may be patients, incidents, tasks, forms – any of which may be relevant to an aspect of performance. Common methods for selecting a population sample are listed below.

- Simple random sampling. Every patient or event in the process has an equal chance of being sampled. For example, all clinic patients have an equal chance of being selected for wait time measurement.
- Stratified sampling. Groups, or strata, are identified and a random sample selected from each group. For example, clinic wait time data are collected for a random sample of pediatric patients and a random sample of geriatric patients at different times throughout the week.
- Systematic sampling. Events are periodically measured. For example, wait time data are gathered for every tenth clinic patient.
- Cluster sampling. A typical group is selected and a random sample is taken from that group. For example, a random sample of clinic patients seen on Tuesday is chosen for measurement of wait times.

When measurement results are being reported to an external group (for example, measures required by CMS or the Joint Commission) the population and allowable sampling techniques are documented in the measurement specifications. These data collection requirements must be consistently applied. When there is no externally defined sampling requirement for a measure and you would like to use sampling then be sure to get a statistically valid sample. Only when the sample data truly represent the whole population can sample-based performance measure data be meaningful and useful. The sampling guidelines in Exhibit 3.7 are suggested because of their statistical significance and relative simplicity in application.

Exhibit 3.7. Sampling Guidelines

Population Size	Sample Size
30 or less	Entire population
31-100	30
101-500	50
More than 501	70

To apply these sampling guidelines, first determine the period of time being covered by the sampling, e.g. one week, one month, one quarter, etc. Next identify the number in the population for that period, e.g. number of admissions per week, month, quarter, etc. Select your sample size based on that population. See the two examples below.

Example 1
Period of time: 1 month
Number of admissions per month: Approximately 290
Sample size: 50 cases

Example 2
Period of time: 1 week
Number of admissions per week: 72
Sample size: 30 cases

Data Collection Plan

Once questions relevant to data collection have been answered the decisions should be documented. A well-defined data collection plan is essential because it standardizes the various processes required to capture all necessary data for each measure. When the roles and responsibilities of data gatherers and time frames for collecting data are clear, it decreases the risk of disruption during staff transitions. Documenting the data collection methodology for each measure helps ensure you have reliable and reproducible data over time.

When measuring performance requires data from various systems, a process for capturing data from these different sources needs to be created. Documenting the procedures for compiling the data eliminates re-learning the process next month. In Exhibit 3.8 is an excerpt from a data planning tool used to document data collection plans for measures used to evaluate performance in the HIM department.

Exhibit 3.8. Data Collection Plan for HIM Department Measures (excerpt only)

Measure	Measure Specifications	Data Source	Collection Frequency	Responsible Person
Percent of inpatient records accurately coded	**Numerator**: Number of accurately coded records	Coding audit form	Monthly random sample of 20% of records	Coding supervisor
	Denominator: Number of inpatient records reviewed	Inpatient records that have been coded		
Average time from patient request for health records to provision of requested copies	**Numerator**: Total time (hours) to respond to all requests	Electronic release of information log	Monthly. All requests measured.	Release of information supervisor
	Denominator: Total number of patient requests for health records	Electronic release of information log		

Data sources and methods of data capture can change over time requiring periodic evaluation of the data collection plans. For instance, with greater use of EHRs more data will be available electronically. In addition to the structured data in EHRs, new methods such as natural language processing can derive meaning from unstructured data, permitting capture of clinical information found in clinical notes (Shah, Steyerberg, & Kent, 2018). Yet despite these technological advances and innovations, some manual capture of data may continue to be necessary.

Summary

When planning the performance measurement data collection strategy, evaluate existing data sources to determine where information needed to create each measure can be found. First determine if the necessary data are available in existing information systems – automated or paper-based. If the data are available, then check to be sure the data definitions in those systems are consistent with what is needed to create the measure. Although it may seem as if all possible data elements are now being gathered somewhere in an organization, there are times when data needed to calculate a particularly important measure are not readily available. In these situations new ways of capturing the data must be identified.

The accuracy and completeness of information in the data source determine the level of confidence in measurement results. Performance measurement results are only useful if the data collection yields valid information. Assess the reliability and effectiveness of the data gathering process before finalizing the collection plan. It may be necessary to conduct periodic audits of the collected data to confirm its accuracy.

Every data source has advantages and drawbacks. For instance, electronic patient databases in pharmacies and health insurance companies may lack pertinent clinical details needed for process and outcome measures. Billing databases in provider organizations have been designed primarily for financial and administrative uses and often lack clinical information needed to measure quality (Tang et al., 2007). Patient records, both paper-based and electronic, may also lack the data needed to measure performance. As an example, clinic records almost always contain names of new medications prescribed by the physician yet documentation indicating patients were counseled about medication side effects is often missing. If the clinic is measuring how often counseling occurs an alternative data source – such as patient surveys – would be required. Surveys, however, are time-consuming activities and they do not always produce a complete set of data for performance measurement. No data source is perfect; there are always trade-offs to consider.

Student Activities

1. Select three Joint Commission accountability (core) measures from different categories. For each measure identify the data sources for the numerator and denominator. The measures and measurement specifications are available on the Joint Commission website (www.jointcommission.org)
2. Review the Consumer Assessment of Healthcare Providers and Systems (CAHPS®) Home Health Care Survey used to measure the experiences of people receiving home health care from Medicare-certified home health agencies. Discuss how the survey is administered, the sample size requirements, and extent to which survey results will provide actionable information. Current CAHPS® survey information is available at: https://homehealthcahps.org/

Website Resources

CMS Electronic Clinical Quality Improvement Resource Center: eCQMS.
https://ecqi.healthit.gov/ecqms

Data Governance Handbook: Implementing Data Management Practices in Health Centers (2017)
Center for Care Innovations, Oakland, CA
www.careinnovations.org/wp-content/uploads/2017/11/CCI-Data-Governance-Handbook.pdf

Journal of the American Medical Informatics Association (many open access articles)
https://academic.oup.com/jamia

Managing a Data Dictionary (2016), Practice Brief of the American Health Information Management Association (HIM Body of Knowledge available only to members)
www.ahima.org

Measure Authoring Tool (MAT) for creating electronic clinical quality measures
www.emeasuretool.cms.gov/

Sample Size Calculator
www.surveysystem.com/sscalc.htm

Specifications Manual for Joint Commission National Quality Measures
www.jointcommission.org/specifications_manual_joint_commission_national_quality_core_measures.aspx

SurveyMonkey
www.surveymonkey.com

TypeForm
www.typeform.com

References

Benin, A., Fenick, A., Herrin, J., Vitkauskas, G., Chen, J., & Brandt, C. (2011). How good are the data? Feasible approach to validation of metrics of quality derived from an outpatient electronic health record. *American Journal of Medical Quality, 26(*6), 441–51.

Casalino, L.P. et al. (2016). US physician practices spend more than $15.4 billion annually to report quality measures. *Health Affairs, 35(*3), 401-406.

Centers for Medicare and Medicaid Services (CMS). (2018). Electronic Clinical Quality Improvement Resource Center: eCQMS. [Online document; retrieved 6/23/2018.] https://ecqi.healthit.gov/ecqms

Shah, N.D., Steyerberg, E.W. & Kent, D.M. (2018). Big data and predictive analytics: Recalibrating expectations. *Journal of the American Medical Association, 320(*1), 27-28.

Tang, P., Ralson, M., Arrigotti, M., Qureshi, L., & Graham, J. (2007). Comparison of methodologies for calculating quality measures based on administrative data versus clinical data from an electronic health record system: implications for performance measures. *Journal of the American Medical Informatics Association, 14(*1), 10-15.

West, D., Radcliff, T., Brown, T., Cote, M., Smith, P., & Dickinson, W. (2012). Costs associated with data collection and reporting for diabetes quality improvement in primary care practices: A report from SNOCAP-USA. *Journal of the American Board of Family Medicine, 25(*3), 275-282.

EVALUATING PERFORMANCE

Reader Objectives

After reading this chapter and reflecting on the contents, you will be able to:

1. Demonstrate an understanding of the role of evaluation in quality management activities.
2. Compare and contrast different formats for displaying measurement data.
3. Apply methods for interpreting healthcare performance measurement data.
4. Explain the role of comparative performance data in performance evaluation.
5. Recognize performance results warranting further investigation.

Key Terms

Bar graph: Graphical representation of data showing the relative size of different categories of a variable with each variable represented by a bar, usually with a gap between the bars.

Benchmarking: Structured process for comparing an organization's own performance and work practices to those of other comparable organizations judged to be the best for the purpose of learning how to create better performance.

Box plot: Graphical representation of data showing the lowest value, highest value, median value in a data set and the size of the first and third quartile.

Common cause variation: Instability in performance representing random variation inherent in the process being measured.

Control chart: Line graph that includes statistically calculated control limits.

Control limits: Statistically calculated limits on a control chart used as criteria for signaling the need for action.

Dashboard: The metaphor of an automobile dashboard is used to describe a set of performance measures displayed in a concise manner that allows for easy interpretation.

Histogram: Graphical representation of data showing the center, dispersion, and shape of the distribution of a data set.

Horizontal axis: The x-axis on a graph.

In-control process: Processes in which the performance measure(s) being evaluated are in a state of statistical control; performance variations are attributed to a constant system of chance causes.

Line graph: Graphical representation of a time ordered sequence of data with a centerline drawn horizontally through the chart.

Lower control limit: The lower line on a control chart below which random variation is not expected; mathematically represented by the average minus one, two, or three standard deviations.

Out-of-control process: Processes in which the performance measure(s) being evaluated are not in a state of statistical control; performance variations cannot be attributed to a constant system of chance causes.

Performance trend: Pattern of gradual change in performance or an average or general tendency of performance data to move in a certain direction over time.

Performance variation: Fluctuations in performance results.

Pie chart: Graphical representation of data showing each unit of data represented as a pie-shaped piece of a circle.

Radar chart: Graphical representation used to display the difference between actual and expected performance for several measures in a defined time period; sometimes called a spider diagram.

Sigma: A statistical term for a measure denoting how much a process varies from perfection.

Special cause variation: Instability in performance results that would not be predicted by chance alone.

Standard deviation: A measure of the dispersion of a collection of values.

Statistical process control: Application of statistical techniques to control performance of a process.

Tabular report: Numeric performance data organized in a multi-column, multi-row format.

Tampering: Occurs when something is done in reaction to a particular performance result without knowing whether it is due to natural variation in performance or something out of the ordinary.

Time-series data: Quantities representing performance measurement results over a calendar period such as a week, month, quarter, or year; the same measurements are recorded on a regular basis.

Upper control limit: The upper line on a control chart above which random variation is not expected; mathematically represented by the average plus one, two, or three standard deviations.

Vertical axis: The y-axis on a graph.

Performance Evaluation

Performance evaluation is an important quality management activity. The purpose is to evaluate measurement results, as illustrated in Exhibit 4.1. Collected data are processed and synthesized so people can make informed decisions about what is happening, why performance might vary from expectations, and what corrective action might be required. Put another way, the purpose of evaluation is insight. Measures selected by healthcare organizations provide people with a meaningful performance profile of the department or service to which the measures apply.

Exhibit 4.1. Assessment – A Quality Management Evaluation Activity

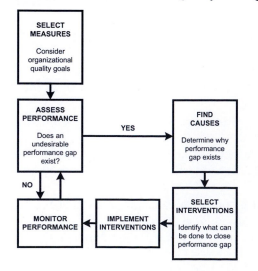

Performance measurement data are used to evaluate success in meeting established goals and assist in identifying areas needing attention. Before data can be used for quality management purposes, it must be analyzed and interpreted. Analysis is problematic or wrong conclusions reached if data are inadequately summarized or poorly displayed. The performance evaluation activity involves two steps:

- Organize and present data
- Evaluate results

Organize and Present Data

This step starts with confirming the accuracy and reliability of the raw data you want to organize and report. Before data gathering there were efforts made to assure quality of the data. Effectiveness of these efforts is checked at this step. Ask yourself the questions below:

- Have all cases that were to be included in the study population been identified and reviewed?
- If data were gathered manually, have all required data fields on the data collection tool been completed?
- If data were gathered manually, did the data gatherers follow the explicit data collection instructions?
- If data were obtained from electronic data systems, did edit/validation checks confirm accuracy of the input?
- If data were obtained from electronic data systems, did edit/validation checks confirm accuracy of the output?

It should be possible to answer *yes* to each question. Any *no* answers must be addressed before proceeding. It is important to purge the raw information of inaccuracies before people evaluate the measurement results.

After correctness of the raw data is verified it is often necessary to organize the information for reporting purpose. The data can be put into a data file (sometimes called a data set or, if electronic, a database). A data file organizes the information like a spreadsheet. Each column represents a different variable and each line represents a different case. A number in a data set represents the value of a particular variable for a particular case. The data file is built by copying information from the manual data collection tool onto a paper template or into an electronic database using one line per case. It may be necessary to synthesize data from different sources into the data file – for instance, download some information from electronic data systems and obtain some from manual data collection instruments.

Once data are organized into a data file (whether on paper or in an electronic file) it is much easier to view relationships between different variables. In Exhibit 4.2 is a portion of the data file from a study of pain management for patients who have undergone surgery. The variables collected during the study are listed across the top. The results for each case are added, one line per case. You may choose to input the case data in no particular order if entering into an electronic spreadsheet or database where sorting is easily accomplished. If building a manual data file the information can be arranged by case number or the answer to a specific variable (for example, level of reported pain).

Exhibit 4.2. Excerpt of Data File from Pain Management Study

Case No.	Patient taught relaxation techniques?	Total mg of Demerol (1st 24 hours postop)	Total mg of Morphine (1st 24 hours postop)	Level of pain reported by patient at 24 hours postop (0= no pain; 10= worst pain)
03-75-32	Y	400		0
15-38-81	Y		40	1
43-51-09	Y	500		1
31-00-65	Y		30	2
01-45-87	Y		60	1
42-76-32	N	700		3
21-44-91	N		55	3
19-55-17	N		85	5
45-61-39	N	650		2

Data files should facilitate ease of entry, storage, editing, and preparation of results for analysis. Electronic data files (statistical, spreadsheet or database program) are best for this purpose. When automated, the data file can be easily queried and sorted, can interface with other electronic information systems, and can be made flexible enough to respond to data field modifications.

The next step is deciding how you are going to present or display the measurement information. It is beneficial to understand some key issues when deciding on how to report measurement results.

- Who are the audience for the data?
- What are the intended uses of the data?
- Will the data be used to support decisions and take actions or is it just for monitoring performance?
- What basic message do you want to communicate?
- What is the presentation format (written report, oral, visual presentation)?
- What is the underlying nature of the data and any assumptions?

The data should be grouped in a way that makes it easier to draw conclusions. This grouping or summarizing can take many forms, the most common being data tables and graphs. Sometimes a single data grouping will suffice for the purposes of decision-making. In complex situations, and especially when larger amounts of data must be dealt with, multiple groupings are necessary to create a clear picture of performance.

Tabular Reports

To create a tabular report (sometimes called a data table) the raw data are translated into performance rates so people can monitor trends. Illustrated in Exhibit 4.3 is an example of a tabular report showing patient satisfaction trends. For each quarter, the percent of patients reporting being 'very satisfied' with items on the ambulatory surgery center survey is displayed in addition to the 12-month average.

Exhibit 4.3. Tabular Report of Ambulatory Surgery Patient Satisfaction Information

	Percent of Patients Reportedly 'Very Satisfied'				
	1st Qtr	2nd Qtr	3rd Qtr	4th Qtr	12 Month Avg
Number of survey respondents	185	127	141	157	610
Information given to you prior to surgery	89%	90%	91%	88%	90%
Information given to family prior to surgery	86%	89%	89%	85%	87%
Information given your family after your surgery	88%	88%	90%	85%	87%
Explanation given for any delays	82%	85%	84%	82%	83%
How well staff kept your friends/ family informed	85%	84%	90%	83%	86%

In Exhibit 4.4 is an excerpt from a performance measurement report prepared for an outpatient wound care clinic. The report combines tabular reports and narrative information. The performance objectives are clearly defined and the measurement results reported together with relevant comments.

Exhibit 4.4. Tabular and Narrative Wound Care Clinic Performance Measurement Report (excerpt)

Quarterly Performance Measurement Report: Wound Care Clinic

This quarter: 10/1 through 12/31   **Last quarter:** 7/1 through 9/30

Overall: Year-to-date and last year's average

Important Process: Provision of care that satisfies patient's expectations.

Goal: 100 percent of patients have an overall satisfaction score rating of 8 (out of possible score of 10).

Patient Satisfaction Results (0-10 scale. 10 = Extremely Satisfied.)

	Average Score for All Patients	Met Goal	Average score for Medicaid patients
This Quarter	7.9	No	7.0
Last Quarter	7.5	No	6.8
Overall	7.6	No	7.1

Comments: We are not reaching our patient satisfaction goal. This can be a delicate balancing act, particularly with regard to the Medicaid population. In the last 3-4 months, we have been using a Treatment Agreement form that is reviewed in the first session or two to facilitate a friendly, open discussion of treatment goals and procedures. This can serve as a vehicle to either solidify a treatment alliance or, at minimum, clarify in a friendly way that we cannot provide what the patient wants at the current time.

Dashboards are special types of tabular reports that use symbols and/or colors to draw people's attention to performance concerns. In Exhibit 4.5 is an excerpt from dashboard style format used to report organization-wide quality measurement results to a hospital governing board and senior leaders. Stars and colors are used to signify the hospital's actual performance. A key to understanding the meaning of the number of stars used to report results is provided at the bottom of the report. The actual report is printed in color with the stars reported in different colors. Not only can people see how well the organization is doing by counting the stars they can also judge results by the color-coding.

Exhibit 4.5. Dashboard Tabular Report of Quality Measures

Quality Measures	Actual Year-to-Date Performance	Performance Goal
Infection Control		
Hospital-wide infection rate	✶ ✶ ✶ ✶	✶ ✶ ✶ ✶
Surgical site infection rate	✶ ✶ ✶ ✶	✶ ✶ ✶ ✶ ✶
Inpatient Mortality Rate	✶ ✶ ✶ ✶	✶ ✶ ✶ ✶ ✶
Performance Measurement Sets		
Heart failure care	✶ ✶ ✶	✶ ✶ ✶ ✶
Heart attack care	✶ ✶ ✶ ✶	✶ ✶ ✶ ✶ ✶
Pneumonia care	✶ ✶ ✶	✶ ✶ ✶ ✶
Surgical care	✶ ✶	✶ ✶ ✶ ✶
Pregnancy care	✶ ✶ ✶ ✶	✶ ✶ ✶ ✶ ✶
Patient Incidents		
Falls	✶ ✶ ✶	✶ ✶ ✶ ✶
Medication Errors	✶	✶ ✶ ✶ ✶

Key   Exceptional = ✶✶✶✶✶ (Blue)   Above Normal = ✶✶✶✶ (Blue)   Normal = ✶✶✶ (Yellow)

Below Normal = ✶✶ (Red)   Marginal = ✶ (Red)

Creating a performance dashboard that relies on symbols and color to denote performance results requires some behind-the-scenes decisions. People must decide on numeric levels that equate to the performance ratings. For example, what is an 'Exceptional' infection rate versus a rate in the 'Normal' category? These decisions must be made for each measure with input from all stakeholders and the decisions must be revisited when performance expectations are revised.

Graphic Representations

There are many ways to communicate performance information through graphical means and the same set of measurement data can often be displayed in different ways. The hard part is determining the best graph to emphasize the point you want to make and also accurately tell the story in the data. In the next section are common graphic displays together with explanations of how to create the graph and when to use it.

Bar Graph (also known as a bar chart)

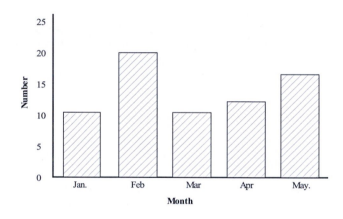

Development Steps:
1. Draw an x-axis and y-axis. The x-axis (horizontal) shows the time periods or items you are comparing. The y-axis (vertical) shows the quantities associated with each of the items on the x-axis. Label the x-axis and y-axis.
2. Establish a scale for the y-axis. The scale should start with zero and go at least as high as the largest quantity you'll be showing. The rest of the scale should be divided into equal increments.
3. Set the x-axis scale. This requires nothing more than showing each of the items you are comparing. Allow for a little space between the items if you do not want the bars to be touching one another.
4. Show the quantities associated with each item by drawing a bar from the zero on the x-axis to the quantity associated with the item on the y-axis.

When to Use: To show performance results from different time periods or different sites (e.g. results from different providers). If several time periods or sites will be shown, it's better to use a line graph.

Box Plot (also known as a box-and-whisker diagram)

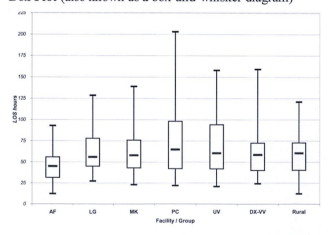

Development Steps:
1. Collect the data and arrange it into an ordered set from lowest value to highest.
2. Calculate the depth of the median, the depth of the first quartile, the depth of the third quartile, the interquartile range, the upper adjacent limit and the lower adjacent limit.
3. Draw and label the axes of the graph. The scale of the vertical axis must be large enough to encompass the greatest value of the data sets. The horizontal axis must be large enough to encompass the number of box plots to be drawn.
4. Construct the boxes, insert median points, and attach upper and lower adjacent limits. Identify outliers (values outside the upper and lower adjacent limits) with asterisks.

When to Use: To show the data sets lowest value, highest value, median value, and the size of the first and third quartile. Useful for analyzing small performance data sets that do not lend themselves easily to histograms. Can be used to show changes in variation of the same variable over different time periods.

Histogram

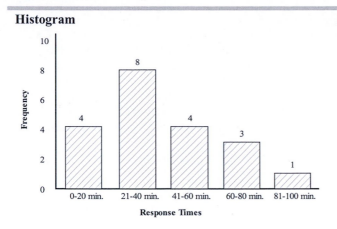

Response Times

Development Steps

1. Collect numerical data on the number of occurrences, errors, or other phenomena observed and count the data points.
2. Determine the range of your group of data. Decide how many bars your histogram will have and divide the range by the number of bars to determine how many intervals each bar in the histogram will cover.
3. Decide on the scale for the y-axis (vertical).
4. Decide on the width for the bars then draw each bar.

When to Use: To show the frequencies of certain events or categories of data values in a set of data from one time period. Data are plotted in increasing or decreasing order based on the frequency count for each data categories. Not used to show performance over time

Line Graph (also known as a run chart)

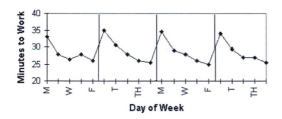

Development Steps:

1. Choose a measure and place the measure on the vertical axis. The measure could be the numerical value for a performance measure, the number of errors, percent injuries, dollars saved, or whatever.
2. Choose a time interval for taking measurements and place the interval on the horizontal axis.
3. Enter your measurements (data points or dots) chronologically. Data can be entered as it becomes available. Then draw a line connecting the points.

When to Use: Best for showing changes in performance measurement data over several time periods. Also used for displaying several groups of continuous measurement data simultaneously.

Pie Chart

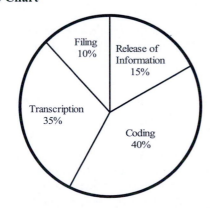

Development steps:

1. Make sure you have 100% of the data on whatever you are reporting.
2. Organize the data from the largest quantity to the smallest and calculate the percentage of each item to the total of all items. (Hint: Divide the quantity for each item by the total of all items added together and then multiply by 100.)
3. Draw a circle using something round as a guide.
4. Starting at the 12 o'clock position and going clockwise draw a wedge (pie slice) representing the percentage of the pie for the largest item.
5. Label each slice and show the percentage of the whole pie the slice represents.

When to Use: To show the contribution of parts to a whole. Reports a snapshot of performance from one time period. Not used to show performance over time.

Radar Chart (also known as a spider diagram)

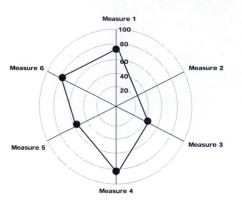

<u>Development steps:</u>
1. Assemble the data to be analyzed.
2. Determine appropriate scales for the "rings" in the diagram. If the diagram is intended to be used to judge performance against a standard, the outer most ring should represent the goal.
3. Plot the data on the chart. Position each data point with respect to the performance standard represented by the outlier ring.
4. Draw a line connecting the points.

<u>When to Use</u>: To visually show the comparative rankings of several related measures. Can be used to show changes in performance, however if several time periods will be shown, it's better to use a line graph.

Graphs can be drawn by hand, however most people use data analysis or spreadsheet software programs to create graphs. The choice of which program to use is often based on personal preference or company policy. However, it is still up to you – not the software program – to select the best graph for presenting performance measurement data.

Visual representation of numbers as bars, lines, pies, and the like are what makes graphs so powerful. Make the charting area as prominent as possible without squeezing other chart elements off the page. If you can get the point across without footnotes, axis titles, or legends, do it so you can make the charting area bigger. Remember graphs should communicate enough information to be stand-alone reports. Keep the following tips in mind when creating graphic performance measurement reports.

- *Less is more.* Do not put too many data series in a graph. Line graphs are especially intolerant of overcrowding. More than three or four lines, particularly if the lines follow much the same direction, are visually confusing. The only exception to this rule is when creating a line graph of several data series that people would not expect to be similar.

- *Group bars to show relationships.* Group bars together tightly if you are trying to suggest they belong together. If you are showing a group of bars over a series of years, for example, it makes sense to cluster the bars for each year and leave a little extra space between years. If there is no need to do this, put more space between your bars and make them a little wider so they are easier to see.

- *Add definition with black outlines.* Give the bars in bar charts, the slices in pie charts, and the risers in 3-D charts a little definition by making their outlines black, or a dark, brilliant color. If you are making your chart into a slide, the people at the back of the room will appreciate being able to distinguish the elements.

- *Use grids in moderation.* When using grid lines in your charting area, use only as many as are needed to get an approximate idea of the value of any given data point in the chart. Too many grid lines create visual clutter. Balance horizontal and vertical grid lines so they are not too long and narrow or tall and narrow. Use soft colors, such as gray, for grid lines. Once you have defined the color and weight of the grid lines, make sure the chart frame (the frame around the charting area) is black or a dark, brilliant color and heavier than the grid lines.

- *Choose colors carefully.* If you create a colored graph for a PowerPoint™ presentation in a large room, use strong, coordinating colors to attract attention and help people at the back of the room distinguish individual series. If your graph is going in a paper report where it will be examined at close range, keep the colors softer so readers are not overwhelmed.

- *Limit use of typefaces.* Use one typeface, or at most two, on a graph and use the same size and weight for similar elements such as the axes and legend text. A recommended setting is 12 to 18 points and bold.

If you use the bold and italic fonts in a typeface, as well as different sizes, you can generate enough typographic variety without going outside one type family.

- *Choose legible typefaces*. Pick a typeface that looks clear in smaller sizes and in bold, especially if your graph will be in a small size in a publication or if it will be viewed by a large audience in a big room. If the graph title is big enough, you can use just about any typeface for it and it will be legible. However, for legend text, axes, footnotes and the like, take more care. Use typefaces that are neither too light nor too heavy.
- *Set type against an appropriate background*. Be careful about the background behind the type. Some color combinations, such as pink or violet type and a medium or dark blue background, could make the audience feel a little dizzy. If you are using a dark background color, your type must be bright enough to be readable; it should not look as if the background is trying to swallow it up. If you are using light type on a dark background, use a bold weight, especially with smaller type sizes. Complex fill patterns in the background can also make type hard to read, particularly smaller items like legend text and axis scales.
- *Use pattern fills with moderation*. Graph creation software packages can produce just about any kind of color combination or fill pattern you can imagine. However, don't get carried away with color and patterns without thinking about your output device. Sophisticated fill patterns take up more disk space and take longer to print on color printers.

Analyzing Measurement Results

There are several ways to answer the question, is current performance acceptable? A simple comparison of current performance with the performance goal may be sufficient. If the goal is met, no further investigation is needed. Measurement data continues to be gathered and reported to ensure quality doesn't deteriorate. If the data reveal a gap between actual and expected performance, the quality management process advances to the investigation and performance improvement phase.

In addition to simply comparing actual and expected performance, there are other methods to evaluate measurement results. Common assessment approaches are trend analysis, statistical process control, and comparing performance with other organizations.

Trend Analysis

It is often useful to analyze performance trends. Is quality improving, declining, or remaining about the same? Simply reviewing measurement data from a single time period, without considering previous results, can be misleading. People may over-react to what seems to be a performance concern when it is just a one-time aberration. On the other hand, people may not notice quality is slowly eroding or wrongly think real progress is being made toward a performance goal. To effectively assess measurement results, both performance trends and goal attainment should be evaluated.

The purpose of trend analysis is to detect significant changes in performance using time-series data. By evaluating performance trends people are able to more accurately answer these questions:

- Is our performance goal achievable by how things are now done?
- Is current performance stable (in a predictable range)?
- Is progress being made toward reaching goals or is the performance gap widening?

Performance rarely remains constant from month to month. Trend analysis provides a way of determining whether patterns in measurement data are due to random fluctuations (sometimes called *noise*) or whether there are important changes requiring action.

Trend Analysis Tools

Tabular reports can be used to display time-series performance data, but this type of report is not the best format for identifying significant changes over long time periods. A line graph is the simplest tool for detecting patterns or trends in performance data that should be investigated. Either time itself, or something that changes with time, is impacting performance. Below are examples of significant patterns or trends that might be apparent when time-series performance data are plotted on a line graph. The rules developed by statistical analysts to identify significant shifts in performance are not absolute – there are differing opinions from one analyst to the next (Mohammed, Worthington, & Woodall, 2008). To identify significant patterns or trends in data displayed on a line graph you should have a minimum of 15 data points and some statisticians suggest a minimum of 20 data points (Woodall, 2000).

Exhibit 4.6. Significant Data Patterns and Trends

Example:

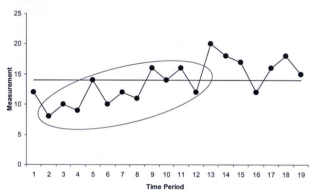

Zigzag Pattern

A significant pattern is present when data points alternatively "move" up and down eight times (some prefer up to fourteen). If the values of two or more data points are the same, the pattern is considered to be broken.

Example:

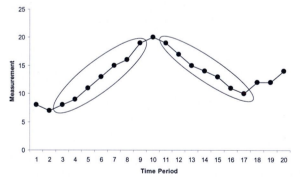

Performance Trend

A significant performance trend is present when six (some prefer seven) or more successive points show either a consistent increase or a consistent decrease in value. If two successive data points are the same, this does not break the trend.

Example:

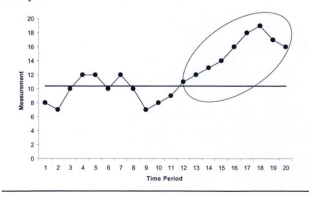

Long Run

A long run is present when seven (some prefer eight) consecutive data points are either above or below the median. Ignore data points falling on the median. This is a signal the average or median performance rate is shifting.

Statistical Process Control

Statistical process control was developed as a feedback system to help workers in manufacturing industries prevent defects rather than fix them after they occur. One element of this process control system is a control chart. Dr. Walter Shewhart, a statistician, developed the control chart during his work in the 1920s at Bell Laboratories. When measuring output of the telephone manufacturing process Dr. Shewhart found a certain amount of variation was always present – even when the process was repeated in exactly the same way. By measuring process output and plotting it on a control chart Dr. Shewhart was able to distinguish between expected and unexpected performance variations (Shewhart, 1925).

A control chart is special type of line graph that provides people with a statistical method for monitoring variation in performance measurement data. Although its origins are in manufacturing, today it is used to measure performance in all industries including healthcare. Since 2000 Joint Commission standards have recommended accredited organizations use control charts to identify undesirable performance variations. The NCQA encourages health plans to use control charts for monitoring HEDIS™ measurement results.

A control chart graphically depicts performance variations and helps people distinguish between what Dr. Shewhart called common cause and special cause variation. Common cause variation (also called nominal, chance, or random variation) occurs in every process. The source of common cause variation is derived from how work is done. Common cause variation is predictable – unless something about the process is changed, future performance will most likely fall within a predictable range. When performance stays within a predictable range the process output is considered stable. Stable performance is not necessarily good or bad; it just means performance rates are in a state of statistical control.

Special cause variation (also called abnormal or assignable cause variation) is not predictable. This type of performance variation is caused by something unusual or abnormal affecting the process. Unstable processes periodically and suddenly produce erratic output. When special cause variation is detected, the source of this variation should be investigated and eliminated.

The value of using a control chart to evaluate performance is in the knowledge gained from learning whether performance is stable or unstable. People can find and eliminate special causes of variation. A stable process can be improved by making changes to the process itself. If people wrongly react to random variation in a stable process as if it were due to special causes, it is called tampering and leads to further complexity, increasing variation, and performance problems.

Creating control charts for performance assessment purposes is an advanced topic beyond the scope of this book. However, a few basics are covered for introductory purposes.

Control Chart Elements

All control charts have two essential elements: the current performance measure results (what's happening right now) and an estimate of what performance is likely to be in the future. Control charts have three mathematically calculated parameters:

- centerline value – which is usually the average or median value of current performance
- upper and lower control limits – which are derived from the probability distribution of the data

The upper and lower control limits identify the expected range of random variation present in a process. Generally, a three-sigma limit is used (99.7% of all expected values). Tighter limits, such as a two-sigma (95.5%) limit, may be set for some critical processes.

In Exhibit 4.7 is a C-chart used in a large healthcare organization to plot the daily number of employees who are absent from work due to illness. The average number of daily absences (25.6) for the 3-week time period is shown as the centerline. The centerline also provides an estimate of the number of employees who will be absent in the future. An estimate is nothing more than an educated guess about what is likely to happen, based on past experience.

Exhibit 4.7. C-chart: Number of Illness-Related Employee Absences

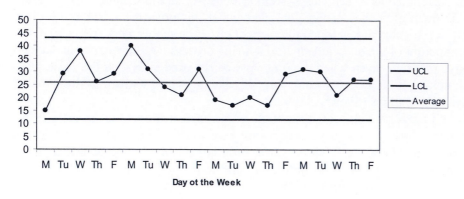

The second element of a control chart is its ability to statistically predict performance in the future, for instance, how many employees will be absent each day next week? The extent to which a prediction is likely to be correct depends on the type of variation in absentee rates. If there are a lot of special cause variations in the number of absent employees, then an estimate of future absentee rates rests on a shaky foundation. If there is only common cause variation, then people can be more confident their estimate is fairly close.

As shown in Exhibit 4.7 the number of absent employees during the 3-week period falls within the statistically calculated UCL (upper control limit) and LCL (lower control limit) lines. Thus, the variation exhibited in absentee rates is considered to be due to random or common cause variation. Because performance is in a state of statistical control (no values fall outside of the control limits) a more confident prediction of future absentee rates can be made. If special cause variations had been present (one or more data points falling above or below the upper or lower control limits), a reasonably reliable estimate of future absentee rates could not be made.

There are several kinds of control charts and the type of data to be plotted influences which control chart is used. There are two types of data: variable and attribute. Variable data are quantitative data that can be measured. Some examples are patient weight or test turn-around time. Attribute data are qualitative data that can be counted. Some examples are counts of compliance with patient management criteria or counts of errors in a document. Characteristics of common types of control charts used to graph healthcare performance data are listed in Exhibit 4.8.

Exhibit 4.8. Types of Control Charts and Characteristics

Type	Control Chart Characteristic
C-chart	Used to show attribute data (sometimes referred to as a *count* chart). C-charts are used in dealing with counts of a given event over consecutive periods of time.
P-chart	Used to show the fraction of nonconformance for a nonstandard sample size over a constant area of opportunity (sometimes referred to as a *proportion* chart). This type of control chart accounts for changes in the sample size and is effective for small as well as large samples.
U-chart	Used is used to show event counts when the area of opportunity is not constant during each period (sometimes referred to as a *rate* chart). The control limits are computed for each individual quarter because the number of standard units varies.
X-charts	Used to show individual measured quantities for indications of process control or unusual variation (sometimes referred to as an *individual* chart). The standard deviation for X-charts is calculated using a moving range.
X-bar and R-bar charts	Used in conjunction with each other to show variables data. The measurements describe a process characteristic and are reported in small subgroups of constant sizes (usually two to five measurements per subgroup). The average (X-bar) and the range R of each subgroup are plotted on the control chart.

Some general comments about construction and use of control charts in statistical process control are offered in the next section. However, students will want to learn more about the types of charts and how to interpret results before using them to plot measurement data.

Constructing a Control Chart

The steps in constructing a control chart are summarized below.
1. Plot the data point points (as is done with a line graph).
   - If samples were taken, first compute and record the mean for each sample and then plot each sample mean in order. For individual observations, simply plot the values in order.
2. Plot the average or mean.
   - After you have plotted individual values and connected them with lines, then compute the mean by summing the values and dividing the sum by the total number of values. Plot the mean value and extend a line horizontally across the graph (some types of control charts plot the median as the centerline). This centerline represents an estimate of what is actually happening on average.
3. Establish control limits
   - Control limits are estimates of the standard deviation computed from the data and placed at equal distances on both sides of the centerline. The control limits are used to judge the extent of variation in the process. If the process remains consistent, the performance data are expected to remain within the control limits.
   - The UCL and the LCL for different types of control charts are calculated using special formulas beyond are the scope of this book. See the website resources at the end of this chapter for more information about these formulas.
   - In general, control limits are set by computing an estimate of the standard deviation (known as *sigma*). A sigma (σ) unit is a measure of scale for the data. Sigma units express the number of measurement units, which correspond to one standard unit of dispersion. The control limits are usually set at 3-sigma to reduce the number of false alarms. If control limits are set at 1 or 2 sigma the reviewer may wrongly presume some random variations are due to special causes.

Interpreting the Results

The region enclosed by the control limits is the area within which predictions of future performance can be made. Process variation within the control limits is said to represent common cause variation. If performance falls outside this region (a signal of special cause variation), the reviewer knows that an extraordinary situation is causing variation from the established process. These situations should be immediately investigated.

Exhibit 4.9. Percent of Incomplete Charts 30 Days after Discharge

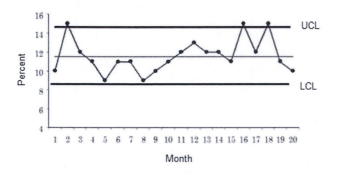

In Exhibit 4.9 is a P-chart showing the percent of patient charts not completed by physicians or clinical staff within 30 days of hospital discharge. As shown in the chart, the percentage occasionally exceeds the UCL (upper control limit); meaning it is a statistically unstable process. The situations causing this instability need to be resolved to bring the process into a state of statistical control. Until that happens, the monthly results will continue to be unpredictable.

Another situation warranting attention is when data plotted on a control chart shows a significant pattern or trend in performance. Evidence of a pattern or trend suggests something in the process is changing or is unstable and requires further analysis. The same statistical principles used to identify trends or patterns in data plotted on a line graph also apply to control charts. Even when data points remain within upper and lower control limits, there may be trends indicating something is happening in the process that needs investigating.

In Exhibit 4.10 is a control chart showing the average number of days it takes for HIM department staff to code the diagnoses and procedures for discharged patients.

Exhibit 4.10. Control Chart of Inpatient Record Coding Times

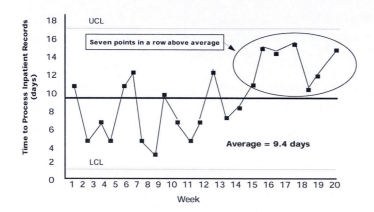

The task of coding records does not exhibit special cause variation (no data points outside of control limits); however there is a trend of seven data points in a row above the centerline suggesting a significant change may be occurring in the process. It is in the detection of situations where the process appears to act differently from its predicted pattern that the control chart proves its value in performance monitoring.

Exhibit 4.11. Reacting to Data Variation on Control Chart

Once performance rates remain within the control limits and are considered stable, it does not necessarily mean the process is acceptable. It only means that process output is more predictable and further reduction of variation will require process improvements. The decision tree in Exhibit 4.11 illustrates issues to consider when responding to special and common cause variation.

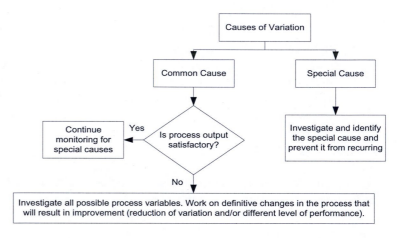

Comparing Performance

Healthcare providers and purchasers have many opportunities to see how the organization is performing compared to others. Several sources of publicly available performance data were listed in chapter 2. In addition to performance data available publicly, there are performance comparison projects that distribute data just to participants. For example, participants in the Premier Quality Improvement Solutions (www.premierinc.com) can benchmark clinical and financial outcomes against peers and easily analyze the effect of quality measures on patient outcomes and cost.

It is possible for an organization's performance results to be well within internal expectations yet performance is sub-optimal when compared to what other organizations can achieve. An example of a comparative data report is illustrated in Exhibit 4.12. This comparison chart (a variation of a box plot graph) shows 12-month mortality rates for patients with heart failure at six hospitals in one U.S. metropolitan area. The national and statewide mortality rates for the time period are reported at the top. The total number of patients and mortality rate is reported for each hospital. The hospital's average mortality rate is also displayed as a point on a line. These lines represent the amount of random variation in the data. The middle line represents the statewide average mortality rate of 4.6%.

Exhibit 4.12. Comparison of Heart Failure Mortality Rates

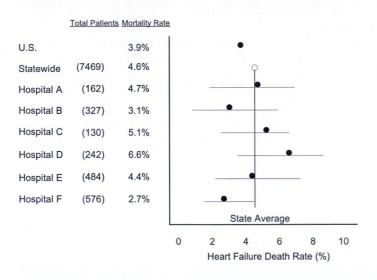

	Total Patients	Mortality Rate
U.S.		3.9%
Statewide	(7469)	4.6%
Hospital A	(162)	4.7%
Hospital B	(327)	3.1%
Hospital C	(130)	5.1%
Hospital D	(242)	6.6%
Hospital E	(484)	4.4%
Hospital F	(576)	2.7%

Physicians at Hospital D (highest mortality rate at 6.6%) might discount the data saying, *our patients are sicker and that's why mortality rates are higher than the average.* To counteract this argument, outcome measure comparison projects often use severity of illness risk-adjusted data.

The purpose of risk adjustment is to get more even-handed statistical comparisons between disparate populations or groups. By reconciling key differences among patients, risk adjustment permits comparisons of 'apples with apples.' Studies have shown that failure to adjust appropriately for patient risk produces outcome comparisons that are flawed, misleading and, sometimes, meaningless (Gregg et al., 2014). The mortality rates shown in Exhibit 4.12 are adjusted to account for patients' age, sex and severity of condition. Other factors – for example, some hospitals may transfer out the most severe cases – are not accounted for in the risk-adjustment method used to report the data in Exhibit 4.12.

Whenever comparative patient outcome data are used to evaluate performance providers should become familiar with the risk adjustment methodologies used by groups producing the reports. Some methods of risk-adjusting patient outcome rates are based solely on data found in administrative databases, such as the Medicare claims files that contain information collected by Medicare to pay for health care services provided to beneficiaries. Administrative databases include patient demographic data, payer information, principal and other diagnoses and procedures codes, admission source, and discharge disposition. These data elements are used to risk-adjust patient outcome reports.

Missing in administrative databases are data on patient physiological findings, diagnostic test results and patient treatment preferences. These factors were not taken into account when reporting the mortality data in Exhibit 4.12. When the quality department at Hospital D reviewed the records of patients with heart failure who had died it was discovered that 60% of the patients had do-not-resuscitate (DNR) orders written on their first or second hospital day. A DNR order indicates the patient does did not want to be revived should their heart stop. This factor alone may explain the higher rate of deaths at Hospital D.

Exhibit 4.13. Expected Versus Observed Mortality at 8 Hospitals

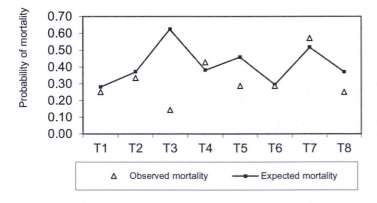

The graph in Exhibit 4.13 illustrates the predicted (expected) versus actual (observed) mortality for patients at eight different hospitals. The patients' expected mortality is based on risk factors such as comorbid diagnoses (e.g., hypertension, chronic renal failure, diabetes), demographic characteristics (e.g., age and sex), and specific procedures (where relevant). A statistical test may be conducted to determine whether the difference between the expected and actual values is statistically significant. This test is performed to make sure differences are very unlikely to be caused by chance alone.

It may not be possible to get detailed information on the severity of illness risk adjustment methodology used by groups publishing outcome data. If there are too many unanswered questions about the data, it should not be used as a basis for assessing performance.

The term *benchmarking* is often used to describe any type of performance comparison. However, benchmarking is not merely comparing performance to just any organization. Benchmarking involves using the level of performance achieved by an exemplary or so-called 'world-class' organization as the standard for comparison (Sower, Duffy, & Kohlers, 2007). This standard may come from an exemplary healthcare organization or from a company outside of the healthcare industry recognized as superior with respect to a particular aspect of performance. For instance, comparison data from a hotel or a car rental company with an excellent check-in procedure can be used to assess the efficiency of the patient registration process in a hospital or clinic.

Summary

The purpose of performance evaluation is to judge whether current levels of quality are adequate. If quality is found to be satisfactory, performance monitoring continues and data are periodically analyzed to ensure quality does not deteriorate. If performance data reveal improvement opportunities, the third step of quality management is undertaken – quality improvement. In this step, the cause of undesirable performance is identified and actions taken to improve performance. The activities of quality improvement are covered in chapters 5 and 6. Warning signs that may be evident in performance measurement data indicating the need for quality improvement activities include:

- Performance goals are not met.
- Performance goals are met, however there are significant patterns/trends or evidence of special cause variation in the trended measurement results.
- Performance goals are met and there are no significant patterns/trends or evidence of special cause variation in the trended results, however performance in other organizations is better.

To determine if any of the above performance warning signs exist, several factors must be evaluated:
- Difference between actual performance and performance goals
- Evidence of patterns and trends in time-series measurement data
- Amount and type of variation in time-series measurement data
- Gap between the organization's performance and what other organizations are experiencing

Student Activities

1. Select the graphic data display best to use for reporting performance measurement data for the following situations:
   - Rate of patient falls in two consecutive time periods
   - Rate of patient falls in one time period for four different facilities
   - Rate of patient falls over several consecutive time periods
   - Rate of patient falls during one time period, categorized by age group
2. Identify an online source of comparative performance data for the following performance measures:
   - Percent of patients receiving home care services who need urgent or unplanned medical care
   - Percent of patients with a myocardial infarction (heart attack) who receive a thrombolytic agent within 30 minutes of arrival at the hospital
   - Percent of nursing home residents who are physically restrained

3.   Identify five Joint Commission performance measures that include a risk adjustment. For each measure, list the data elements used to risk adjust the measurement results. For instance, for the measure, *acute myocardial inpatient mortality*, the following patient-specific data elements are used to risk adjust the measurement results: Admission source, Age, Other Diagnosis Codes, and Sex. Current measures with the data specifications can be found on the Joint Commission website (www.jointcommission.org)

Website Resources

Agency for Healthcare Quality and Research. (2013). *Statistical Process Control: Possible Uses to Monitor and Evaluate Patient-Centered Medical Home Model*
https://pcmh.ahrq.gov/sites/default/files/attachments/StatisticalProcess_032513comp.pdf

Agency for Healthcare Quality and Research, Examples of Research Data Infographics
www.ahrq.gov/data/infographics/

American Health Information Management Association. 2011. *Health Data Analysis Toolkit.* (Available to AHIMA members only)
http://library.ahima.org/PdfView?oid=103453

Arthur, J. (2008, June). Statistical process control for healthcare. *Quality Digest.*
www.qualitydigest.com/june08/articles/03_article.shtml

Guidelines for Effective Presentations. Kaiser Foundation Tutorial.
www.kff.org/interactive/guidelines-for-effective-presentations-tutorial/

Health Care Data Analytics (online book)
www.charuaggarwal.net/HDA-TOC.pdf

Health Resources and Services Administration (HRSA), Department of Health and Human Services. 2011. Part 3 & 4 in: "Managing Data for Performance Improvement."
www.hrsa.gov/quality/toolbox/508pdfs/managingdataperformanceimprovement.pdf

Lance, P., A. Guilkey, A. Hattori & Angeles, G. (2014). *How Do We Know If a Program Made A Difference? A Guide to Statistical Methods for Program Impact Evaluation.* Chapel Hill, North Carolina: MEASURE Evaluation.
www.cpc.unc.edu/measure/resources/publications/ms-14-87-en

Process or Product Monitoring and Control, Chapter 6 in online *Engineering Statistics Handbook*
www.itl.nist.gov/div898/handbook/

Using Benchmarking Measurement to Improve Performance over Time (2018). White paper of the AAAHC Institute for Quality Improvement
www.aaahc.org/wp-content/uploads/2018/12/aaahc_whitepaper_single-sheets_final.pdf

"Using Run and Control Charts to Understand Variation" a video presentation sponsored by the Institute for Healthcare Improvement (available on YouTube)
https://youtu.be/j4ZYHYJ0XUo

References

Gregg, C., Fonarow, G.C., Alberts, M.J., Broderick, J.P.,.Jauch, E.C., Kleindorfer, D.O., Saver, J.L., Solis, P., Suter, R., & Schwamm, L.H. (2014). Stroke outcomes measures must be appropriately risk adjusted to ensure quality care of patients. *Stroke. 45(*5), 1589-1601.

Mohammed, M., Worthington, P., & Woodall, W. (2008). Plotting basic control charts: Tutorial notes for healthcare practitioners. *Quality and Safety in Healthcare, 17(*2), 137-145.

Shewhart, W. A. (1925). The application of statistics as an aid in maintaining quality of manufactured product. *Journal of the American Statistical Association,* 20, 546-548.

Sower, V., Duffy, J., & Kohlers, G. (2007). *Benchmarking for Hospitals: Achieving Best-in-Class Performance without Having to Reinvent the Wheel*. Milwaukee, WI: ASQ Quality Press.

Woodall, W.H. (2000). Controversies and contradictions in statistical process control. *Journal of Quality Technology*, *32(*4), 341-350.

Chapter

5

IMPROVING PERFORMANCE

Reader Objectives

After reading this chapter and reflecting on the contents, you will be able to:
1. Demonstrate an understanding of how improvement projects are formed.
2. Compare and contrast common performance improvement models.
3. Describe steps of common performance improvement models.
4. Recognize how to select project objectives and team participants.
5. Explain stages of improvement team development.

Key Terms

Gantt chart: Type of bar chart used to illustrate a project schedule.

Improvement project team: Group of individuals sharing a common performance improvement goal and the responsibility for achieving it.

Kaizen: Japanese word for continuous and incremental improvement.

Kaizen events: Improvement projects often conducted over 4-5 days with the goal of rapid change.

Lean: Performance improvement model that seeks to create efficient processes with zero waste.

Performance improvement model: Systematic process used to make healthcare improvements.

Plan-Do-Check-Act (PDCA): Performance improvement model in which improvements are planned, tried, and checked to see if they deserve to be implemented or abandoned.

Plan-Do-Study-Act (PDSA): A modification of the PCDA model originated by W. Edwards Deming

Prioritization: Application of an explicit set of criteria to establish the order in which problems will be resolved or actions will be implemented.

Rapid cycle improvement: Performance improvement model based on the PDSA model that relies on small process changes and careful measurement of the effects of these changes.

Six Sigma: Performance improvement model that seeks to create nearly defect free processes; also used in statistics to denote a 99.9997% defect-free yield for a process.

Storyboard: Report format using pictures, diagrams and short narratives to illustrate the major steps of a completed improvement project.

Team dynamics: Motivating and driving forces that can hinder or help an improvement team achieve project objectives.

Performance Improvement

Continual improvement of performance should be a primary goal for all healthcare organizations. To support this goal, improvement actions are initiated when there is a gap between what is actually happening and what is desired. Improvement opportunities may be discovered in a variety of ways, including:

- Assessment of performance measurement data
- Findings from regulatory and accreditation surveys
- Feedback from patients/clients and other customers
- Reports of physician and employee concerns

As illustrated in Exhibit 5.1, performance improvement involves three major steps: (1) find causes of performance gaps; (2) select interventions; and (3) implement interventions.

Figure 5.1. Improvement – A Quality Management Activity

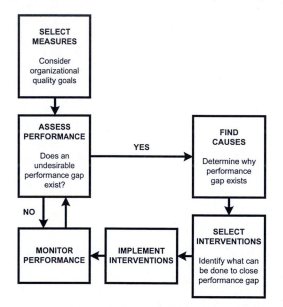

Opportunities for improvement and improvement actions occur at every level of the healthcare system. Some improvement initiatives are undertaken at the department level. For example, a HIM department can conduct an improvement project aimed at reducing the time it takes to respond to external requests for copies of completed patient records. All tasks involved in this process are under control of the HIM department. Changing the release of information process will not affect what is happening in other departments. Only people working in the HIM department would need to be involved in this improvement activity.

Improvement projects can involve people in more than one unit or department. When the improvement project crosses unit or department boundaries people from all involved areas should be represented on the improvement team. For example, a team involved in reducing nursing home resident falls might include physicians, nurses, and representatives from departments such as pharmacy, physical therapy, housekeeping, and occupational therapy.

Improvement projects are resource intensive. Departments and organizations can often support only a limited number of projects at any one time. When several opportunities for improvement are identified, choices must be made. The following criteria can be used as a guide for selecting high priority improvement projects:

- The problem is important. It has been a problem for some time and is widespread. The benefits of solving the problem are obvious.
- Support for change exists. People recognize the need for change either because of personal experiences or because performance measurement data have persuaded them a change is needed.
- The project has emotional appeal or visibility. People are motivated to work on solving the problem.
- The status quo has some risks. There are hazards associated with not addressing the problem. If something is not done, it may create other problems – for example: patient care may suffer, staff morale may drop, physicians may no longer admit patients, or there may be negative publicity.

Joint Commission (2017) standards require leaders set priorities for performance improvement, giving priority to high-volume, high-risk, or problem-prone processes and changes in the internal or external environment. CARF standards for rehabilitation facilities indicate performance improvement priorities should be based on how the persons served will be affected. Standards of other healthcare accreditation bodies have similar patient- or client-focused requirements for selecting improvement priorities.

Improvement Models

When a decision is made to improve performance, a systematic improvement project is undertaken. There are several improvement models – roadmaps – that guide people through the steps of a project. Improvement roadmaps have similar steps. The models covered in this chapter are: Plan-Do-Check Act, Rapid Cycle Improvement, Six Sigma, Lean, and Lean Sigma.

Plan-Do-Check-Act Model

Healthcare organizations are not required to use any particular improvement model. Thus, several different models are used. Most of these are variations on the Plan-Do-Check-Act (PDCA) cycle developed in the 1920s by Walter Shewhart, originator of the concepts and techniques of statistical process control (Best & Newhauser, 2006). Shewhart was one of the first process improvement experts to discuss using a systematic model for continuously improving performance.

The PDCA model, illustrated in Exhibit 5.2, is shown in a circle because it is intended to be used for ongoing improvement with the steps repeated again and again.

Exhibit 5.2. Plan-Do-Check-Act Cycle

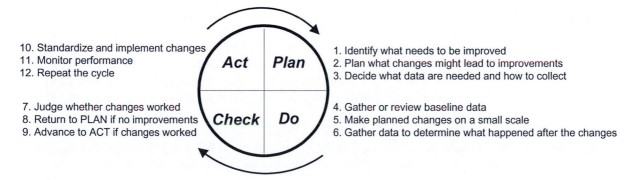

Renowned statistician, W. Edwards Deming, went to Japan as part of the occupation forces of the allies after World War II to teach the Japanese industrial quality improvement methods such as statistical process control and systematic process improvement (Best & Newhauser, 2005). Deming modified Shewhart's original model to Plan-Do-Study-Act (PDSA), while retaining the same basic concepts. Today the PDCA and PDSA project roadmaps are the most widely recognized four-step improvement models.

Rapid Cycle Improvement Model

Rapid cycle improvement (RCI), illustrated in Exhibit 5.3, is an improvement model based on the Shewhart and Deming improvement models. The RCI model entails four steps:
1. Set the aim (the goal). This involves answering the question: What are we trying to accomplish?
2. Define the measures (the expected improvements). This involves answering the question: How will we know that a change is improvement?
3. Design changes (action plan). This involves answering the question: What changes can we make that will result in improvement?
4. Implement and test changes (the solution). This involves completing a P-D-S-A cycle.

Exhibit 5.3. Rapid Cycle Improvement Model

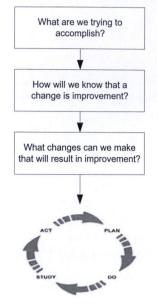

Setting the aim involves taking a clear and deliberate look at what is to be accomplished. Questions to help the improvement project team determine what they want to accomplish include:

- Is it measurable? Will we know if it was achieved?
- Is it a 'stretch' goal?
- Is it right for the project time frame?
- Is it consistent with the organizational mission?
- Does it matter to patients and families?
- Does the project team match the aim?
- Is it outcome-oriented?

The aim or goal of the RCI project influences the second step – define measures. The measures describe how the team will know that a change has resulted in improvement? For example, if the goal is to improve patient satisfaction in a surgical unit, a key measure would be, *average time from assessment of patient's pain to administration of pain medication.*

The third step is to select process changes expected to achieve the aim. Suggestions for process changes can come from many sources including project team members, frontline staff, the literature, other organizations, and professional colleagues. The last RCI step is to test the changes using a rapid-cycle PDSA process. The process is considered 'rapid cycle' because the team designs and implements small, concrete changes that can be quickly put into action in a pilot situation. Thus the success of action plans can be evaluated in a very short time (for example 1-2 weeks). If the changes don't work another PDSA cycle is initiated until successful solutions are found.

Rather than conduct a comprehensive (and often time intensive) analysis of a process, RCI relies on small process changes and careful measurement of the effects of these changes. The RCI approach uses an accelerated method (usually less than 4 weeks per improvement cycle) to collect and analyze data and make informed process changes based upon this analysis. This is then followed by another improvement cycle to evaluate success.

Ongoing repetition of improvement cycles serves as the basis for incremental improvements and allows for creation of internal performance benchmarks. The RCI performance improvement model has been successfully applied to the operational aspects of healthcare delivery as well as clinical patient care processes.

Six Sigma Improvement Model

Six Sigma is a disciplined, data-driven improvement model aimed at near-elimination of process defects. Improvements are intended to enable healthcare organizations to do things better, faster, and at lower cost while offering superior consumer satisfaction.

Motorola started the Six Sigma movement towards manufacturing excellence in the mid-1980s when they adopted a new goal of zero defects. Motorola worked toward this goal by thoroughly reviewing customer needs, analyzing internal processes and the abilities of suppliers. By conducting this thorough analysis Motorola was able to produce reliable products that meet customer needs. The philosophy, measure, and methodology of Six Sigma form a framework to help healthcare organizations focus on reducing defects while improving processes and reducing costs.

One of the major contributions of Six Sigma is a reorientation of the definition of what constitutes acceptable healthcare quality. *Sigma* is a statistical term that measures the variability of a data set (population) about its mean (μ) (see Exhibit 5.4).

Exhibit 5.4. Normally Distributed Bell-Shaped Curve

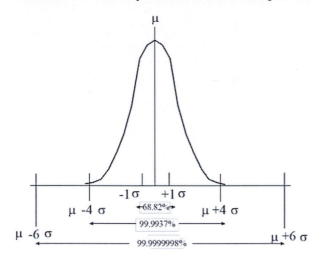

In a normally distributed bell-shaped curve, approximately 69% of the data points will fall within one standard deviation, or one sigma, of the mean; 95% within two sigma; 99.73% within three sigma; 99.9937% within four sigma; and 99.9999998% within six sigma. When a process has achieved Six Sigma, defects will occur only 3.4 times in one million opportunities.

For all practical purposes, Six Sigma represents defect-free work. The goal of a Six Sigma project is to reduce process variation, which leads to fewer errors and improved outcomes.

Initiation of a Six Sigma improvement project is similar to any performance improvement activity. Leaders select projects based on the organization's strategic goals and likelihood the project will lead to significant improvements. Six Sigma projects for improving existing processes often follow a highly structured and disciplined roadmap known as DMAIC (pronounced as *dee-MAY-ick*) methodology. This process improvement model involves five phases, each with defined goals and critical checkpoints. Primary activities occurring during each phase are summarized in Exhibit 5.6.

Exhibit 5.6. Six Sigma DMAIC Improvement Model

Phase	Primary Activities
DEFINE	Establish the focus • Review initial project charter • Form the team • Identify and describe the performance gap using data
MEASURE	Examine the current situation • Review the process in detail • Describe the current situation in detail with data
ANALYZE	Analyze the causes of performance gap • Brainstorm and prioritize root causes • Use data to verify the causes • Select root causes to address
IMPROVE	Act on the causes • Brainstorm possible actions to take • Select actions to take • Develop and implement action plans on a small scale Evaluate the results • Study the results • Modify actions plans as indicated
CONTROL	Standardize the changes and draw conclusions • Implement actions on a large scale and standardize actions • Identify benefits, difficulties and lessons learned • Discuss future improvement plans

Lean Improvement Model

For several years manufacturing industries have been using the Lean improvement model to improve productivity, eliminate waste, enhance product quality, and lower costs. Now this model is being applied to process improvements in healthcare organizations. Recognizing and eliminating waste are fundamentals of lean thinking. Seven types of waste often found in healthcare are listed below.

- Unnecessary human movement
- People waiting for something needed to do their work
- Doing more than is needed to meet customer requirements (over-processing)
- Poor quality work and rework to fix mistakes
- Excessive inventory
- Unnecessary movement of supplies or equipment
- Doing something that doesn't add value (over-production)

A Lean improvement project typically follows these six steps.
1. Form and train a team of process experts
2. Map the process
3. Gather data and identify waste
4. Identify causes and solutions
5. Implement solutions
6. Measure results

During step three of a Lean project, the improvement team asks the question, where does waste reside? There may be only a small percentage of work that adds value to the process. For example, in the operating room (OR) the actual work of the surgery starts with the incision. All around that work are processes that may or may not add value. One of the best ways to identify waste is through direct observation. Here is an example from the OR: An orthopedic surgeon agrees to let a member of the OR Lean project team observe him during his case turnover activities. The team member follows the surgeon with a device that measures the distance he walks between cases. The surgeon likes a particular style of surgical cap not stored near his OR. Before each case, he walks across the entire surgical suite to get a cap; a round trip of about 1,000 feet. The simple fix to eliminate this wasted activity: stock the surgeon's cap close to his OR.

Lean is best described as the relentless pursuit, identification, and elimination of waste in all processes. Processes over time tend to become fat – steps are added to processes and these become ingrained in the way things are done. Later other new steps are added. After a matter of years, unnecessary process steps and waste become 'the way we do things' without constant re-evaluation of the value of each activity. The Lean improvement model focuses attention of the improvement team on reduction of waste.

Some healthcare organizations sponsor Lean or Kaizen events which are condensed improvement projects conducted over a 4-5 day period. Kaizen is the Japanese word for continuous and incremental improvement. The goal of these projects is to achieve rapid change by intensely focusing on a specific process needing redesign (Lavallee, 2011). Kaizen events are similar to rapid cycle improvement projects as the intent is to make small changes that can be quickly implemented and evaluated.

During the first day of a Kaizen event, team members walk through the entire process targeted for improvement. This hands-on observation allows team members to experience the process and make note of any constraints, areas of waste, or issues that may lead to unsafe or inefficient care. The remaining project days involve creating a detailed map of the process to further highlight constraints and error prone situations. Ideas for improving the process are generated by the team and prioritized for implementation. Once process improvements have been defined and agreed to, the team begins to make process changes. Within just a few short days, the team initiates improvements and assesses the impact of the changes on workflow and outcomes. This real-time evaluation allows the team to rapidly make adjustments that might be necessary to ensure the redesigned process is working well.

Lean-Six Sigma

Since introduction of Lean and Six Sigma improvement models, it is common to find organizations using a combination of both models to conduct improvement projects. The most effective aspects of each model are combined to get even better performance results than would have typically been achieved by Lean or Six Sigma individually. These projects start with removal of waste from the targeted process (a Lean strategy) and then defects resulting from the process are eliminated using Six Sigma strategies. For instance, a Lean-Sigma project involving an emergency department patient registration process would start by examining the process steps. Wasted, non-value added activities would be removed and the process streamlined. Next, outputs from the more efficient process would be examined for defects (for example, computer input errors, duplicate patient record numbers). Using Six Sigma techniques the source of these defects would be uncovered and corrective actions taken.

Steps Common to All Models

Whatever performance improvement models may be used, improvement projects have common steps.

1. Identify improvement opportunity

    The improvement opportunity is clearly defined at the start of the initiative. For example, the leadership group in a nursing home formulated the following improvement goal: *There is an opportunity to decrease the incidence of urinary tract infections in our residents.* The leaders decided to work on making changes in patient management processes because they had noticed a steady increase in the number of urinary tract infections (UTIs). In addition, comparative data revealed other nursing homes with similar residents had lower UTI rates. The leaders then set a specific target or end point for the improvement project, stating: *UTIs will be reduced to a level of less than 5% within 6 months.* For some improvement initiatives, multiple targets are defined.

2. Organize a team

    A team of people is brought together to evaluate the current way of doing things and identify ways to achieve desired goals. If the issue under investigation crosses departmental boundaries, then an inter-departmental team is formed. For a project involving reduction of nursing home resident UTIs, the team might include licensed nurses, certified nurse assistants, housekeepers and the infection control nurse. When the process under investigation is within the boundaries of a single department, then only people in that department are typically on the team. A team leader is designated; generally someone who has training or experience in performance improvement models and techniques. In some organizations, a quality department representative serves on all inter-departmental improvement teams.

3. Gather information

    Initial team meetings are devoted to gathering information to determine what needs changing in the process to achieve the project goal. This step may involve the use of various data collection tools and other improvement tools. A step-by-step map of the process is often drawn to help the team visualize what tasks are currently done and where changes are needed. It may be necessary to talk with or observe the people actually doing the work to find out exactly what's happening. The team may employ other group decision-making techniques. Commonly used improvement tools are described in chapter 6.

4. Select actions

    Once the team understands what needs changing in the current process to achieve goals, corrective actions are selected. Corrective actions are process revisions intended to improve performance or rectify undesirable conditions. Action plans choices are influenced by what the team discovered during step three. Before making process changes, actions are thoroughly reviewed by the team, people intimately involved in the process, and a leadership group. The team must be sure any changes made to the process will not cause new problems or be resisted by process owners. Process changes are implemented as a pilot project or in only a small area so the effect of the changes can be closely monitored. Techniques for successfully improving reliability of performance are detailed in chapter 6.

5. Test the effect

     Data are gathered to determine the effect of actions taken to improve performance. The team wants to know if the project improvement goals have been achieved. The problems identified in step three may be fully or only partially resolved; or the actions may have had no effect. Perhaps the intervention actually caused more performance problems. Baseline performance data collected by the team during step three are used for 'before and after' comparisons of performance. If process changes do not achieve desired results, then it's back to the drawing board! It may be necessary to gather more information or repeat some of the analyses in step three. New actions are then developed and piloted (step four).

6. Adopt the change

     If preliminary analyses of process changes show actions have been successful (as defined by the project goals in step one), the changes are made on a permanent basis. This may require rewriting of procedures, educating and training physicians and staff, formal communications, or other strategies designed to incorporate the new way of doing things into daily practices. During this step, the team also determines how performance will be periodically measured to determine if desired results are sustained.

7. Monitor performance

     All improvement projects include a follow-up phase; that is, data are gathered to determine the effectiveness of action plans. In some instances, already existing performance measures can be used to evaluate results. In other situations, special studies of performance may be necessary. Healthcare organizations must be able to demonstrate to themselves and others that improvement activities have resulted in better performance. The CMS and the accreditation standards of most groups require the effectiveness of improvement actions be measured.

     An improvement project can take anywhere from a few days to several months to complete. The duration of a project varies according to the scope and complexity of the process selected for improvement. An improvement project is complete when there is objective evidence goals have been met or problems no longer exist and process changes have been incorporated into routine practices.

Improvement Project Reports

Senior leaders of the organization are kept informed of the status of all inter-departmental improvement projects. For intra-departmental projects, it may be sufficient for only the department director to stay informed. A one-page form, such as the one shown in Exhibit 5.7, can be used to update leaders on the current status of projects. As each step is completed, more information is added to the report.

Exhibit 5.7. Performance Improvement Project Report

Improvement Goal:		
Team Members:	Relevant Process:	
Analysis:		
Action Plan	Implementation Date	Results

Gantt Chart

To keep improvement action plans on track toward completion, some organizations use Gantt charts to display the anticipated time schedule for implementing actions. The chart is also useful for estimating the time and resources required to implement each action plan. An illustration of a simple Gantt chart is found in Exhibit 5.8. Some software programs have Gantt chart creation capabilities.

Exhibit 5.8. Gantt Chart

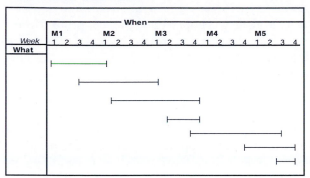

A Gantt chart is created by first defining a time line across the top of the chart. The time line can be days, weeks, months, years or any time interval appropriate for the particular activity (when). Next, the actions or tasks to be performed are listed in sequential order down the left side of the chart (what). People knowledgeable in the process change steps are involved in developing this list of tasks. Lines are drawn lines from the time that an activity is expected to be started to the time when the activity is predicted to end (the deadline).

Storyboard

A storyboard is a tool for reporting what happened during an improvement project. It is created when the project is done and *tells the story* of the entire project often using visual depictions such as bulleted points, charts, and graphs. A storyboard is like the Cliff Notes of a project – it contains only the bare essentials. The story begins with the Plan phase of the project. It is followed by information describing the Do phase, then the Check and Act phases. In Exhibit 5.9 is an example of a storyboard for an improvement project in the clinical laboratory.

Exhibit 5.9. Storyboard of a Clinical Laboratory Improvement Project

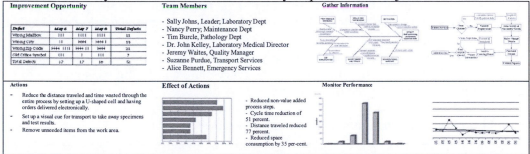

Only key charts and graphs are included in the storyboard. People reading the story understand what was accomplished, but not necessarily every step taken by the team. Using a storyboard to summarize a project has many advantages:

- It is short and simple to read
- It is easy to display on bulletin boards, overhead presentations or handouts
- It contains all pertinent data and information about the project
    - The baseline data and demonstrated need for improvement
    - The implemented changes (both what was implemented and how change was managed)
    - Communicates to others what the team did, why, and how others may be impacted

Improvement Project Teams

A team effort is necessary to effectively improve the quality of healthcare services. When a process needs improving – even if only one person is doing that job – everyone involved and affected by the process should have a voice in what needs changing and how to make those changes. The improvement project focused on reducing UTIs in nursing home residents was initiated by leadership, but it is the frontline staff members that will investigate and solve problems. People personally involved in the process being improved are often the best people to know what is not working well and how to fix it.

The challenges for improvement teams are many, starting at their inception. For instance, project teams may lack a clear understanding of the improvement goal. Unclear goals can result in project delays or implementation of process changes that don't achieve improvement expectations. Described in the next section are important considerations when creating and leading improvement project teams.

Select Team Members

Once a decision is made by senior leaders or managers to proceed with an improvement project, the next step is formation of an improvement team. The improvement team should include representatives from all groups involved in the process to be improved. However, it is important the team not get too large. The optimum size of an improvement team is somewhere between six and ten people. If the process to be improved is complex or crosses the entire organization, it may be necessary for people to represent more than one stakeholder group. If this is not an option, input from groups not represented on the team can be gathered through questionnaires or special work sessions.

It is essential to involve the right people in an improvement initiative because successful implementation of actions will depend on ownership. Ownership is more likely to occur if the people being asked to do something differently have a voice in the design of improvement actions. For instance, if the project team involved in reducing nursing home UTI rates does not include a certified nurse assistant representative it may be hard to get this group of employees to change the way they care for residents.

It is useful to clearly define the start and end point of the process to be improved to clarify the stakeholders needing to be represented on an improvement team. For instance, in Exhibit 5.10 is a high-level flowchart of the blood transfusion administration process in a hospital. The hospital wants to improve the entire process – starting with a physician's order for transfusion and ending with administration of blood at the patient's bedside.

The team for this improvement project would include representatives from the medical staff, nursing services, laboratory and the blood bank. Because some steps in the process are computerized, someone from information technology (IT) might also be included on the team.

Exhibit 5.10. High-Level Flowchart of Hospital Blood Transfusion Process

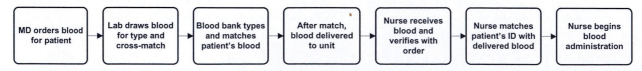

An improvement team needs a leader able to engage all the different players in completing the project. This person is usually appointed by the individual or group requesting the project be done. The team leader should have training in the use of improvement tools and be familiar with the improvement model guiding the project. Ideally, the team leader is of sufficient stature to be able to resolve any difficulties that may arise. The leader is responsible for planning meetings, circulating agendas and minutes, and ensuring the project stays on track toward meeting its objectives. In some organizations improvement project teams are also assigned a facilitator – an individual skilled in process measurement and improvement and teambuilding.

Clarify Objectives and Project Focus

Improvement projects need clear objectives. At the first team meeting, the leader clarifies the reason for the improvement project, expected results, and how project success will be judged. All team members are involved in refining the objective statements – key words or expressions which describe the purpose for the improvement project. In Exhibit 5.11 are the objectives, desired end results, and success measures for an improvement project involving processing of patient prescription refills in an internal medicine clinic.

Exhibit 5.11. Improvement Project Objectives, Desired Results, and Measures of Success

Improvement Project Objective:
Maximize patient satisfaction by reducing the wait time for prescription refills.

Desired End Results:
- Process prescription refill requests within 24 hours of receipt.
- Improve patient satisfaction scores.

How Success will be Measured:
- Percent of prescription refills processed within 24 hours
- Percent of patients rating the clinic staff as 'very responsive to my health needs'

Everyone on the team should agree to the project objectives, end results and measures of success. The leader keeps the objectives at the forefront during the improvement project and progress toward meeting objectives is periodically reviewed.

Team Dynamics

Team dynamics are a major consideration during improvement projects. Dynamics are motivating and driving forces that can hinder or help the group achieve project objectives. The team leader must manage the team dynamics appropriately to increase the likelihood of project success.

Every improvement team is a bit different. Sometimes team members already know one another. They may have worked together on other projects. In other situations, the team members may just be getting acquainted with one another. There may be conflict between members who have had past disagreements. Some team members may want to advance their own ideas while discrediting the ideas of others. Whatever the circumstance, it is up to the team leader (with help from a facilitator, if available) to handle disruptive team dynamics.

Improvement teams mature in stages. Designating a group of people to function as an improvement team is only the first step in team development. Creating synergy between individual team members takes some time. To become effective, improvement project teams must establish common objectives and their individual focus must be on those objectives, ahead of personal needs. In the 1960s psychologist, B.W Tuckman (1965) identified four distinct stages all teams goes through in order to be productive. The Tuckman model defines four identifiable stages of team development.
1. Forming,
2. Storming,
3. Norming, and
4. Performing

Forming

In this stage, members of the improvement team are polite to each other. They are assessing one another and how they fit into the group. They often test the limits of tolerance of other team members. During this time the leader can get the group to agree on project goals and establish ground rules for how the team will work together. However other tangible improvement work will have to wait until people get to know each other. The group 'being on its best behavior' characterizes the forming stage.

Storming

In the storming stage, team members begin to let down their guard and disagree with each other. If the leader does not channel the conflict in a productive fashion, the project is at great risk of failure. Unhealthy conflict may form within the team. To prevent this from happening, the team leader must encourage constructive controversy and respect for differing opinions. Creativity should be fostered to allow for evaluation of a wide range of views. All improvement teams experience the storming phase.

Teams that don't work through the conflict which naturally occurs at this phase will, in the end, be less successful. The team leader and perhaps one or two individuals on the team will end up setting the direction for the entire group, thus limiting creativity. Additionally, discontent team members may later undermine the success of improvement actions.

Norming

In this stage, members accept and appreciate the differences of individuals, learn to productively work through conflict and focus on the tasks at hand. There may be a risk of 'group think' if individuals go along with ideas to maintain harmony rather than introduce differences of opinion.

Performing

In the performing stage, team members are trusting of one another. The group transforms into a productive, fun, and rewarding improvement team. During this stage, creativity is fostered and ideas, rather than personal agendas, are debated. The improvement team takes collective pride in project accomplishments. Creative confrontation and innovative problem solving characterize this stage.

Managing Team Stages

An improvement team that is familiar and comfortable with one another may move through the four stages fairly quickly. It doesn't take long and the group is in the performing stage. The team leader merely needs to ensure everyone is on the same page with regard to how things are to get done. An improvement team that is familiar but uncomfortable with one another may get stuck in one of the early stages without skillful facilitation and teambuilding by the leader.

Regardless of the team composition conflict is a natural part of any improvement project. Discussion of differing viewpoints promotes team growth and development which leads to a successful improvement project. However, the team leader must intervene when this discussion leads to conflict. Conflict resolution requires open communication as well as a focus on issues not individuals. The team must be encouraged to search for win-win improvements benefiting everyone. Approaches a team leader can use to successfully manage team conflict are summarized in Exhibit 5.12.

Exhibit 5.12 Team Leader Approaches to Resolving Improvement Team Conflict

- Welcome conflict; use it as potential for change. Address data, facts, assumptions and conclusions.
- Clarify the nature of the problem as seen by all team members.
- Try to identify areas of agreement. Focus on common interests, not positions.
- Deal with one problem at a time, beginning with the easier issues.
- Listen with understanding. Reflect and clarify when communicating.
- Use objective criteria when possible.
- Invent new problems solutions where all parties gain.
- Evaluate and review the improvement process after implementing the action plans.

Summary

During the third step of quality management – improvement – causes of undesirable performance are identified and improvement actions taken. Quality improvement is not a random process. Distinct steps, or improvement models, are followed to achieve better performance. Some organizations expect everyone to use the same improvement model for most projects. In other organizations, the improvement model chosen for a project is dependent on the project objectives. For instance, a hospital team charged with eliminating defects in chemotherapy administration might use the Six Sigma improvement model. Another team charged with improving patient flow in the emergency department might use the RCI model to implement several small process changes and test the effects. A Kaizen event might be done when an outpatient laboratory wants to quickly improve efficiency of the blood collection process.

Teams are formed when performance needs improving or a problem needs to be solved. This is best accomplished using the collective experience, skills, and knowledge of a group of individuals. At the start of an improvement project the team gains a better understanding of the cause of undesirable performance by gathering and analyzing data about process performance and problem situations. Once it becomes clear what needs changing to achieve improvement goals, the team implements improvement actions and measures to see if the actions are effective at accomplishing project objectives.

Improvement team members should have job knowledge and technical, problem solving and interpersonal skills. With the exception of specific job knowledge and technical skills, most people can develop the skills they need after joining a team. The team leader plays a crucial role in managing the group dynamics and keeping the project on track.

Student Activities

1. Explore the website of the Institute for Healthcare Improvement (www.ihi.org). Select one of the quality improvement projects described on the site. For the project you select, describe what happened during each step of the project.
2. When completing the student activities in chapter one, you were asked to describe a personal situation in which you received inferior quality healthcare services. Design a rapid cycle improvement project to improve the quality of services you received. Start the project by answering three improvement questions:
   - What am I trying to accomplish? (the aim)
   - How will I know the change is an improvement? (measures of success)
   - What change can I make that will result in an improvement within 7 days? (actions)

   Also identify the groups (departments, units, positions, etc.) that should be represented on the improvement team for this project.
3. Research the stages of team development – forming, storming, norming, performing – and the leader's role in successfully managing teams during each stage. Report what you find.

Website Resources

American Society for Quality. Quality in healthcare case studies (free registration)
http://asq.org/healthcare-use/why-quality/case-studies.html

Centers for Medicare and Medicaid Services. Home health quality improvement resources.
www.homehealthquality.org/Education/QAPI-Resources.aspx

Centers for Medicare and Medicaid Services. *Quality Assurance and Performance Improvement (QAPI) at a Glance: A Step by Step Guide to Implementing QAPI in Your Nursing Home.*
www.cms.gov/Medicare/Provider-Enrollment-and-Certification/QAPI/Downloads/QAPIAtaGlance.pdf

Clinical Quality and Safety, Office of the National Coordinator for Health IT
www.healthit.gov/topic/clinical-quality-and-safety

Getting Better All the Time: Working Together for Continuous Improvement (manual on quality improvement approaches for nursing home caregivers)
www.nhqualitycampaign.org/files/gettingbetterall-the-time.pdf

The ABCs of PDCA (Plan-Do-Check-Act cycle). This paper demonstrates the PDCA cycle of quality improvement as it relates to public health.
www.phf.org/resourcestools/Pages/The_ABCs_of_PDCA.aspx

Video: *Lean at Miami Children's Hospital*
https://youtu.be/TvpweB9cigA

Video: *Lean Healthcare. Why Lean? Why now?*
https://youtu.be/bSF9Ro7HBIc

Video: *The Domestic Lean Goddess - Clothing Processing Center - Eliminating the 7 Wastes*
https://youtu.be/JkXUqxO0FEA

Video: *The Eight Wastes in Health Care*
https://youtu.be/7mA1L_a_FX4

References

Best, M., & Newhauser, D. (2006). Walter A Shewhart, 1924, and the Hawthorne factory. *Quality and Safety in Healthcare, 15(*2), 142-143.

_____. (2005). W Edwards Deming: father of quality management, patient and composer. *Quality and Safety in Healthcare, 14(*8), 137-145.

Joint Commission, The. (2017). Leadership standards. In *Comprehensive Accreditation Manual for Hospitals, 2018.* Oak Brook Terrace, IL: The Joint Commission.

Lavallee, D. (2011). Improve patient safety with lean techniques. In P. Spath (Ed*.) Error Reduction in Health Care, 2*nd ed. (pp. 246-264). San Francisco, CA: Jossey-Bass.

Tuckman, B. (1965). Developmental sequence in small groups. *Psychological Bulletin, 63(*6), 384-389.

IMPROVEMENT TOOLS AND TECHNIQUES

Reader Objectives

After reading this chapter and reflecting on the contents, you will be able to:
1. Demonstrate an understanding of tools and techniques used to improve performance.
2. Describe frequently used quantitative and qualitative improvement tools.
3. Choose improvement tools to use during different steps of an improvement project.
4. Explain techniques used to achieve more reliable performance.
5. Recognize process changes that improve efficiency and reduce mistakes.

Key Terms

Affinity diagram: Improvement tool used to organize detailed information into more general categories.

Brainstorming: Improvement tool used to generate ideas and make group decisions.

Cause and effect diagram: Improvement tool used to organize the origins or factors that produce a result.

Decision matrix: Improvement tool used to systematically rate and prioritize sets of information.

Flowchart: Improvement tool that provides a graphic representation of a process.

Force field analysis: Improvement tool used to understand competing forces that increase or decrease the probability of successfully implementing changes.

Human factors engineering: The study of human vulnerabilities and limitations to create systems that reduce the likelihood of human error and increase process efficiency and effectiveness; sometimes called reliability science.

Human factors principles: Work system improvements based on human factors engineering research.

Improvement tools: Diagrams, charts, techniques, and methods used in the work of quality improvement.

Multi-voting: Narrows a large list of possibilities to a smaller list of the top priorities or to a final selection; allows an item favored by all, but not the top choice of any, to rise to the top.

Nominal group process: See multi-voting.

Pareto diagram: Improvement tool used to apply the Pareto principle; helps differentiate the significant few problems from the trivial many.

Pareto principle: Named after 19th-century economist Vilfredo Pareto, the principle suggests that most effects come from relatively few causes; that is, 80% of the effects come from 20% of the causes.

Process reliability: Probability that a process will function satisfactorily over a period of time without failure.

Qualitative tools: Improvement tools used for generating ideas, setting priorities, providing direction, understanding problem causes, and helping to understand processes.

Quantitative tools: Improvement tools used for measuring performance, collecting and displaying data, and monitoring performance over time.

Redundancy: Duplication of activities or interventions to prevent errors or system failures from affecting performance.

Reliability science: See human factors engineering.

Scatter diagram: Improvement tool used to analyze the relationship between two performance variables.

Stratification: Technique used in combination with other data analysis tools; separates data into categories and sub-categories so patterns can be seen.

Value Stream Map: A visual depiction of work system steps from beginning to end showing workflow, information flow, and process cycle time.

Workflow diagram: Improvement tool used to visually represent the movement of people, materials, paperwork or information within a process; sometimes called a spaghetti diagram.

Performance Improvement Tools

Performance improvement tools are statistical analysis and decision-making instruments used during an improvement project. Don't confuse performance improvement models with the tools and techniques used during application of the model. During the life of an improvement project many different tools may be used. Some of the tools are quantitative; meaning they are used to quantify or count customers, a process, or a circumstance. Some of these tools are qualitative; meaning they used to describe customers, a process, or a circumstance.

Quantitative Tools

In chapters 3 and 4 you learned about tools used to gather and report performance measurement data. An improvement team often uses the same quantitative tools (for example, line graphs, histograms, bar graphs) to report data for analysis purposes during the project. In addition to the quantitative improvement tools described earlier, other quantitative tools commonly used during an improvement project are Pareto charts and scatter diagrams.

Pareto Chart

A Pareto chart graphically displays the relative importance of differences among groups of data within a set. It is used by an improvement team to apply the Pareto principle, named after the Italian economist Vilfredo Pareto (1848-1923). The Pareto principle, often referred to as the 80-20 rule, postulates that in any series of variables (problems or errors), a small number will account for most of the effect. For example, 80% of patient complaints stem from 20% of the problems.

A Pareto chart provides the project team with information to help focus improvement efforts on the vital few problems rather than the trivial many. For instance, the Pareto chart in Exhibit 6.1 shows the top three causes of patient dissatisfaction: the testing process, noise, and parking. A team working on improving patient satisfaction would use this information to focus improvement actions on the top three problems. If these problems are eliminated, the data suggest almost 80% of the causes of patient dissatisfaction will be removed.

A Pareto chart shows a snapshot of performance from one time period. It is never used to show performance over time.

Exhibit 6.1. Pareto Chart

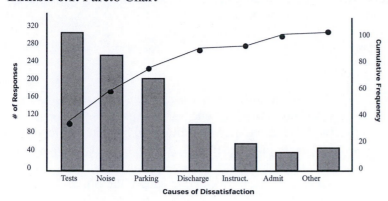

Below are the steps for creating a Pareto chart:

1. Define the categories and the units of comparison for the data, such as frequency, time or cost.

2. Sort data into the defined categories and arrange the categories in descending order from largest to smallest. If there is an 'other' category, show it on the far right of the graph.

3. Calculate the percent of the total that each category represents.

4. Working from the largest category to the smallest (or other) category, calculate the cumulative percentage for each category with all previous categories.

5. Draw and label the left vertical axis with the unit of comparison. Scale this axis from zero to the grand total of all categories.

6. Draw and label the horizontal axis with the categories, largest to smallest, left to right.

7. Draw bars for each category. Each bar's height should be the category sum as measured on the left axis.

8. Optional: Draw and label the right vertical axis from 0 to 100 percent, with the 100 percent value at the same height as the grand total mark on the left vertical axis. Draw a line graph of the cumulative percentage, beginning with the lower left corner of the largest category.

Scatter Diagram

A scatter diagram (sometimes called a *scatter plot*) is a simple visual form of graphical analysis. If the improvement team is investigating a potential relationship between two variables, then a scatter diagram is a good quantitative tool to use. It shows a snapshot of performance from one time period and is not used to show performance over time.

Suppose a team in the urgent care clinic is charged with improving customer satisfaction. They want to dig deeper into the factors influencing high satisfaction levels. The team guesses staff helpfulness has a positive impact on overall customer satisfaction. To test this theory the scatter diagram in Exhibit 6.2 is created using data from 20 satisfaction surveys. The overall satisfaction score (ranging from 1 to 10) is shown on the y-axis and the score given to staff helpfulness (ranging from 1 to 10) is shown on the x-axis.

Exhibit 6.2. Scatter Diagram

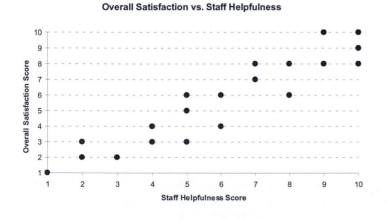

The scatter diagram in Exhibit 6.2 reveals a strong correlation between overall customer satisfaction and staff helpfulness. Armed with this data the team now suspects that efforts to improve staff helpfulness may improve overall customer satisfaction scores. This theory will be tested when action plans are implemented and success evaluated.

A scatter diagram is meant to be a visual quantitative tool. If there appears to be a pattern, such as a line or a curve then you have a relationship. The scatter diagram in Exhibit 6.2 shows pretty clear evidence there is a positive correlation between the two variables. However, correlation is not the same as causation. In Exhibit 6.3 are common scatter diagram patterns and the meaning of these patterns.

Exhibit 6.3. Scatter Diagram Patterns and Interpretation

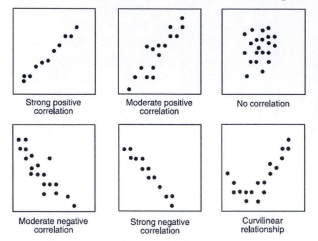

Just because you see a relationship in a scatter diagram doesn't mean one variable is the only cause of the other. Both may be influenced by other factors. For instance, just because staff helpfulness scores and overall satisfaction scores appear to increase at the same rate doesn't mean one causes the other. The indication of a relationship only suggests additional investigation would be worthwhile.

Below are the steps for creating a scatter diagram:

1. Select two variables you believe have a causal relationship – one variable is thought to affect the value of the other variable.
2. Draw the x-axis (horizontal) and the y-axis (vertical). Data for the suspected causal variable is usually shown on the x-axis; the caused variable on the y-axis.
3. Set the scales for both axes. The scales should range from the lowest number to the highest number of data you will be plotting. You don't have to begin with zero. Divide the scale into smaller, equal increments, and label the increments. The increments for the x-axis don't have to be the same as the increments for the y-axis.
4. Plot the two variables from each case on the diagram. To plot the points, just take the paired values, go to the left on the X-axis to the point corresponding to the X value, and then up to the point corresponding to the Y value. Do this for each pair of measures.

Digging Deeper

Sometimes project teams must dig deeper into the measurement data to better understand what needs changing to achieve improvement goals. This technique of digging deeper is known as stratification. This is not an improvement tool. It is technique used to break down data into categories or subcategories to make better sense of it. The case study in Exhibit 6.4 illustrates how a project team might use stratification.

Exhibit 6.4. Case Study of HIM Department Improvement Project

An improvement team in the HIM department is trying to understand its relatively high rate of coding errors. Someone asks whether there are certain time periods when the problem is worse. The team stratifies coding error data by week and produces a control chart of the weekly data, only to find random variation. Further stratification by day of the week and time of day also fails to pinpoint the problem source. The team asks whether it is possible only certain employees account for the high error rate. To answer this question, error data are stratified by coder. Again, the team finds nothing unusual. Finally, someone comes up with the theory that coding errors occur more often in the records of physicians with poor documentation habits. When the team stratifies coding error data by the physician of record, they find this theory is in fact correct.

The improvement team stratified – broke down, categorized and separated – measurement data several different ways to get closer to the root cause of the problem. They could have stratified the numbers in many other ways, as performance is often affected by several factors. Team members' knowledge of the system is useful when selecting ways of stratifying data to uncover sources of quality problems.

Qualitative Tools

Qualitative improvement tools are used for generating ideas, set priorities, provide direction, understand root causes, and help understand work processes. The most common qualitative improvement tools used during improvement projects are:

- Brainstorming
- Cause and effect diagram
- Affinity diagram
- Prioritization tools

- Flowcharts
- Value stream map
- Workflow diagram
- Force field analysis

Brainstorming

Brainstorming is a way for a group of people to generate as many ideas as possible in a very short time by tapping into group energy and individual creativity. It is particularly useful when generating ideas about problems, areas of improvement, possible causes, solutions, and resistance to change. By bringing out many creative ideas in a short period of time and encouraging all team members to participate, this useful tool opens up people's thinking and broadens their perspectives. It allows ideas to build on one another. However, brainstorming is not a substitute for quantitative data when it comes to decision-making. Suppositions made during brainstorming need to be validated with data.

How to Use It
- Write the question or issue to be explored on a flipchart or any place where everyone can see. Make sure everyone is clear about the topic.
- Give people a few minutes to think of some ideas before starting.
- Invite everyone to call out his or her ideas or have each member in turn offer an idea about the topic. Other team members should listen carefully and build on each other's ideas.
- Have one person record the ideas (all of them) on a flipchart so the whole group can easily scan them, pausing only to check accuracy.
- Continue the process until the team feels it has run out of ideas on the topic. End the session when people begin taking a long time to come up with ideas.
- Discuss and clarify the ideas on the flipchart.

Cause and Effect Diagram

Cause and effect diagrams are structured brainstorming tools. The diagram is used as a framework for generating and sorting ideas or hypotheses about possible causes of problems. Items are listed in a graphic display sometimes called a fishbone diagram (because of its shape) and sometimes called an Ishikawa diagram, after the inventor of the tool, Kaoru Ishikawa, who first used the technique in the 1960s.

Shown in Exhibit 6.5 is a cause and effect diagram for the problem of computer downtime. The problem or main effect – computer downtime – is entered in the box at the right of the diagram. The causes brainstormed by the improvement team are sorted into cause categories. When creating a fishbone diagram, the improvement team chooses categories most relevant to the problem or effect and may add or drop categories as needed. The diagram in Exhibit 6.5 uses the cause categories: software, environment, users, and hardware. Below are often-used cause categories:

- Manpower, methods, materials, measurement, and equipment
- Clients, workers, supplies, environment, and procedures
- What, how, when, and where
- Equipment/supplies, environment, rules/policies/procedures, and staff/people

Exhibit 6.5. Cause and Effect Diagram

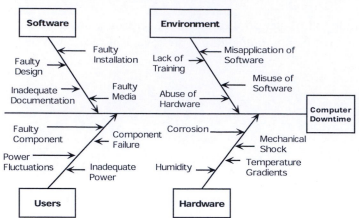

The completed cause and effect diagram is used by an improvement team to spot linkages between problems and potential causes. The graphic display, with major branches reflecting categories of causes, stimulates and broadens thinking about potential or real causes and facilitates further examination of individual causes. It helps focus the team's attention on possible causes. However the brainstormed causes must be proven before taking any actions.

A cause and effect diagram is merely a structured way of expressing hypotheses or 'best guesses' about the causes of a problem or why something is not happening as desired. The team should not begin solving the problem until data are gathered to validate or reject each hypothesis.

How to Use It

1. Agree on the problem or desired state and write it in the *effect* box. Be as specific as possible. Cause and effect diagrams can reflect either causes that block the way to the desired state or helpful factors needed to reach the desired state.
2. Define the major categories of steps or causes. Add or drop categories as needed when generating causes. Each category is written into the box. Generally, using three to six categories works best.
3. Identify specific causes and add them to the correct branches or sub-branches (sticky-notes work well for this exercise). Use simple brainstorming to generate a list of ideas before classifying them on the diagram. If an idea fits into more than one category, place it on both.
4. Each major branch should include three or four possible causes. If a branch has too few, the group should find some way to explain this lack or ask others who have some knowledge in that area to help.
5. The team then selects several areas they agree are the most likely causes. These choices can be made by voting, based on the team members' best collective judgment.

Before advancing to the solution phase, use quantitative tools to gather data to prove (or disprove) the team's choice of most likely causes. If data confirms none of the likely causes, go back to the cause and effect diagram and choose other causes for testing.

Affinity Analysis

Affinity analysis helps an improvement team brainstorm and organize large amounts of information based on *affinities* or natural relationships. Affinity analysis allows the ideas to determine the categories or groupings, rather than allowing pre-determined groupings (such as those on a cause and effect diagram) to determine or constrain the generation of ideas.

An affinity analysis can help a team quickly organize many different ideas or topics. It is also useful for making sure the lone idea does not get lost in the shuffle. Affinity analysis is especially useful when issues appear too large or complex, when consensus is desired, or when creative ideas are needed. It helps develop team consensus because everyone's idea is included and the idea groupings are done by the team.

How to Use It

1. State the issue or question to be considered and make sure all participants are clear on what is being asked.
2. Generate and record ideas on slips of paper. Each idea or item should be recorded on its own slip. Sticky-notes or note cards, if available, are good to use for this exercise. Ideas can be generated through brainstorming or each person can record his or her ideas on slips of paper.
3. Place the slips of paper in any order in a manner so everyone to see them (e.g., on a wall or table). See example in Exhibit 6.6.

Exhibit 6.6. Issues in Implementing Continuous Quality Improvement

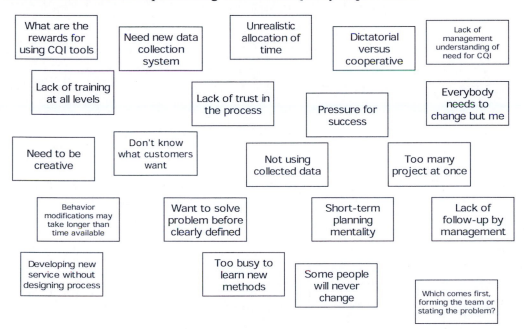

4. Ask team members to sort the ideas on the slips of paper into related groups by having them move the slips of paper around, but without discussion. After a while, the team members will no longer be moving items around. If a slip of paper is constantly being moved back and forth between two groupings, either clarify the meaning or place it in both groupings by adding another paper. See example in Exhibit 6.7.

Exhibit 6.7. Issues Sorted into Columns of Related Groups

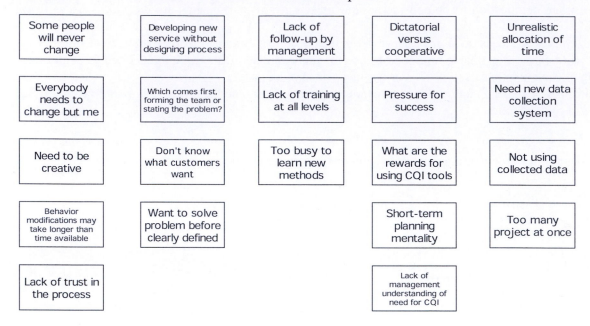

5. For each grouping, develop a name or category reflecting the meaning of that group and write it on a slip of paper. These become the header cards for each category. Place the header cards at the top of each grouping. If necessary draw lines around the groupings so it is clear where each idea is categorized. See example of the completed affinity diagram in Exhibit 6.8.

Exhibit 6.8. Completed Affinity Diagram for Issues in Implementing Quality Improvement

Breaking through old way of thinking	Lack of planning	Organizational issues	Old management style	Lack of CQI knowledge
Some people will never change	Developing new service without designing process	Lack of follow-up by management	Dictatorial versus cooperative	Unrealistic allocation of time
Everybody needs to change but me	Which comes first, forming the team or stating the problem?	Lack of training at all levels	Pressure for success	Need new data collection system
Need to be creative	Don't know what customers want	Too busy to learn new methods	What are the rewards for using CQI tools	Not using collected data
Behavior modifications may take longer than time available	Want to solve problem before clearly defined		Short-term planning mentality	Too many project at once
Lack of trust in the process			Lack of management understanding of need for CQI	

6. Once the ideas are categorized in the completed affinity diagram the team uses prioritization tools to sort through the ideas in each group.

Prioritization Tools

Prioritization tools are used when a team needs to make decisions among several options. Group methods for narrowing down and ranking a list of ideas include simple voting or use of priority-setting matrices. Both methods allow individuals to express their opinions or choices in order to reach group consensus. Voting is a relatively unstructured technique in which people make choices, using either implicit or explicit criteria. A priority-setting matrix allows the team to review options against a standard set of explicit criteria.

Voting is most useful when options are fairly straightforward or when time is limited. Improvement teams can structure voting in several ways, but they all have the purpose of letting each individual state his or her preferences. Regardless of the type of voting used, all group members must understand the various options being voted on.

- Straight voting: All options are listed and each person in the group is given one vote. All votes are weighted equally. This is the easiest method for a group to use.
- Multi-voting: All options are listed and each person is allowed to vote for a limited number of items (for example, three or five). Each person ranks their top three to five choices and assigns a value to these rankings, for example: highest priority = 3; next priority = 2; last of three priorities = 1; not a priority = 0. The rankings are added up for each item, and the one with the highest score is the top priority for the group. Multi-voting is sometimes referred to as 'nominal group process.'
- Weighted voting: All options are listed and each person is given the chance to give more weight to some choices than to others. One way of doing this is to give each person a fixed amount of hypothetical money to spend. They can distribute it any way they wish among the alternatives, e.g., if given $5, one could spend all $5 on a single item one felt very strongly about, or one could distribute it evenly over five items, or any other combination. This method allows the voting to reflect the strength of the individual's conviction about various choices.

A decision matrix (sometimes called a priority-setting matrix) helps focus team member decisions on explicit criteria. The group discusses and agrees on the criteria by which each participant should base their judgment. The decision matrix is used to record the participant's votes. In Exhibit 6.9 is a matrix used by the organization's leaders to choose which improvement opportunities will be worked on first. Six selection criteria have been defined:

- Success (probability of solving problem)
- Time necessary to solve problem
- Cost of solving problem
- Impact on organization's vision/mission
- Impact on customer satisfaction
- Acceptance by people involved

Exhibit 6.9. Decision Matrix

Selection Criteria

Improvement Opportunities	Success	Time	Cost	Impact on Mission	Impact on Satisfaction	Acceptance	Your Total	Group Total

Ranking Key: 3 = Good, Easy, Short   2 = Average   1 = Poor, Hard, Long

Team members individually vote, using the ranking key shown at the bottom of the matrix. An individual's total is shown together with the sum for the group. The opportunity statements receiving the highest group vote totals are selected for improvement projects.

Flowcharts

A flowchart is a graphic representation of how a process works that shows, at a minimum, the sequence of steps. A flowchart helps the improvement team clarify how things are currently working and how they could be improved. This qualitative tool also assists the team in finding the key elements of a process, while drawing clear lines between where one process ends and the next one starts. Creating an accurate flowchart requires people with strong knowledge of the current process.

Flowcharts can be used to examine processes for the flow of patients, information flow, flow of materials, clinical care processes, or any combination of these processes. The basic symbols used in most flowcharts are found in Exhibit 6.10.

Exhibit 6.10. Flowchart Symbols

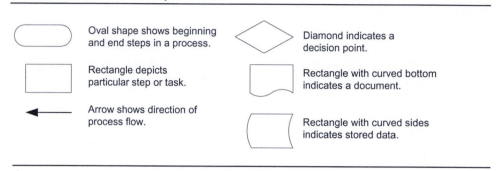

Several types of flowcharts may be used by improvement teams.

- High-level or first-level flowchart (the most simple)
- Top-down flowchart (shows sub-steps)
- Detailed flowchart (shows all steps, including delays and decisions)
- Matrix or deployment flowchart (shows the people involved in the steps)
- Value stream map

High-Level Flowchart

A high-level flowchart shows the major steps of a process. By limiting the amount of information displayed, high-level flowcharts force people to narrow their thinking to only those steps absolutely essential to the process. An example of a high-level flowchart showing patient flow in an outpatient clinic is found in Exhibit 6.11.

Exhibit 6.11. High-Level Flowchart of Patient Flow in Outpatient Clinic

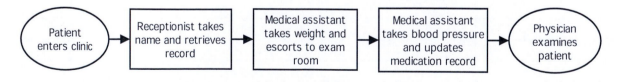

A high-level flowchart is generally used by an improvement team to gain a basic picture of the process and to identify any changes taking place in the process. It is also useful for identifying appropriate team members for a performance improvement project and for developing measures to monitor the process.

Top-Down Flowchart

A top-down flowchart starts with the major steps drawn horizontally. The detail is provided in numbered subtasks under each major task. A top-down flowchart does not show decision points, reworks and so on. Steps in creating a top-down flowchart:
1. List the most basic steps in the process being studied.
2. List steps across the top of the page. You should end up with no more than six or seven steps.
3. Below each step list the major sub-steps, again no more than six or seven.

In Exhibit 6.12 is a top-down flowchart of the process of transferring a nursing home (NH) resident to the hospital – from the time it is recognized the resident should be taken to the hospital until information is provided to the receiving hospital.

Exhibit 6.12. Top-Down Flowchart of Nursing Home Resident Transfer to Hospital

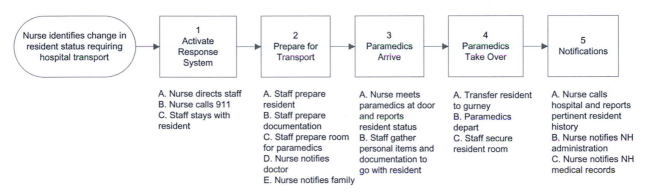

Matrix or Deployment Flowchart

A matrix flowchart (sometimes called a deployment flowchart or swim lane diagram) maps out a process in terms of the resources completing the steps. Resources can be anything but are often things like departments, people, locations, etc. It is in a matrix form, showing the various resources and the flow of steps among these resources. Exhibit 6.13 illustrates a sample matrix flowchart showing the movement of process steps between three different departments.

Exhibit 6.13. Sample Matrix Flowchart.

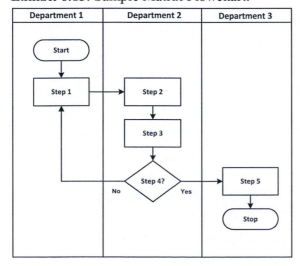

A matrix or deployment flowchart is chiefly useful for identifying who (a person or department) is providing inputs or services to whom, as well as finding situations where different people or departments may needlessly be doing the same task. The flowchart is drawn with each process step placed in the swim lane belonging to the appropriate resource used. Matrix flowcharts are useful for displaying the flow of information or materials between resources at a glance.

A deployment flow chart is a special type of matrix flowchart developed by Dr. W. Edwards Deming. A typical deployment flowchart would show the process steps, roles and interdepartmental interactions required to roll out a product or complete a complex process.

Detailed Flowchart

A detailed flowchart indicates the steps or activities of a process and includes such things as decision points, waiting periods, tasks frequently needing to be redone, and feedback loops. In Exhibit 6.14 is a detailed flowchart showing how a clinic schedules patient appointments. Detailed flowcharts are useful for conducting in-depth process examinations to look for problems or areas of inefficiency.

Exhibit 6.14. Detailed Flowchart Showing Clinic Scheduling Process

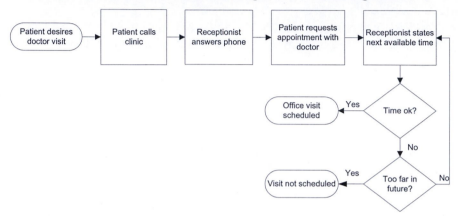

There are several basic steps to the construction of a flowchart and these are applicable to most types of charts.
1. Agree on the purpose of the flowchart and which format is most appropriate.
2. Determine the beginning and end points of the process to be flowcharted. Get agreement from the group on these points.
3. Identify the elements of the flowchart by asking the following questions:
   • Who provides the input for this step? Who uses it?
   • What is done with these inputs? What decisions need to be made?
   • What is the output to this step? Who uses it to do what?
4. Review the final product to be sure it represents the actual steps in the process, not what people would like the process to look like.

Value Stream Map

Value stream maps are commonly created during Lean projects. This specialized type of flowchart provides a detailed map of all tasks needed to deliver a particular service to a customer, including the time needed to complete each task as well as wasted time. The map is used to improve the process through step-by-step review and identification of connections, activities, information, and flow. Exhibit 6.15 illustrates a high-level value stream map of the process of obtaining blood specimens for hospitalized patients. This is the current state of the process. A new value stream map will be drawn after process changes are made. Below are the steps for creating a value stream map (ASQ, 2016).
1. Identify the service of interest.
2. Gather a team of experts and people with strong knowledge of the service.
3. Draw the current process with all of the steps, delays, and information flows required to deliver the service of interest.
4. Assess the current process in terms of flow and waste and collect data on value added activities, cycle times for each activity, etc.
5. Calculate the total process time and value added time.
6. Identify and list all areas of waste (e.g., unnecessary waits, over-processing, redundant steps, etc.).
7. Develop a list of opportunities for improvement based on these observations.

Exhibit 6.15. Value Stream Map of Phlebotomy Process (Current State)

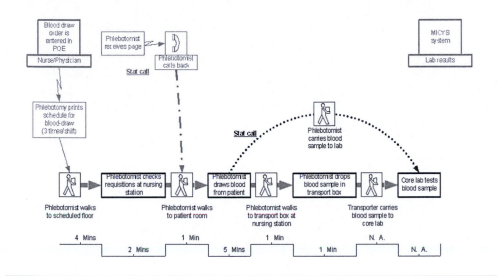

Value stream maps can become very complex if delivering the service involves multiple tasks performed by different individuals and departments. A facilitator trained in value stream mapping is often needed to assist the Lean project team in completing the map.

Workflow Diagram

A flowchart is a visual representation of the sequential steps of a process. A workflow diagram is a visual representation of the movement of people, materials, paperwork or information within a process. A workflow diagram can also illustrate general relationships or patterns of activity among various inter-related processes (such as all processes occurring in the HIM department). Workflow diagrams are also called spaghetti diagrams because the completed product resembles a plate of spaghetti. The more messy the spaghetti strands, the more messy and inefficient the process.

Workflow diagrams are used to document how work is carried out and to find opportunities for improvement. These diagrams are especially useful for identifying waste – the primary purpose of a Lean improvement project. There are four basic steps to the construction of a workflow diagram.
1.   Draw the area to be studied.
2.   Draw a line for each movement.
3.   Brainstorm how the movement can be decreased.
4.   Improve workflow and repeat.

This case study illustrates how a workflow diagram is used in an improvement project. An urgent care center is looking for ways to reduce the movement of patients. They decide to use a workflow diagram to represent the current state. The quality manager draws a map of the building and then watches a few patients from the time they enter the office to when they leave, drawing a line on the map for every movement they make. In Exhibit 6.16 is the result for one patient.

Exhibit 6.16. Workflow Diagram Showing Movement of Patient in the Urgent Care Center

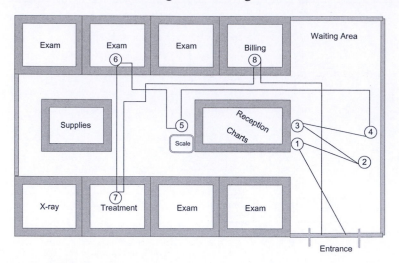

Force Field Analysis

Force field analysis is used by an improvement team to identify the forces that help and the forces that hinder reaching a desired outcome or solution to a problem. It depicts the situation as a balance between two sets of forces: one that tries to change the status quo and one that tries to maintain it. This analysis method can focus the team's attention on ways of reducing the hindering forces.

Force field analysis compels the improvement team to think together about what is working for and against the status quo. The diagram created from this discussion allows team members to view factors as two sets of offsetting issues. Illustrated in Exhibit 6.17 is a force field analysis depicting the driving and restraining forces for implementing an electronic health record in a clinic.

Exhibit 6.17. Force Field Analysis

Driving Forces		Restraining Forces
Reduce duplicative documentation in patient records	→ ←	People not trained in the use of computers
Improve transfer of information among caregivers	→ ←	Employees' fear of changing the status quo
Need to provide online access to clinical practice guidelines and protocols	→ ←	Lack of time for people to be involved in developing computerized guidelines/protocols
Need to reduce adverse drug events caused by illegible handwriting and lack of access to patient-specific information	→ ←	People's memories of past IT projects that have not been successful

Force field analysis is used to study existing problems and to anticipate and plan more effectively for implementing process changes. When used in problem solving, force field analysis is especially helpful for identifying more subjective issues, such as employee morale, management, effectiveness, and work climate.

To conduct a force field analysis, first state the problem or desired state and make sure everyone understands it. Next, team members brainstorm all factors influencing movement toward the desired state and those hindering movement toward that state.

Once the lists are complete, the team reviews and clarifies each force or factor by asking: what is behind these factors? what works to balance the situation? The team then determines how great the hindering forces are (high, medium, low) on the desired state. Factors with the biggest impact become the focus of plans to reduce resistance to change. The team develops actions plans to address the largest hindering forces.

Selecting Improvement Tools

Various quantitative and qualitative tools may be used during an improvement project. The decision to use a particular tool hinges on whether it will help support team activities at that point in the project. For instance, sometimes the team needs to understand what is causing undesirable performance. Brainstorming, a qualitative tool, could be used to generate as many ideas as possible. It can be helpful to use more structured brainstorming tools, such as a cause and effect diagram or an affinity analysis, to sort possible causes into categories.

Actions are not taken based solely on brainstorming results. Data are needed to confirm assumptions. A quantitative tool, such as a survey, might be used to gather data from the people involved in the process to verify the exact areas of concern. Queries of electronic databases may be done to gather even more information. Quantitative tools such as a Pareto chart or control chart could be used to display the results of data collection. By flowcharting the process the team often finds opportunities to reduce errors or inefficiencies. A flowchart of the new process might be created by the team during the action planning phase of a project. Ideally, the project team leader has some experience in using improvement tools and can assist in selecting the best tool to use during a particular project step.

Summarized in Exhibit 6.18 are some common improvement tools that might be used during the steps of an improvement project. When selecting tools consider what is needed by the team during each project step. Do they need to expand their thinking about problems or possible solutions? Do they need to gather or analyze data? Do they need to evaluate various alternatives? Find the best tool for accomplishing what is needed by the team.

Exhibit 6.18. Quick Reference Guide to Improvement Tools

Project Step	Examples of Tools to Use		
Define issues that need evaluating to achieve improvement goals	Affinity diagram Bar graph Box plot Brainstorming	Cause and effect diagram Control chart Dashboard Flowchart	Line graph Pareto chart Pie chart Scatter diagram
Collect information to further understand and validate the issues	Checksheet Flowchart	Questionnaire Survey	Value stream map Workflow diagram
Analyze what is known about the causes of undesirable performance	Affinity diagram Bar graph Cause and effect diagram	Control chart Histogram Line graph	Pareto chart Scatter diagram
Generate solutions intended to achieve improvement goals	Brainstorming Cause and effect diagram Decision matrix	Flowchart Force field analysis Gantt chart	Prioritization tools Value steam map
Measure performance to determine if solutions achieved desired goals	Bar graph Box plot	Control chart Dashboard	Line graph Radar chart

Performance Improvement Techniques

The most important part of an improvement project is the action planning and implementation phase. Improvement goals will not be achieved if solutions are not effective. When choosing how best to change current processes to improve performance, teams often start by brainstorming ideas and getting input from other departments or organizations that have tackled similar problems. Healthcare organizations are now implementing improvement actions found to work well in other industries. These improvement techniques, based on human factors engineering, are intended to reduce mistakes and improve performance reliability.

Human factors engineering (HFE) is the study of human vulnerabilities and limitations for the purpose of creating processes that are less error-prone and more efficient (Boston-Fleischhauer, 2008). This analysis was first applied to military tasks during World War II. Since then the research has branched out to include any activities involving human-system interfaces. An application of HFE that may be familiar to students is usability testing of technology. Human factors principles are used to optimize the relationship between technology and humans with the goal of making the technology easy to use and a good fit for the people who use it (Carayon, Xie, & Kianfar. 2014).

What we have learned from human factors research is that people cannot be expected to function flawlessly. The systems in which people work must be a good fit – designed to better accommodate natural human frailties. Healthcare is a complex system. While performing routine daily activities people make occasional mistakes. Errors occur because of any number of personal and environmental factors, including:

- inattention
- memory lapse
- failure to communicate
- poorly designed equipment

- fatigue
- inexperience
- distracting working conditions
- multi-tasking

When designing improvement actions, project teams must consider human factors principles. Solutions should increase the consistency with which tasks are completed as required to achieve desired performance goals. Because more reliable process output is the goal, HFE is sometimes called reliability science (Luria et al., 2006).

Human Factors Principles

Years of research in the design of interactive systems involving people, tools, and technology have resulted in an understanding of how best to optimize performance. Applying this research requires a project team carefully examine the system they want to improve to determine how best to achieve quality goals. For instance, what tasks must get done? What skills are needed to complete the tasks? How are handoffs accomplished between people doing different tasks? What is the work environment like? In essence, team members must learn how the system works in actual practice and propose changes that will optimize performance.

Several general work system improvement recommendations have come out of human factors studies. These principles are listed in Exhibit 6.19 (Karsh et al, 2006). These principles are not unique to a particular improvement model. They can be applied when designing actions during any type of improvement project.

Exhibit 6.19. Human Factors Principles for Work System Improvements

• Simplify the process	• Use constraints and forcing functions
• Standardize	• Design for errors
• Reduce reliance on memory	• Adjust the environment
• Improve information access	

Simplify the Process

Simple processes are easier for people to follow. By simplifying processes – eliminating unnecessary steps (waste) – it is more likely each task will be completed as required. A recent study of protocols for verifying patient surgical sites found that significant personnel time was required for multiple redundant checks without clearly added benefits (Kwaan et al., 2006). Authors of the study suggested that simplification of the protocols would improve adherence and efficiency.

When a project team proposes changes in the way work gets done a flowchart of the new process should be created and analyzed for possible simplification before it is implemented. Detailed and matrix flowcharts are particularly useful for identifying redundant or unnecessary steps that can be eliminated.

Standardize

If tasks are done the same way every time by everyone there is less chance for error. Unnecessary variation can also be found in equipment, supplies, and the location of equipment and supplies. Standardization improves performance reliability by creating predictability and consistency in the process. HCA Healthcare used standardization techniques to improve patient care and coordination among physicians, nurses, technicians and others involved in delivering babies. Highly specific, checklist-driven protocols and procedure documentation templates were created for use by caregivers. By standardizing the care provided to obstetric patients, HCA improved perinatal outcomes, reduced the primary cesarean delivery rate, and lowered the incidence of maternal and fetal injuries (Clark et al., 2008).

Initial process simplification and standardization actions need not be perfect. A project team may use small tests of change to quickly learn what works best. A small change is made in the process and within one week the effects of the change are measured. Was the change accepted by staff members? Did it achieve desired performance goals? If the change didn't work out, the team studies the reason for failure and uses this knowledge to redesign the process for the next small test of change. This cycle of testing small changes to the process is commonly used in the rapid cycle improvement model but can also be used during the action planning phase of any type of improvement project.

Reduce Reliance on Memory

Sometimes poor performance is caused by people merely forgetting to do required tasks. Unintentional memory slips can be reduced by adding easy-to-use reminder systems to the work environment. Checklists, protocols, preprinted patient assessment tools, and computerized pop-up decision aids are examples of techniques used to reduce people's reliance on memory.

The improvement project team can be innovative in designing reminder mechanisms. For example, nurses at OSF St. Francis Medical Center in Peoria, IL were asked to turn bed-ridden patients every two hours to reduce the incidence of pressure ulcers (AHA, 2009). Several reminder aids were built into the patient care systems to help nurses remember to do this required task:

- Play part of the song 'Roll Over Beethoven' over the hospital speaker system every 2 hours during the day and evening as a reminder to nurses to reposition their patients
- Place 'Save Our Skin' signage on the doors of patients at-risk for pressure ulcers

Whenever possible, improvement teams should seek ways to make it easier for people to remember what tasks are to be done and how to perform these tasks. Often several actions are necessary to achieve performance goals. An improvement team in an oncology clinic made several changes to the chemotherapy administration process to achieve desired quality and patient safety goals. The actions included:

- Change location of chemotherapy preparation to reduce staff interruptions during preparation
- Create a standardized chemotherapy preparation checklist for pharmacists and nurses
- Create a chemotherapy medication administration record that is sequenced the same as actual administration

Improve Information Access

Good decisions require good information. People must have ready access to relevant and complete information or faulty decisions can occur. The right information must get to the right people at the right time. To achieve this goal, the improvement team should identify the process steps where information needs to be communicated from one place to the next and then determine how best to make information flow efficient. A workflow diagram is a useful tool for showing how information flows in the work environment system and where communication problems exist.

Here's an example of how improved information access resulted in better performance. While evaluating ways of reducing nosocomial infections, a hospital improvement team discovered infection control practitioners waited up to 48 hours to receive information about patient cultures testing positive for bacterial or yeast organisms. The hospital's enterprise IT system was revised to enable regular extraction of information from the microbiology database with the infection control department receiving an email every morning alerting them to the presence of 'red flag' microorganisms present in patient cultures. This allowed infection control practitioners to act quickly in consulting with caregivers on these cases.

Not only must information be accessible, it must also be up-to-date. The importance of having current information during patient hand-off communications is emphasized by Joint Commission standards. Accredited organizations are to ensure the process for transitioning patient care from one caregiver to the next includes up-to-date information regarding the patient's care, treatment and services, condition and any recent or anticipated changes (Joint Commission, 2017). To accomplish this, organizations often develop a standardized approach for hand-off communications to ensure consistency.

Use Constraints and Forcing Functions

Constraining and forcing functions are barriers that make it easier for people to do the right thing. For instance, the 'Are you sure?' prompt that follows hitting the delete key in a computer program makes it more difficult to inadvertently delete a file you want to keep. You can't start your car when in reverse gear; a physical restraint that keeps you from having an accident. Bar-coded patient identification is a forcing function used in medication administration to eliminate errors caused by failure to comply with traditional medication recipient identification protocols.

Forcing functions are often integrated into the computer-user interface. For example, at some facilities an MRI procedure cannot be scheduled without first confirming the patient has no contraindications such as a metallic implant. To make sure patients on opiate medications also receive stool softeners or laxatives, one hospital added a forcing function to the computerized order entry system. When a physician orders an opiate the system automatically defaults to a stool softener ordering screen. At this point the physician can opt out, however the rationale for doing this must be documented (Luria et al., 2006).

Design for Errors

Human factors research has proven that we should not expect people to perform flawlessly. Consequently, improvement teams must design systems that encourage reliable performance but also allow for quick error detection and correction. An example of a process designed for errors involves discontinuing patients' urinary catheters after surgery. Prolonged catheterization increases the risk of urinary tract infections and caregivers must be alert to the need for timely catheter removal. In one hospital several reminders are built into the care systems to ensure a patient's catheter is removed as soon as it is no longer needed. First, a pink sticker with the surgery date is placed on the urine collection bag in the postoperative recovery unit. In addition, a catheter alert reminder is incorporated into the EHR. Within 24 hours of a patient's surgery, the physician must document why a urinary catheter is still needed or order removal of the catheter. Every day the unit charge nurse conducts urinary catheter surveillance checks to ensure all patients with catheters have a medical need for one. The many reminders and redundancies built into this system are intended to ensure that caregivers do not let surgical patients remain catheterized any longer than medically necessary.

When designing for errors be careful not to make the process unnecessarily complex. Remember, the more simple the process the more likely people will consistently perform correctly. Another caution when adding reminders and redundant steps to a process is the risk of complacency. When people are aware that others are duplicating their efforts, redundancy can diffuse responsibility and lead individuals to overlook important tasks. For example, physicians may over-ride the catheter alert reminder in the EHR if they know that each day a charge nurse will be verbally reminding them to discontinue the catheter.

Adjust the Environment

Human factors engineers have long recognized the error-producing factors in work environments; for example: noise, poor lighting, glare-producing surfaces, heat, clutter, electrical interference, humidity, and moisture. When designing actions to improve performance, a project team may need to physically visit the worksite to identify human performance problems related to workstation design, workplace layout, equipment, supplies, and procedures. The result of this analysis can be used to identify possible performance barriers and develop solutions for eliminating or controlling them.

Changes to the work environment can result in some significant improvements in performance. For instance, the Veterans Health Administration found the incidence of patients wandering away from nursing facilities was greatly reduced by environmental changes such as adding alarms to fire escape doors that could not be disconnected by staff and placing black floor tiles in front of each door area leaving a perception of a dark hole. After measuring the success of various actions aimed at reducing the number of wandering patients, environmental and equipment changes were found to be 2½ times more successful than other performance improvement actions (DeRosier et al., 2007)

Summary

During an improvement project, quantitative tools are used to gather, display, and analyze numeric or count information about process performance. Qualitative tools are used to gather, display, and analyze descriptive information about process problems or circumstances contributing to undesirable performance. These tools are also used to develop improvement actions and measure whether actions are effective at achieving project objectives.

Achieving improvement goals requires more than artful use of improvement tools. Teams must identify how best to change current practices to improve performance. Human factors research has provided insights into why people make mistakes and how work systems must be configured to achieve reliable performance. Rather than quickly jumping to conclusions about what is needed to fix performance problems, improvement teams should carefully analyze the work system and then apply human factors principles when making changes.

Student Activities

1. Explore the website of the Institute for Healthcare Improvement (www.ihi.org) and the website of the AHA Hospitals in Pursuit of Excellence (www.hpoe.org). Select one of the quality improvement/case study projects described on the site. For the project you select, list the improvement tools used by the team during each step and what the tool was used for.
2. A high level flowchart of the process of buying, cooking and eating microwave popcorn is shown below. Using human factors principles, explain how the process could be improved to make sure no mistakes are made during each step.

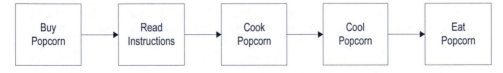

Website Resources

Advancing Excellence in America's Nursing Homes
www.nhqualitycampaign.org

ASQ Quality Tools: A to Z
http://asq.org/learn-about-quality/quality-tools.html

Agency for Healthcare Research and Quality. (2008). *Becoming a High Reliability Organization: Operational Advice for Hospital Leaders*.
https://archive.ahrq.gov/professionals/quality-patient-safety/quality-resources/tools/hroadvice/hroadvice.pdf

Agency for Healthcare Research and Quality (2019). The CAHPS Ambulatory Care Improvement Guide: Practical Strategies for Improving Patient Experience
www.ahrq.gov/cahps/quality-improvement/improvement-guide/improvement-guide.html

Hospitals in Pursuit of Excellence improvement project case studies
www.hpoe.org

IHI Quality Improvement Essentials Toolkit
www.ihi.org/resources/Pages/Tools/Quality-Improvement-Essentials-Toolkit.aspx

Improving Clinical Microsystems
http://clinicalmicrosystem.org/

Isabella Geriatric Center and Cobble Hill Health Center. *Working Together for Continuous Improvement: A Guide for Nursing Home Staff.*
www.isabella.org/Isabella/Resources/APerformanceImprovementManual.aspx

Society for Health Systems
www.iienet2.org/shs/

References

American Hospital Association (AHA). (2009). Save our skin: preventing pressure ulcers in *Hospitals in Pursuit of Excellence*. [Online document; retrieved 7/25/2018.]
        www.hpoe.org/Case_Studies/OSFStFrancisMedCenter_Ulcers.pdf
American Society for Quality (ASQ). (2016). Value stream map. [Online information; retrieved 8/1/2018.]
        http://asqservicequality.org/glossary/value-stream-map/
Boston-Fleischhauer, C. (2008). Enhancing healthcare process design with human factors engineering and reliability science, part 1: Setting the context. *The Journal of Nursing Administration, 38*(1), 27-32.
Carayon, P., Xie, A., & Kianfar. (2014). Human factors and ergonomics as a patient safety practice. *BMJ Quality and Patient Safety, 23*(2), 196-205.
Clark, S.L., Belfort, M.A., Byrum, S.L., Meyers, J.A., & Perlin, J.B. (2008). Improved outcomes, fewer cesarean deliveries, and reduced litigation: results of a new paradigm in patient safety. *American Journal of Obstetrics and Gynecology, 199*(2), 105.e1-105.e7.
DeRosier, J.M., Taylor, L., Turner, L., & Bagian, J.P. (2007). Root cause analysis of wandering adverse events in the Veterans Health Administration. In A. Nelson & D.L. Algase (Eds.), *Evidence-based Protocols for Managing Wandering Behaviors* (pp. 161-180). New York: Springer Publishing Co.
Joint Commission, The. (2017). *2018 Comprehensive Accreditation Manual for Hospitals.* Oakbrook Terrace, IL: The Joint Commission
Karsh, B.T., Holden, R.J., Alper, S.J. & Or, C.K.L. (2006). A human factors engineering paradigm for patient safety: Designing to support the performance of the healthcare professional. *Quality and Safety in Health Care, 5*(Suppl I):59-65.
Luria, J. W., Muething, S. E., Schoettker, P. J., & Kotagal, U. R. (2006). Reliability science and patient safety. *Pediatric Clinics of North America, 53*(6), 1121-1133.

MANAGING PATIENT SAFETY AND RISK

Reader Objectives

After reading this chapter and reflecting on the contents, you will be able to:
1. Demonstrate an understanding of the relationship between patient safety and risk management.
2. Describe measures of patient safety.
3. Identify techniques to evaluate and improve the safety of healthcare processes.
4. Describe the impact of information technology on patient safety.
5. Recognize risk management activities.

Key Terms

Adverse drug event (ADE): An injury resulting from medical intervention related to a drug.

Adverse patient event: Unexpected occurrences related to medical treatment resulting in patient death or serious disability; not related to the natural course of the patient's illness or underlying disease condition

Claim: In risk management, a patient's demand for payment for injury, or lost or damaged property resulting from alleged negligence by the facility, the physician, or the employees or agents of either.

Common formats: Common definitions and reporting formats that allow healthcare providers to collect and submit standardized information regarding patient safety events to PSOs.

Damages: Monetary compensation for an injury.

Error: Unintended act producing an undesired result or significant potential for an undesired result (sometimes called a mistake).

Failure: The way in which a function or intended action is compromised.

Failure mode: Different ways a process step or task can fail to achieve anticipated results.

Failure mode and effects analysis: An improvement model involving systematic assessment of a process to identify the location, cause, and consequences of potential failures for the purpose of eliminating or reducing the chance of failures occurring.

Incident: Any happening not consistent with the routine operation of the facility or routine care of a particular patient that could have or did lead to an undesired result.

Malpractice: Improper or unethical conduct or unreasonable lack of skill by a holder of a professional or official position; often applied to physicians, dentists, lawyers, and public officials to denote negligent or unskillful performance of duties when professional skills are obligatory.

National Patient Safety Goals: Expectations for patient safety improvement established annually by The Joint Commission for accredited facilities.

Near miss: A situation that could have resulted in a patient death or disability but did not, either by chance or through timely intervention.

Negligence: Failure to use that degree of care a reasonably prudent person would use under similar circumstances.

Never events: Preventable adverse patient events that should not ever occur.

Patient safety: Actions undertaken by individuals and organizations to protect healthcare recipients from being harmed by the effects of healthcare services.

Patient Safety Organizations (PSOs): Groups with expertise in identifying risks and hazards in the delivery of patient care, determining the underlying causes, and implementing corrective and preventive strategies.

Potentially compensable event: A patient injury or death that could be attributed to acts of negligence by healthcare practitioners or other involved individuals.

Risk: Probability and magnitude of harm from a hazard.

Risk management (RM): Process of defining and analyzing risks and then deciding on the appropriate course of action to minimize risks.

Root cause: Fundamental reason for an actual or potential adverse event.

Root cause analysis (RCA): An improvement model involving investigation of a sentinel event or other undesirable incident to identifying the fundamental problems that, if corrected, would reduce the likelihood of future similar events.

Sentinel event: An unexpected occurrence, involving a patient's death or serious physical or psychological injury or risk thereof.

Serious reportable events (SREs): Preventable adverse events that should never occur and should be reported if they occur.

Trigger tool: Method of using 'signals' or clues in patient records to identify adverse events that may not have been reported through traditional mechanisms.

Managing Risk of Harm and Liability

Each day people are exposed to risks. Some of these risks create the potential for harm. For example, college students face a risk during every exam. There is a risk the student will not pass the test. Flunking the exam could mean the student won't pass the course. If too many courses need repeating, the student may not graduate. Students can't eliminate these risks – it is doubtful instructors will quit giving exams – however students can reduce the likelihood of harm by carefully studying the subject matter before taking a test.

Individuals also face the risk of being sued in a court of law for their actions (or lack of action). For example, if there are broken steps leading up to the front door of your house and a visitor stumbles on a broken step and is injured, the visitor might file a lawsuit to recover damages associated with your failure to repair the stair steps. To reduce the chance of accidents, we try to identify and fix hazards before they cause harm to someone. We also purchase liability insurance to protect our financial assets in case we inadvertently injure another individual.

Businesses, including those providing healthcare services, also face risks caused by internal or external vulnerabilities. These risks include potential damages, injuries, liabilities or financial losses, and other negative consequences. For a healthcare organization these risks can come from clinical processes when a patient is harmed during the delivery of healthcare services. Risks can also come from the business side of healthcare services. For example, an ambulatory surgery center can be fined for improper medical waste disposal.

For an individual, managing risk involves two primary activities: reducing the chance of harm and minimizing liabilities associated with harming others. Managing risk in a healthcare organization involves similar activities. Using quality management techniques, healthcare processes are made safer – with the goal of reducing unintended patient harm. In addition, healthcare organizations use risk management strategies to identify and control business liability risks.

Historical Overview

It wasn't until the 1960s that hospitals could be sued for patient injuries. Prior to that time, the legal system viewed hospitals as charitable organizations existing for the benefit of physicians. The courts held physicians accountable for their actions and nurses and other hospital employers were considered to be acting on behalf of the physician. In the landmark 1965 case of Darling vs. Charleston Community Hospital legal liability for patient injuries were extended to the hospital and its employees. In Exhibit 7.1 is a brief description of this case.

Exhibit 7.1. Darling v. Charleston Community Hospital

Summary of the 1965 case decided by the Illinois Supreme Court:

A young football player suffered a fractured leg and was taken to the emergency room of a nearby hospital. The physician on call was a general practitioner who had not treated an injury of this type for several years. The physician reduced the fracture, applied a cast, and admitted the patient to the hospital. While in the hospital the patient complained of continuing pain and showed signs of compromised blood flow in the affected limb. The patient ultimately developed gangrene and was transferred to another hospital for amputation.

Charleston Community Hospital was found to be negligent for allowing a physician who lacked current clinical competence to care for the patient without obtaining an appropriate consultation. The hospital was also held liable for the actions of the nurses, who had observed the patient's deteriorating condition but had not challenged the manner in which the attending physician was managing the patient. The Darling case was significant because it expanded the hospital's liability to include responsibility for the actions of medical staff physicians, previously considered by the courts to be independent contractors. Another first in the Darling case occurred when the court allowed submission as case evidence the hospital's medical staff bylaws, standards of the Joint Commission, and standards of government licensing agencies.

Today all healthcare organizations, including health plans, have the same legal duty as any other business; that is to make sure individuals working in or for the organization are competent to perform their responsibilities and customers won't be harmed by the actions and decisions of these individuals.

Since Hippocrates said 'First, do no harm' over 2000 years ago, healthcare professionals have sought to minimize errors resulting in patient injury or death. Until recently, the occasional harmful error was considered an unfortunate but inevitable byproduct of modern medicine or it was blamed on a 'bad apple' individual. This attitude began to change with publication of *To Err is Human: Building a Safer Health System* (Institute of Medicine [IOM], 1999). This publication generated unprecedented media attention when it reported that an estimated 44,000 to 98,000 Americans die each year from medical mistakes. A range of recommended to improve patient safety were made and some ambitious safety improvement goals were set for all parts of the healthcare system.

Public pressures following the IOM report resulted in development of patient safety improvement initiatives in all sectors of the healthcare industry. Consumers, as well as regulatory and accreditation groups, now expect healthcare organizations to investigate the cause of errors and design safer patient care processes.

To encourage hospitals to take steps at making care safer for patients the Medicare program has implemented financial penalties for lesser quality care. If a hospitalized patient develops what is considered by Medicare to be a preventable complication – often called a *never event* – no additional payment will be made to cover the added cost of caring for the complication. Never events include situations such as surgery on the wrong body part, foreign body left in a patient after surgery, and certain types of hospital-acquired pressure ulcers and infections (Agency for Healthcare Research and Quality [AHRQ], 2018). Most Medicaid programs and many private health plans have implemented similar financial disincentives for never events.

This chapter describes how quality management techniques are used in healthcare organizations to improve patient safety. Also described are organizational risk management strategies to address various types of legal jeopardy.

Patient Safety Improvement

Safe healthcare is one of the key dimensions of healthcare quality identified in the IOM report, *Crossing the Quality Chasm* (2001). Safe healthcare is defined as "avoidance of unintended patient injuries." To achieve safe healthcare, organizations are working to better protect healthcare recipients from being harmed by effects of healthcare services. These initiatives, often labeled patient safety improvement, are a subset of an organization's overall quality management program. It is sometimes difficult to differentiate between what is being done to improve patient safety versus quality improvements made for other purposes. In truth, there are no clear-cut distinctions. Almost all healthcare processes – clinical and non-clinical – impact some aspect of patient safety.

Patient safety improvement involves the familiar quality management activities: measurement, assessment, and improvement. Much of what was described in previous chapters also applies to patient safety improvement activities. In this chapter, you are introduced to some additional concepts and techniques often associated with making healthcare safer and less risky.

Measurement

Measures of patient safety allow organizations to identify unsafe or unreliable processes needing improvement. Some measures alert an organization to occurrence of an adverse patient event. These are reactive measures; reporting after-the-fact something undesirable happened. Some measures alert an organization to potentially risky conditions or situations. These are proactive measures; reporting an opportunity for improvement that, if not acted on, could possibly result in an adverse event. Listed in Exhibit 7.2 are examples of patient safety measures.

Exhibit 7.2. Patient Safety Measures

- Number of adverse events occurring during anesthesia use
- Number of medication errors per 1000 doses dispensed
- Number of surgical patients discharged with foreign body accidentally left in during procedure
- Ratio of transfusion reactions to total units transfused
- Number of patient falls per 1000 patient days
- Percent of patients not identified using two identifiers prior to medication administration
- Percent of staff not compliant with hand-hygiene requirements
- Number of hospital patients with identification band missing or in an inappropriate location
- Percent of behavioral health patients not adequately searched after returning from a leave of absence

Annually the Joint Commission announces National Patient Safety Goals that accredited organizations are expected to meet. These goals influence the safety measures chosen by organizations. For example, to evaluate compliance with patient safety goals related to accurate patient identification, a hospital would periodically measure:

- Percent of blood draws in which the patient name and date of birth was confirmed by phlebotomist prior to the blood draw
- Percent of surgical procedures in which a final verification of the patient's identification and surgical site was done prior to the start of the procedure

Data for patient safety measures are gathered in the same manner as all performance measurement information. Some data are obtained by reviewing patient records and querying electronic databases. Some data are gathered during random observation reviews of people doing a job. Organizations also rely on incident reports completed by people working on the front lines of patient care. In addition, patient records are searched to find clues or triggers that may indicate the presence of an adverse event.

Incident Reporting

Incident reports are a primary source of information on patient safety. These reports are used to document events resulting in some type of patient harm. In addition, many organizations encourage reporting of near-miss events – occurrences that could have caused patient harm, but did not. Here's an example of a near-miss: A patient is about to be given a medication to which they have an allergy. The patient speaks up and alerts the nurse, who had overlooked the allergy alert in the patient's record. An adverse drug event is prevented – yet it could have been disastrous. Near-miss events represent a weakness in the system of care that, if not remedied, could lead to significant future consequences. The benefit of reporting both harmful events and near-misses are obvious. The safety pyramid (Exhibit 7.3) developed by H.W. Heinrich reinforces the value of near-miss reporting (1931).

Exhibit 7.3. Heinrich Safety Pyramid

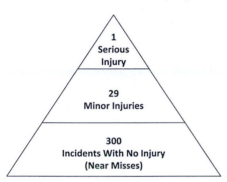

Heinrich's work has long been held as the model for safety and accident prevention theory in all industries. His study of industrial accidents revealed that for each serious-injury incident, a company could expect 29 minor injury and 300 near-miss incidents.

Near-misses, which constitute the base of the pyramid, occur much more frequently than more serious accidents. Usually each significant adverse patient event can be linked back to a number of near-miss incidents that happened earlier. By correcting the causes of near-misses, harmful patient events may be avoided. The cause of near-misses can only be investigated and corrected if leaders are made aware of them through an incident reporting system.

Most healthcare organizations have procedures governing the completion of incident reports, including definitions of the type of events to be reported and by whom. At the present time there are no national mandates requiring reporting of specific types of events however the National Quality Forum (NQF) has published a suggested list of serious reportable events (SREs). The work of the NQF in developing and endorsing performance measures was described in previous chapters. The list of SREs published by the NQF (2011) is found in Exhibit 7.4. These events can potentially occur in any healthcare environment.

Exhibit 7.4. Serious Reportable Events

1. Surgical or Invasive Procedure Events
   a. Surgery or other invasive procedure performed on the wrong site
   b. Surgery or other invasive procedure performed on the wrong patient
   c. Wrong surgical or other invasive procedure performed on a patient
   d. Unintended retention of a foreign object in a patient after surgery or other invasive procedure
   e. Intraoperative or immediately postoperative/post-procedure death in an ASA Class 1 patient
2. Product or Device Events
   a. Patient death or serious injury associated with the use of contaminated drugs, devices, or biologics provided by the healthcare setting
   b. Patient death or serious injury associated with the use or function of a device in patient care, in which the device is used or functions other than as intended
   c. Patient death or serious injury associated with intravascular air embolism that occurs while being cared for in a healthcare setting
3. Patient Protection Events
   a. Discharge or release of a patient/resident of any age, who is unable to make decisions, to other than an authorized person
   b. Patient death or serious injury associated with patient elopement (disappearance)
   c. Patient suicide, attempted suicide, or self-harm that results in serious injury, while being cared for in a healthcare setting

4. Care Management Events
   a. Patient death or serious injury associated with a medication error (e.g., errors involving the wrong drug, wrong dose, wrong patient, wrong time, wrong rate, wrong preparation, or wrong route of administration)
   b. Patient death or serious injury associated with unsafe administration of blood products
   c. Maternal death or serious injury associated with labor or delivery in a low-risk pregnancy while being cared for in a healthcare setting
   d. Death or serious injury of a neonate associated with labor or delivery in a low-risk pregnancy
   e. Patient death or serious injury associated with a fall while being cared for in a healthcare setting
   f. Any Stage 3, Stage 4, and unstageable pressure ulcers acquired after admission/presentation to a healthcare setting
   g. Artificial insemination with the wrong donor sperm or wrong egg
   h. Patient death or serious injury resulting from the irretrievable loss of an irreplaceable biological specimen
   i. Patient death or serious injury resulting from failure to follow up or communicate laboratory, pathology, or radiology test results
5. Environmental Events
   a. Patient or staff death or serious injury associated with an electric shock in the course of a patient care process in a healthcare setting
   b. Any incident in which systems designated for oxygen or other gas to be delivered to a patient contains no gas, the wrong gas, or are contaminated by toxic substances
   c. Patient or staff death or serious injury associated with a burn incurred from any source in the course of a patient care process in a healthcare setting
   d. Patient death or serious injury associated with the use of physical restraints or bedrails while being cared for in a healthcare setting
6. Radiologic Events
   a. Death or serious injury of a patient or staff associated with the introduction of a metallic object into the MRI area
7. Potential Criminal Events
   a. Any instance of care ordered by or provided by someone impersonating a physician, nurse, pharmacist, or other licensed healthcare provider
   b. Abduction of a patient/resident of any age
   c. Sexual abuse/assault on a patient or staff member within or on the grounds of a healthcare setting
   d. Death or serious injury of a patient or staff member resulting from a physical assault (i.e., battery) that occurs within or on the grounds of a healthcare setting

More than half of the states have implemented mandatory incident reporting programs for healthcare facilities and several states have voluntary reporting systems. The NQF list of SREs is often used as a basis for these reporting requirements. State-specific regulations have yet to be standardized nationwide, however this could eventually change.

The mechanisms for reporting incidents and information required to be reported vary from one organization to the next. Some facilities must use the incident report format designed by their liability insurance carrier. Other organizations use self-designed formats. Some incident report forms are multi-page documents with lots of detail about an incident. Other report forms contain just a few key questions for people to answer about the incident. Many facilities have electronic incident reporting capabilities.

In 2005, President Bush signed into law the Patient Safety and Quality Improvement Act (Patient Safety Act). The Patient Safety Act authorized HHS to facilitate creation of a national network of patient safety databases to accept, aggregate, and analyze adverse events involving patients and make information on trends and patterns in healthcare errors available to the public (AHRQ, 2005). The Patient Safety Act allowed for creation of Patient Safety Organizations (PSOs) to maintain the databases, which contain standardized patient incident information. Organizations meeting PSO inclusion requirements are listed on the PSO website maintained by AHRQ (www.pso.ahrq.gov). As of this writing, there are 85 approved PSOs.

The AHRQ is coordinating development of common formats, which refers to the common definitions and reporting formats that allow healthcare providers to collect and submit standardized information regarding patient safety events to PSOs. AHRQ's common formats include:

- Event descriptions (descriptions of patient safety events and unsafe conditions to be reported),
- Specifications for patient safety aggregate reports and individual event summaries,
- Delineation of data elements to be collected for different types of events to populate the reports,
- A user's guide and quick guide, and
- Technical specifications for electronic data collection and reporting.

Much of this work can be found on the AHRQ Patient Safety Organization Privacy Protection Center website (www.psoppc.org/psoppc_web/).

Unlike some state regulations that mandate reporting of incidents to a state agency, reporting of incidents to an independent PSO is voluntary. Healthcare organizations choosing to submit patient incident data to a PSO may need to revise their internal incident reporting process to ensure compatibility with the PSO common data definitions and reporting formats.

Trigger Tools

Studies by public health researchers have established that only 10-20% of errors made during delivery of health services are ever reported (Noble & Pronovost, 2010; Levinson, 2012). Focused in-depth patient record review can capture significantly more adverse events than voluntary reporting but it can be time consuming and expensive to review all records. Researchers at the Institute for Healthcare Improvement (IHI) suggest screening a percentage of records for triggers or clues that need a closer look can help identify more errors (IHI, 2011). For instance, IHI recommends hospitals review a minimum of 20 charts from surgical inpatients each month looking for clues such as:

- Change of anesthetic during surgery
- Insertion of arterial or central venous line during surgery
- Intra-op administration of epinephrine or norepinephrine
- Unplanned x-ray intra-operatively or in post-anesthesia recovery unit

When a closer look at the case reveals an instance of patient harm, the event can be investigated to determine how to prevent repeat events. Efforts are underway to adapt this screening process to queries of electronic patient record databases. In one study researchers used six abnormal laboratory triggers to detect adverse drug events among adults in outpatient care using electronic health records (EHR) as the data source (Brenner et al., 2012). Authors of this study found that adverse drug events (ADEs) could be identified by screening EHR data, however text triggers or more complex automated screening rules which combine data hierarchically may be needed to efficiently screen for ADEs in adults seen in primary care.

Most existing trigger tools have been used to identify adverse events in the inpatient setting. Although some studies have sought to develop trigger tools for ambulatory care, there is relatively little data on the accuracy and reliability of these tools.

Assessment

Evaluation of patient safety measurement data follows the same process as assessment of any performance data. The data are organized and reported and the information is evaluated. Performance assessment techniques described in chapter four – trend analysis, statistical process control, and comparative data – can all be used to evaluate patient safety measurement results.

In Exhibit 7.5 is an excerpt from a tabular report of measures used by a hospital to monitor various aspects of patient safety. The year-to-date (YTD) actual performance can be compared to the goal.

Exhibit 7.5. Tabular Patient Safety Measurement Report

Measure	Goal	YTD
Medication errors resulting in harm (per 1000 patient days)	0.31	0.30
Falls with injuries (per 1000 patient days)	0.67	1.06
Emergency department falls with injuries (per 1000 visits)	0.21	0.22
Two patient identifiers used when taking blood, administering medications or blood products	95%	100%
Critical laboratory results/values reported by Lab within 30 minutes of availability of results	95%	99%
Critical radiology test/procedure results reported by radiologist to ordering physician within one hour of determination/interpretation of test	95%	89%

In Exhibit 7.6 is a combined graphic and narrative report of patient falls in a nursing home. The line graph shows the incidence of falls for 6 months and the narrative summary describes contributing factors together with suggestions on how to prevent falls.

Exhibit 7.6. Six Month Report of Resident Falls

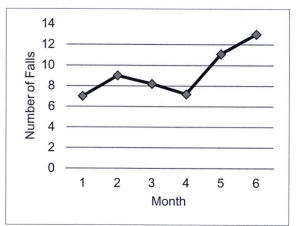

Seven of the resident falls in June were due to slips on wet floors. Appropriately placed "wet floor – caution" signs can help reduce the risk of falls. Please encourage residents and visitors to take special care when walking in areas recently cleaned or where spills are being mopped up.

In every month except February at least one resident fall occurred because of inadequate footwear. Many residents bring their slippers from home to wear in the nursing home. Be sure to check the adequacy of the tread on these slippers before allowing residents to walk around. If necessary, replace the resident's slippers with those available from central supply.

Two resident falls in June occurred because of a faulty lock mechanism on a wheelchair. This equipment has been repaired; however, we still need your help. If a wheelchair does not appear to be completely safe take it out of service immediately! Better to delay the resident transfer than risk an injury. Remember to submit an incident report if you experience equipment related situations (or any situation) which you feel might be potentially hazardous to residents, visitors, or staff.

Instead of using a line graph to show patient fall trends, the nursing home could have created a control chart with statistically calculated upper and lower control limits. This would allow managers and staff to determine if the rate of falls is in a state of statistical control.

Comparative data from other organizations may be available for use in assessing patient safety performance. Before using comparative results for assessment purposes make sure you understand how the data were gathered and the data definitions. For instance, performance measurement results from the Ambulatory Surgery Center Collaboration (ACS QC) are reported online. A safety-related measure in this report is: *number of patients experiencing an unintended burn per 1000 admissions*. In the 2nd calendar quarter of 2018 the rate of burns reported by 1,573 ambulatory surgery centers was 0.015 per 1000 admissions (ACS QC, 2018). Data for this measure are gathered from medical records and incident reports. Burn is defined as, "Unintended tissue injury caused by any of the six recognized mechanisms: scalds, contact, fire, chemical, electrical or radiation, (e.g. warming devices, prep solutions, electrosurgical unit or laser)" (ASC QC, 2016.). If an organization chooses to compare its rate of surgical patient burns with the results reported by the ACS Collaboration, the organization should be using similar data sources and data definitions.

Some patient safety measures reveal information about significant events that should rarely or never happen. Expected performance is zero – meaning just one event triggers an improvement project. The NQF SREs (Exhibit 7.4) are examples of incidents needing immediate investigation and corrective actions.

Healthcare facilities are often required by state regulations and accreditation standards to quickly examine certain types of events whenever they occur. For instance, Maryland state regulations require facilities and residential agencies caring for developmentally disabled individuals evaluate each case of abuse, neglect and death and develop a plan of correction (Maryland Developmental Disabilities Administration, 2013). Joint Commission accredited organizations are required to immediately investigate all sentinel events – unexpected occurrences involving death or serious physical or psychological injury, or the risk thereof. The phrase 'risk thereof' includes any process variation for which a recurrence would carry a significant chance of a serious adverse outcome.

Improvement

If patient safety measurement results reveal improvement opportunities or when an important single event occurs (such as a sentinel event or SRE) the third step of quality management is initiated – quality improvement. In this step, causes of undesirable performance are identified and improvement actions taken.

Any of the improvement models, tools, and techniques described in chapters 5 and 6 can be used for patient safety improvement projects. In Exhibit 7.7 is a bar graph showing changes in healthcare worker compliance with hand hygiene following a hospital-wide rapid cycle improvement project. The project team's action plan – place more alcohol-based hand-rub dispensers throughout patient care areas – significantly increased hand cleaning among all categories of caregivers.

Exhibit 7.7. Bar Graph of Improvement Project Results

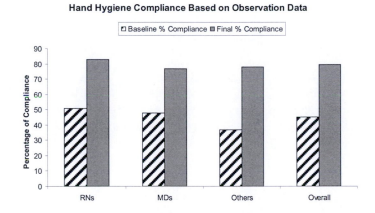

In 2002, The Joint Commission formed an advisory group to develop National Patient Safety Goals (NPSGs) to encourage safety improvement in accredited organizations. The initial six goals recommended by the group took effect in 2003. Each NPSG has one or more associated requirements. Annually, the advisory group re-evaluates the NPSGs and recommends additions, deletions, or modifications to the goals and the specific requirements for the upcoming year. The NPSGs for the current year are found on The Joint Commission website. Often these goals influence what accredited organizations select as topics for safety improvement projects. Since 2004 compliance with the CDC hand cleaning guidelines has been on the list of NPSGs. The hand hygiene rapid cycle improvement project described above was done in support of this goal.

To reduce risks of unintended patient harm during delivery of healthcare services, organizations are also using safety improvement techniques that originated in other industries. The driving forces for adopting these techniques were changes in Joint Commission standards. The first step toward strengthening approaches to improving patient safety began in 1996 when the standards were revised to require thorough and systematic investigations of sentinel events. In 2001 standards were added requiring accredited organizations conduct proactive risk assessments to find and fix safety problems before patients or residents are harmed. The improvement models used for incident investigations and proactive risk assessments are root cause analysis and failure mode and effects analysis.

Root Cause Analysis

Root cause analysis (RCA) is a performance improvement project done following a significant patient incident or sentinel event. The project goals are to identify and eliminate root causes of the event. Root causes are basic deficiencies or process failures that, if corrected, will prevent the event from recurring. Once root causes of the event are identified, improvement actions plans are designed and implemented.

Joint Commission standards require accredited organizations conduct an RCA following occurrence of any serious patient incident considered to be a sentinel event (Joint Commission, 2017). Similar mandatory RCA requirements are found in some state regulations governing healthcare facilities. Examples of sentinel events include:

- Unanticipated death or major permanent loss of function associated with a healthcare–associated infection
- Suicide of any individual receiving care in a staffed around-the-clock care setting or within 72 hours of discharge
- Unanticipated death of a full-term infant
- Abduction of any individual receiving care, treatment, and services
- Discharge of an infant to the wrong family
- Rape of a patient or resident (unconsented sexual contact involving a patient and another patient, staff member, or unknown perpetrator while being treated or on the premises of the healthcare organization)
- Hemolytic transfusion reaction involving administration of blood or blood products having major blood group incompatibilities
- Surgery on the wrong patient or wrong body part or wrong surgical procedure performed on a patient (regardless of the magnitude of the procedure or the outcome)
- Unintended retention of a foreign object in a patient after surgery or other procedure
- Severe neonatal hyperbilirubinemia (bilirubin > 30 milligrams/deciliter)
- Prolonged fluoroscopy with cumulative dose > 1500 rads to a single field, or any delivery of radiotherapy to the wrong body region or > 25% above the planned radiotherapy dose

When a sentinel or adverse event occurs, a project team is appointed by leadership to do the RCA. Events often involve more than one department or professional group so the project is usually a multidisciplinary and inter-departmental. Team members are often the people who were personally involved in the event plus other representatives from the involved units and professions. The RCA follows a systematic process similar to the PDSA improvement model, as shown in Exhibit 7.8.

Exhibit 7.8. PDSA and RCA Steps

PDSA Steps	RCA Steps
Plan	1. Understand what happened. 2. Identify the root causes of the event.
Do Study	3. Design, implement, and evaluate the effectiveness of improvement actions intended to eliminate root causes.
Act	4. Make action plans permanent or revise and re-test improvement strategies.

To comply with Joint Commission standards the RCA team must, at a minimum, consider whether specific factors known to be problematic in healthcare facilities contributed to the incident (Joint Commission, 2017):

- Staffing levels
- Orientation and training of individuals
- Supervision of individuals
- Communication with patient and/or family

- Communication among healthcare team members
- Availability of information
- Adequacy of technological support
- Equipment maintenance and management
- Physical environment
- Security systems and processes

The RCA project often includes use of improvement tools such as graphs, brainstorming, high-level flowcharts, and cause and effect diagrams. Once root causes of the event are well-understood, the team designs improvement actions. Similar to all improvement projects, the action plans are implemented and then evaluated to see if the improvement goal (eliminate root causes) has been achieved. If actions are ineffective, the team goes back to the drawing board; new actions are designed, implemented and evaluated. A summary of an RCA investigation involving a significant hospital adverse event is found in Exhibit 7.9.

Exhibit 7.9. RCA of Hospital Patient Adverse Event
_____

Introduction
A treatment error was investigated in which a patient developed severe neurological complications following removal of a catheter in her jugular vein. In conducting its evaluation, the incident investigation team used various analysis techniques, including a high-level flowchart, brainstorming, and cause and effect diagram. The team reviewed circumstances surrounding the event, conducted extensive physician and staff interviews and document reviews, and performed analyses to determine the factors contributing to the incident, including any management system deficiencies.

Incident Description
A woman with metastatic cancer was hospitalized in the intensive care unit (ICU) for management of congestive heart failure and acute-on-chronic renal failure. The nephrology service initiated continuous venovenous hemodialysis through a large-bore catheter inserted in her right internal jugular vein. Two weeks later, a first-year renal fellow removed the catheter while the patient was seated upright in a chair. The patient became acutely hypoxemic and appeared to seize. Head imaging revealed global central nervous system ischemia suspicious for hypoperfusion. The patient had recurrent seizures and persistent left-sided paralysis, presumably due to air embolus or embolic clot, but the temporal association with removing the central line made air embolism the most likely diagnosis.

Root Causes
1. The institution has no consistent mechanism for ensuring residents and fellows have the necessary competencies to perform various bedside procedures, including removal of central lines.
2. Reluctance of other caregivers to question or correct practitioners when their actions may be inappropriate or could potentially cause patient harm.

Improvement Actions
1. Identify all bedside procedures requiring unique skills and implement training and competency assessments for residents and fellows.
2. Reinforce with staff members the importance of intervening when potentially unsafe situations are identified and clarify the institution's chain of command policy for resolving concerns.

_____

The AHRQ sponsors an online journal and forum on patient safety and healthcare quality, WebM&M (Morbidity and Mortality Rounds on the Web). Web M&M (https://psnet.ahrq.gov/Webmm) features expert analysis of medical errors that have occurred in all types of healthcare settings. Many examples of RCA investigations are found on this site.

Failure Mode and Effects Analysis

Failure mode and effects analysis (FMEA) is a performance improvement project involving an in-depth look at a process to determine where changes are needed to reduce the likelihood of unintended adverse events. The goal of a FMEA project is to improve a process so the risk of failures is greatly diminished. This proactive risk assessment methodology has been used for years in manufacturing, aviation, computer software design, and other industries to conduct safety system evaluations. It is now being used in healthcare organizations to evaluate and improve the safety of patient care activities. The FMEA project team systematically considers the safety of a high-risk process in terms of:

- What could go wrong?
- How badly might it go wrong?
- What needs to be done to prevent failures?

The Joint Commission requires its accredited facilities to periodically conduct proactive risk assessments and FMEA is the most common technique used to fulfill this requirement. However, FMEA projects should not just be done just to comply with Joint Commission standards. Anytime a healthcare organization wants to improve a process to prevent or reduce the likelihood of mistakes, a FMEA project can be conducted. This applies to both clinical patient care processes and support processes such as patient registration or billing.

The process chosen for a FMEA project is often one known to be high-risk or problem-prone (for example, there have been some near miss events or significant mistakes in the past). The team assembled for the project has personal knowledge of how the process now works and what can go wrong. Once the team is formed, the FMEA project follows a systematic process similar to the PDSA improvement model as shown in Exhibit 7.10.

Exhibit 7.10. PDSA and FMEA Steps

PDSA Steps	FMEA Steps
Plan	1. Describe the process by creating a flowchart.
	2. Identify the ways in which the process could break down or fail to perform its desired function
	3. Identify the possible effects a breakdown or failure of the process could have on patients and the seriousness of the possible effects
	4. Prioritize the potential process breakdowns or failures
	5. Determine why the prioritized breakdowns or failures could occur.
	6. Redesign the process and/or underlying systems to minimize the risk of the effects on patients
Do	7. Test and implement the redesigned process
Study	8. Monitor the effectiveness of the redesigned process
	9. Design, implement, and evaluate the effectiveness of risk reduction strategies (action plans).
Act	10. Make risk reduction strategies permanent and monitor the effectiveness of the redesigned process (or revise and re-test strategies).

Here is a case study illustrating the steps of a FMEA project: An ambulatory surgery center has had some intra-operative medication errors. These errors appear to be related to the process used to obtain medications and place them on the sterile operative field. Up to this point no patients have been harmed by these errors, however the mistakes have caused some surgeries to be delayed. The potential exists for a significant drug adverse event and caregivers are doing a FMEA project on this process to prevent such an event.

A team of people representing those involved in the intra-operative medication process is formed to conduct the FMEA. The project starts out with the team defining how the process currently works. A high-level flowchart of the current steps in the process is created. Next the team brainstorms all possible things that could go wrong during each step in the process. These are potential failures modes (things that could go wrong). The high-level flowchart and results of the brainstorming session are illustrated in Exhibit 7.11. The failure modes are listed beneath each process step in the high-level flowchart.

Exhibit 7.11. Medication Procurement and Labeling Steps and Potential Failure Modes

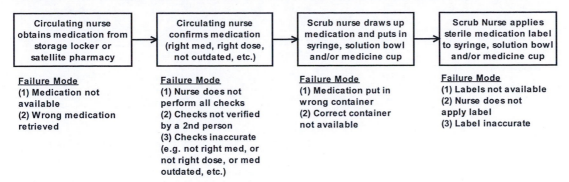

The team then brainstorms the effects of each failure mode, answering the question: what would happen if this failure actually does occur? The effect is described in terms of what the people involved in the process or the patient might experience if the failure occurs. In Exhibit 7.12 are examples of what the team identifies as possible effects for the failure modes identified in two process steps.

Exhibit 7.12. Examples of Failure Modes and Possible Effects

Process Step	Failure Modes	Possible Effects
Circulating nurse obtains medication	Medication not available	• Possible surgery start time delay while medication is obtained • Use alternate medication
	Wrong medication retrieved	• Error identified during double check in next step; possible surgery start time delay while correct medication is retrieved
Circulating nurse confirms medication is correct	Nurse does not do confirmation check	• Error identified during double check; potential delay in surgery
	2nd person does not double check what circulating nurse has done	• Possible wrong or outdated medication administered to patient if first checks were inaccurate
	Initial and double checks are inaccurate	• Wrong or outdated medication administered to patient

Next the FMEA project team selects the failures most in need of being prevented (critical failures). This is done by considering how frequently each failure might actually happen and severity of the consequences should it occur. Process improvement actions will focus on preventing critical failures.

There are several methods the team can use to prioritize critical failures chosen for prevention. This FMEA team uses a scoring system to rank each failure as low, medium, or high based on the failure frequency and its consequences. The risk assessment matrix in Exhibit 7.13 illustrates how the ranking is done. The frequency of each potential failure is scored from 1 to 6 (definitions shown in matrix). Then the consequence of each failure is scored from A to D (definitions shown in matrix). Where the frequency and consequence score intersect on the matrix is the ranking applied to the failure.

Exhibit 7.13. Failure Risk Assessment Matrix

			A Low (Minimal harm)	B Moderate (Short-term harm)	C Severe (Permanent or long- term harm)	D Fatal (Death of one or more people)
Frequency	More than once a day	6	High	High	High	High
	Once a day to once a week	5	Medium	High	High	High
	Once a week or once a month	4	Medium	Medium	High	High
	Once a month to once a year	3	Low	Medium	Medium	High
	Once a year to once every 10 years	2	Low	Low	Low	Medium
	Less than once every 10 years	1	Low	Low	Low	Low
			Consequence			

For example, the team agrees that once-a-week staff members are too busy to do the double checks that catch errors made by the circulating nurse. Thus, this failure, *2nd person does not double check what circulating nurse has done*, is given a frequency score of 5. The effect of such a failure could be significant – it could be fatal for the patient if a wrong medication is administered. Thus, the failure is given a consequence score of D. The intersect point of 5 and D is *High*. Making sure double checks get done is a high priority and this failure is added to the list of other critical failures the team identifies using the same ranking process.

After selecting critical failures, the team identifies the root causes of each failure by determining what would have to go wrong to trigger the failure. Finding the underlying causes of critical failures is an important step toward developing appropriate action plans. The investigation methods used during an RCA project are also used in a FMEA project.

Once root causes of critical failures are identified, the team agrees on how to improve the process so failures are prevented. This is where an understanding of human factors principles, described in chapter 6, is important. There are basically three strategies for making a process safer:

- Eliminate the risk of failure. Process changes are made to prevent failures from occurring. This may involve restructuring tasks so error prevalent behavior is no longer performed. In some situations, automating the process can change the role of human involvement and eliminate the risk of mistakes.

- Make it easier for people to do the right thing. This is the most common improvement strategy. As discussed in chapter 6, it is easier for people to do the right thing when the process steps are standardized. Human errors can be reduced when visible displays of acceptable actions are provided (for example, on-screen reminders and checklists). Decreasing the process steps cuts down the number of opportunities for mistakes. Environmental changes, such as better lighting and less workplace clutter, can also make it easier for people to do the right thing.

- Identify failures quickly and take corrective action. No matter how hard people try, failures will still occur and some of these failures will reach the patient. When redesigning processes to make them safer, the team also considers the potential for unrecognized errors resulting in an adverse event. People may need training in how to be aware of and deal with unusual situations. Adding automation, such as alarms, can provide visual or auditory feedback of off-normal clinical situations.

To eliminate or reduce the risk of critical failures in the intra-operative medication procurement and labeling process the FMEA team designs and implements several action plans. The process changes are tested to be sure desired results actually occur. The FMEA project team may periodically meet to assess how much safer the process has become since implementing the actions or this performance monitoring responsibility may fall to the organization's quality or patient safety committee.

Although RCA and FMEA projects often focus on improving safety of patient care processes, both improvement models can be used to reduce errors in business processes. For example, an RCA could be done following an IT security breach to determine the underlying causes so future breaches can be prevented. A FMEA project could be conducted for the process used to release health record information to patients so critical failures can be prevented.

Risk Management

Risk management (RM) involves defining and analyzing risks and then deciding on the appropriate course of action to minimize these risks. The three basic RM activities are:

- Risk identification
- Risk evaluation
- Risk control

A comprehensive RM program covers all aspects of business and patient care operations. In this chapter the focus of discussion is primarily on management of patient care (clinical) risks however similar strategies are used to manage non-clinical business risks.

Like all quality management activities, the ultimate goal of RM is continuous improvement. The primary reason for continuous improvement, from the RM perspective, is to reduce financial losses associated with negligent performance. Negligence is a legal term used to describe a person's failure to use the same degree of care a reasonably prudent person would use under similar circumstances. Negligence may result from acts of omission or commission, or both.

Structurally the dividing line between quality management and RM activities is blurry. The individual or department responsible for supporting quality management activities may also support RM functions. Small healthcare providers, such as ambulatory surgery centers and physician practices, often rely on one individual – a manager or administrator – to do whatever may be necessary to manage quality and also control liability risks. In larger healthcare organizations it is common to find quality and RM support responsibilities delegated to separate individuals or departments.

When quality management is organizationally separate from RM, the work of continuous improvement is divided up. For instance, patient incident reports may go to the RM department for review and analysis. When the RM department receives notice of an adverse patient incident requiring an RCA, the quality department is notified. Staff in the quality department supports the RCA team, sometimes serving as the team leader. At the same time the RCA is being done, individuals in the RM department are establishing relations with the injured party, evaluating liability risks, and consulting with legal counsel and liability insurers. A representative from the RM department may be a member of the RCA team and may also later be involved in implementing improvement actions. In some facilities people from the RM department lead RCA investigations with the quality department in a secondary role.

Exactly how the work of continuous improvement is divided up between organizationally-separate quality and RM functions is different for each institution. Government regulations and accreditation standards do not differentiate the functions of RM from other quality management activities. Thus, organizations have considerable latitude when integrating the two functions.

Some organizations have an RM plan that describes activities involved in managing organizational risks. The plan generally includes a mission statement, a definition of RM, program goals, and activities involved in the RM function and who is responsible for these activities. When RM functions are conducted separately from quality management functions, the plan defines how information sharing will occur and the mechanism for keeping the organization's leaders informed on risk-related issues.

Risk Identification

Risk identification involves detection of situations, policies, or practices that could result in financial loss for the organization. The goal of risk identification – the proactive component of RM – is to identify problems before injuries or losses occur and take action to prevent or minimize its effects. Healthcare organizations systematically and continuously identify potential liability exposures by several methods. Listed below are common risk identification data sources. Many of these data sources are also used for patient safety and quality improvement purposes.

- Incident reports
- Occurrence reports
- Infection control reports
- Plant safety inspection reports

- Litigation claims and investigations
- Reports of patient dissatisfaction
- Employee comments/suggestions
- Performance measurement results
- Committee minutes
- Equipment problem logs

- Reports of serious deviations from performance standards by physicians or employees
- Safety violation reports
- Attorney requests for patient records
- Inspection reports of regulatory and accreditation groups

Use of incident reports for patient safety improvement is described earlier in this chapter. Incident reports are also used to identify liability risks. When reviewing incident reports, the individual or department responsible for RM is looking for potentially compensable events. An event is considered potentially compensable when it is probable the patient's injury or death could be attributed to acts of negligence by healthcare practitioners or other involved individuals. This determination is made independent of the RCA investigation – which is focused on discovering what caused the system of care to breakdown not whether individuals were at fault. The incident described in Exhibit 7.14 is an example of a potentially compensable event:

Exhibit 7.14. Example of Potentially Compensable Event

A 59-year old female is admitted to the hospital to undergo repair of a right cervical internal carotid artery aneurysm. Prior to surgery a resident starts an IV in the patient's left hand. The surgery lasts approximately 6 hours. During that time a number of parenteral fluids and medications, including continuous Pentothal, are administered through the IV. Throughout the procedure the IV appears to remain patent because it is a gravity infusion and the flow is adequate. The patient's hand is under the surgical drape and is not visualized from the time the surgical drapes are placed until the surgery is completed. When the drapes are removed a significant IV infiltration is noted on the dorsum of the patient's left-hand causing blistering and redness. Within 24 hours of the surgery the patient's left hand is without sensation and remains blistered and ecchymotic. Five days after the surgery it is determined she has full thickness necrosis of the skin on the dorsum of her left hand. The patient requires three additional procedures for debridement and full thickness skin grafts.

When a potentially compensable event happens RM staff begins immediately to control liability risks. This is done by:
- Collecting information (documents, equipment, interviews) to build legal defensibility
- Documenting circumstances as perceived by the patient, family and involved physicians and staff
- Working with facility attorneys and the liability insurer to establish probable cause, scope of liability, and potential financial losses
- Where possible, lessening liability risk by opening lines of communication with the injured party, writing off the bill, offering a settlement, and the like.

The RM department may be responsible for ensuring events are reported to government agencies. In addition to the mandatory adverse incident reporting requirements in some states, events that must be reported include:
- Patient deaths associated with a transfusion of blood or blood components are to be reported to the U.S. Food and Drug Administration (FDA)
- Patient deaths that are or may be attributed to a medical device are to be reported to the FDA and the manufacturer of the medical device
- Serious patient injuries that are or may be attributed to a medical device are to be reported directly to the manufacturer or to FDA if the manufacturer is unknown
- All incidents involving radioactive accidents are to be reported to the appropriate nuclear regulatory agencies of federal and state governments
- Hospital deaths associated with patient restraint or seclusion for behavior management are to be reported to the regional Medicare office

There are also some voluntary external reporting opportunities. Often the RM department is involved in determining whether the facility will share information about a particular event with an external group. Summarized below are two examples of voluntary reporting opportunities.

- The Joint Commission encourages accredited organizations to provide them with information about sentinel events and root cause analysis findings. Reporting is not a condition of accreditation, however. Current sentinel event reporting requirements can be found on the Joint Commission website.
- Actual or potential medication errors can be reported to the FDA's MedWatch program and/or the Medication Errors Reporting Program sponsored by the United States Pharmacopoeia Convention, Inc.

All potential liability risks cannot be identified through incident reports. In addition to identifying risks as events happen, the RM department analyzes historical performance trends looking for signs of potential risk exposure. Examples of performance measures that could be used to identify potential liability concerns are listed below.

- Percent of patient records without adequately documented informed consent
- Percent of new hospital admissions not seen by the primary physician within 24 hours
- Percent of patients who are unexpectedly admitted following an outpatient surgery
- Number of delayed or missed diagnoses
- Percent of full-term live births entering intermediate or intensive care nurseries
- Percent of patients who develop an adverse reaction to a radioisotope agent
- Percent of fire alarms not tested as required by maintenance policies
- Percent of equipment maintenance checks not completed within required time frame

Risk Evaluation

When a potential liability risk is found, the following questions are considered:

- Is there liability exposure? How much?
- Who may be liable?
- What can be done to minimize liability exposure?
- What should be done to avoid similar exposures in the future?
- What are the best defenses if a lawsuit is initiated?

Witness statements are taken following a potentially compensable event to learn more about circumstances surrounding the incident. The patient and their families are engaged by the risk manager to gain their perspective and maintain their trust. How the organization responds to an adverse event can impact consumer confidence in the healthcare system. Open and honest, compassionate discussion of the event by the patient's direct caregiver and RM individuals can help identify improvement opportunities. The goal of patient and family engagement is to disclose accurate, factual information about the adverse event to the patient and family in a timely manner, maintain the trust of the patient and strengthen institutional efforts to improve patient safety (Etchegaray et al., 2014).

It is never appropriate for the physician or the organization to remain silent following a harmful incident as this approach is often perceived as a cover-up by the patient or family. Healthcare RM literature suggests full disclosure of what happened often reduces the risk of liability claims and minimizes the potential for large judgment awards (Saxton & Finkelstein, 2008). Organizations accredited by The Joint Commission are required to inform the patient or surrogate decision maker about unanticipated outcomes of care, treatment, and services relating to sentinel events (Joint Commission, 2017). Several states also require similar notification after an adverse incident resulting in serious harm to a patient.

Risk Control

To reduce future liability risks, lessons learned from past incidents are used to make process changes. For instance, after the incident involving the 59-year old patient whose left hand was damaged during surgery, the following change was made:

> Because the anesthesiologist could not recall if he or the resident started the IV, a new procedure was implemented requiring the name of the person starting an IV be documented in the patient's record and also the name of the person monitoring the patency of the IV during the procedure. Such documentation will help the hospital defend future lawsuits of this type.

Additional process changes resulted from an RCA of the event. These included a change in the regularity of IV monitoring, with more frequent monitoring required during intraoperative administration of irritating medications. To make healthcare safer, human factors principles should be considered when redesigning processes. One of the most effective ways of reducing errors is to standardize the process so people do tasks the same way every time (Bagian et al., 2011).

To control the threat of future patient harm, physicians and staff must understand the importance of RM and their role in problem identification, prevention, and correction. Findings from risk identification activities are shared with physicians and staff to gain support for corrective actions. Through in-service and orientation programs people working in the organization gain a better awareness of risk control issues and everyone's responsibility for reducing patient injuries.

Additional Risk Management Activities

Managing liability risks in a healthcare organization goes beyond clinical, patient care issues. The RM function covers any aspect that might pose legal or financials threat to the institution. It is common to include RM staff in discussions of HIPAA (Health Insurance Portability and Accountability Act) privacy and security issues and during implementation of electronic health records. Risk identification, evaluation and control activities extend into risk categories such as:

- Employee accidents/worker's compensation
- Antitrust
- Fraudulent billing and claims
- Securities violations
- Employee hiring/termination practices
- Breach of contract
- Risk financing
- Electronic data security breaches

Non-clinical RM activities are not usually considered a component of the organization's quality management activities. However, the non-clinical aspects are very much a part of an organization's business practices. The non-clinical RM activities may be done in the RM department or may be delegated to various departments with the organization's legal counsel providing guidance when needed.

Summary

Reducing the risk of patient harm during delivery of healthcare services is an essential element of quality management. Safety is one of the six key dimensions of healthcare quality defined by the IOM. Although patient safety is just a subset of healthcare quality, media attention on medical errors and financial disincentives have greatly elevated the importance of this quality dimension. Today, many quality management activities in healthcare organizations are directed at improving safety.

The same principles and techniques applicable to quality management in general are also used to improve patient safety. The safety of healthcare processes is measured and data are analyzed to identify improvement opportunities. Improvement projects are undertaken to lessen the risk of patient harm associated with healthcare delivery. Two safety improvement models borrowed from other industries – RCA and FMEA – are being used to create safer patient care processes. These same improvement models can also be used to reduce errors in non-clinical business processes.

Patient safety improvement is one aspect of an organization's RM efforts. The purpose of RM is to identify and control potential problems (hazards, threats, and vulnerabilities) that could negatively affect the finances and reputation of the organization. These problems may be clinical or non-clinical in nature. The three primary RM functions are: risk identification, evaluation, and control. Risk and quality management activities intersect when these functions are applied to the clinical aspects of patient care.

Student Activities

1. Explore WebM&M (https://psnet.ahrq.gov/Webmm). Select from the case archives one adverse patient incident discussion. In your own words briefly summarize the incident, list the root causes and recommended improvement actions described by the case study author(s) and identify measures of success for the improvement actions.
2. Tour the Institute for Healthcare Improvement FMEA tool at: http://app.ihi.org/Workspace/tools/fmea/ (you may need to create an IHI account). Discuss how this tool would be used to conduct a FMEA project for a common health information management process.
3. Research the role of information technology (IT) in patient safety. Summarize the potential patient safety benefits and hazards of IT.

Website Resources

All Cause Harm Prevention in Nursing Homes: Change Package to prevent harm (adverse events, abuse, and neglect) for nursing home residents (CMS safety improvement document)
https://qioprogram.org/all-cause-harm-prevention-nursing-homes

American Society for Healthcare Risk Management
www.ashrm.org

IHI/National Patient Safety Foundation
www.npsf.org

IHI (maintains examples of FMEA projects on its website; registration required to view the examples)
www.ihi.org

Joint Commission patient safety resources
www.jointcommission.org/topics/patient_safety.aspx

Patient Safety in Correctional Health Facilities (White paper)
www.ncchc.org/filebin/Resources/Patient-Safety-2016.pdf

Patient Safety Network sponsored by AHRQ
http://psnet.ahrq.gov/

Patient Safety Organizations
www.pso.ahrq.gov

Pennsylvania Patient Safety Authority
http://patientsafety.pa.gov/

RCA²: Improving Root Cause Analyses and Actions to Prevent Harm (report)
https://psnet.ahrq.gov/resources/resource/29089/RCA2-Improving-Root-Cause-Analyses-and-Actions-to-Prevent-Harm

Safety Leaders Organization sponsored by the Texas Medical Institute of Technology
www.safetyleaders.org

Veterans Health Administration Patient Safety Center
https://www.patientsafety.va.gov/

References

Agency for Healthcare Research and Quality (AHRQ). (2018, August). Patient safety primer: Never events. [Online document; retrieved 9/29/2018.] https://psnet.ahrq.gov/primers/primer/3/never-events
_____. (2005). Patient Safety and Quality Improvement Act of 2005 [Online document; retrieved 9/29/2018.] www.pso.ahrq.gov/legislation
Ambulatory Surgery Center Quality Collaboration. (ASC QC). (2018). ASC Quality Collaboration Quality Report: 2nd Quarter 2018. [Online document; retrieved 9/29/2018.] www.ascquality.org/qualityreport.cfm
_____. (2016). *ASC Quality Measures* [Online document; retrieved 9/29/2018.] http://ascquality.org/documents/2016-Summary-ASCQC-Measures.pdf
Bagian, J.P., King, B.J., Mills, P.D., & McKnight, S.D. (2011). Improving RCA performance: The cornerstone award and power of positive reinforcement. *BMJ Quality and Safety, 20(*11), 974-982.
Brenner, S., Detz, A., López, A., Horton, C., & Sarkar, U. (2012). Signal and noise: Applying a laboratory trigger tool to identify adverse drug events among primary care patients. *BMJ Quality and Safety, 21(*8), 670-675.
Etchegaray, J.M., Ottosen, M.J., Burress, L., Sage, W.M., Bell, S.K., Gallagher, T.H., & Thomas, E.J. (2014). Structuring patient and family involvement in medical error event disclosure and analysis. *Health Affairs, 33(*1), 46-52.
Heinrich, H.W. (1931). *Industrial Accident Prevention.* New York: McGraw-Hill.
Institute for Healthcare Improvement (IHI). (2011). Introduction to trigger tools for identifying adverse events. [Online information; retrieved 9/29/2018.] www.ihi.org/knowledge/Pages/Tools/IntrotoTriggerToolsforIdentifyingAEs.aspx
Institute of Medicine (IOM). (2001). *Crossing the Quality Chasm: A New Health System for the 21st Century.* Washington, DC: National Academies Press.
_____. (1999). *To Err Is Human: Building a Safer Health System.* Washington, DC: National Academies Press.
Joint Commission, The. (2017). Sentinel event policies and procedures. [Online document; retrieved 9/29/2018.] www.jointcommission.org/sentinel_event_policy_and_procedures/
Levinson, D.R. (2012). Hospital incident reporting systems do not capture most patient harm. Washington, DC: US Department of Health and Human Services, Office of the Inspector General; Report No. OEI-06-09-00091. [Online document; retrieved 9/29/2018.]. http://oig.hhs.gov/oei/reports/oei-06-09-00091.pdf
Maryland Developmental Disabilities Administration. (2013). *Policy on Reportable Incidents and Investigations.* Baltimore, MD: Department of Health and Mental Hygiene. [Online document; retrieved 9/29/2018.] https://health.maryland.gov/ohcq/dd/docs/10.22.02.01%20FINAL%20PORII%20.pdf
National Quality Forum. (2011). Serious reportable events. [Online document; retrieved 9/29/2018.] www.qualityforum.org/topics/sres/serious_reportable_events.aspx
Noble, D.J. & Pronovost, P.J. (2010). Underreporting of patient safety incidents reduces health care's ability to quantify and accurately measure harm reduction. *Journal of Patient Safety, 6(*4), 247-250.
Saxton, J. & Finkelstein, M. (2008). Enabling patient involvement without increasing liability risks. In P. Spath (Ed.). *Engaging Patients as Safety Partners: A Guide to Reducing Errors and Improving Satisfaction* (pp. 163-200). Chicago, IL: AHA Health Forum.

8

MANAGING HEALTHCARE RESOURCES

Reader Objectives

After reading this chapter and reflecting on the contents, you will be able to:
1. Describe the goals of resource management initiatives.
2. Identify tactics used by providers and health plans to decrease under- and overuse of resources.
3. Recognize the role of case managers and utilization review staff in resource management activities.
4. Identify common measures of healthcare resource use.
5. Demonstrate an understanding of resource management functions.

Key Terms

Bundled Payments for Care Improvement (BPCI): CMS initiative that combines reimbursement for inpatient and professional services delivered during an initial hospital stay as well as services that are received 90 days post-discharge.

Case management: Process whereby people with specific healthcare needs are identified and a plan formulated and implemented to achieve optimum patient outcomes in the most cost-effective manner.

Clinical paths: Care management tools used to organize, sequence, and time major patient care activities and interventions of the entire interdisciplinary team for a particular diagnosis or procedure.

Concurrent review: Assessment of patient care services to ensure appropriate care, treatment, and level of care; assessment performed while patient is receiving services.

Discharge planning: Evaluation of patient's medical and psychosocial needs to arrange for appropriate services after hospitalizations or other extended episodes of care such as home health services.

Disease management: Approach to controlling a defined illness or injury by integrating all components of healthcare to provide the best patient outcomes at the most reasonable and effective cost.

Level of care: The intensity of medical care being provided by the physician or healthcare facility.

Medically necessary: Service or treatment that is appropriate and consistent with a patient's diagnosis, and which, in accordance with accepted standards of practice in the medical community, cannot be omitted without adversely affecting the patient's condition or quality of medical care rendered.

Outcomes management: Process of collecting, analyzing, evaluating, and disseminating results of processes or procedures to improve decision-making and service delivery.

Pay-for-performance (P4P): See value-based purchasing.

Prospective review: An assessment of the medical necessity of services prior to the services actually being rendered.

Protocols: Care management tools describing the process for managing patients with specific clinical conditions.

Retrospective review: Assessment of medical necessity and appropriateness of billing practices for services that have already been rendered.

Standard order sets: Care management tools used to streamline the treatment ordering process and help physicians quickly make appropriate patient care decisions.

Utilization management (UM): The planning, organizing, directing, and controlling of healthcare services in a cost-effective manner while maintaining quality of patient care and contributing to overall goals of an organization.

Utilization review (UR): Evaluation of patient resource use and appropriateness of healthcare services; can be done prospectively, concurrently, or retrospectively.

Value-based purchasing (VBP): Payment model that rewards physicians, hospitals, medical groups, or other healthcare providers for meeting certain quality and efficiency performance expectations; also called pay-for-performance.

Resource Management

Resource management encompasses a diverse set of activities aimed at promoting effective care – one of the six key dimensions of healthcare quality identified by the Institute of Medicine (2001). Effective care refers to services of proven value and for which there are no significant tradeoffs. In other words, the benefits outweigh the risks. These services, such as beta-blocker medications for heart attack patients, are backed by sound medical theory and strong scientific evidence. Ineffective healthcare unnecessarily increases costs.

Resource management activities are aimed at reducing underuse and overuse of services. Underuse occurs when services do not get provided even when they would have been medically beneficial. For instance, women ages 21-65 who received a Pap test in the last 3 years decreased from 87.5% in 2000 to 81.2% in 2015 (AHRQ, 2018). Overuse occurs when services are provided even when they are not warranted on medical grounds or when the costs add no significant benefit. For example, studies suggest that for knee meniscus tears, supervised exercise therapy is just as effective for controlling adult knee pain and improving functional status as arthroscopic partial meniscectomy (Jazrawi, Gold & Zuckerman, 2018).

Achieving effective healthcare is a broad quality management goal. Previous chapters described how healthcare organizations are using quality management techniques to improve all quality dimensions. This chapter focuses on techniques generally associated with resource management, a subset of an organization's wider-ranging quality management efforts.

Healthcare organizations and purchasers employ several tactics aimed at reducing under- and overuse of healthcare resources. These efforts generally fall into five categories.

- Utilization management
- Case management
- Disease management
- Outcomes management
- Pay-for-performance

There is considerable overlap among activities in these categories. The commonalities become apparent throughout this chapter. Some healthcare organizations delegate different aspects of resource management to separate departments or individuals. In other organizations, individuals in one department oversee all resource management activities.

Utilization Management

In the 1980s, the American Hospital Association defined utilization management (UM) as the planning, organizing, directing, and controlling of the healthcare product in a cost-effective manner while maintaining quality of patient care and contributing to the overall goals of the organization. This definition is still applicable today. All types of healthcare organizations have UM programs: hospitals, home health agencies, rehabilitation facilities, long-term care facilities, inpatient and outpatient psychiatric and substance abuse treatment facilities, outpatient clinics, community health service programs, managed and accountable care organizations, and health insurers.

Systems to ensure appropriate use of healthcare services are required by some accreditation groups, however requirements vary. There is no specific mention of UM in Joint Commission standards although throughout the chapters there are requirements to measure, assess, and improve the IOM's six key dimensions of healthcare quality. The UM requirements in the National Committee for Quality Assurance (NCQA) standards for health plans are very specific. In Exhibit 8.1 is an excerpt from these standards. Most states use the NCQA accreditation standards as a basis for state regulations governing UM in commercial and public health plans.

Exhibit 8.1. Partial List of NCQA Utilization Management Standards

To make utilization decisions, the health plan uses written criteria based on sound clinical evidence and specific procedures for applying those criteria in an appropriate manner:

- The criteria for determining medical necessity are clearly documented and include procedures for applying criteria based on the needs of individual patients and characteristics of the local delivery system.
- The health plan involves appropriate, actively practicing practitioners in its development or adoption of criteria and in the development and review of procedures for applying criteria.
- The health plan reviews the criteria at specified intervals and updates them, as necessary.
- The health plan states in writing how practitioners can obtain the utilization management criteria and makes the criteria available to its practitioners upon request.
- At least annually, the health plan evaluates the consistency with which the healthcare professionals involved in utilization review apply the criteria in decision making.

Federal regulations effecting healthcare organizations have specific UM mandates. For instance, the CMS Conditions of Participation require hospitals review Medicare and Medicaid patients with respect to the medical necessity of admissions to the institution, duration of stays, and professional services furnished (CMS, 2011). UM is one of the few requirements in Medicare regulations which are not also included in Joint Commission accreditation standards. Hospitals are required by Medicare to have a written plan detailing how medical necessity reviews will be conducted. This plan must include descriptions of:

- Scope of review activities
- Criteria and information sources used to determine medical necessity
- Processes used to review appropriateness of healthcare and related services

Hospitals must also have a committee to oversee medical necessity reviews. Committee composition and manner of functioning are spelled out in the CMS regulations. For example:

- The committee membership must include at least two doctors of medicine or osteopathy
- Medical necessity reviews may not be conducted by any individual who has a direct financial interest in the hospital (e.g., an ownership interest).
- Medical necessity reviews may not be conducted by individuals professionally involved in the care of the patient whose case is being reviewed

It is rare to find a provider or health plan without some type of UM program, whether done to comply with regulations or simply to improve effectiveness of care. The scope and operations of these programs varies according to the type of organization; however, two basic functions are found in most programs:

- Utilization review
- Improvement of resource use

Utilization Review

Utilization review (UR) involves a formal examination of the appropriateness of healthcare services. This examination is done on a prospective, concurrent, and retrospective basis. The objectives of UR are to assure services are medically necessary and promote delivery of services in the least costly setting.

The process of UR done by healthcare providers is slightly different from UR activities in health plans. Two primary differences are the timing of reviews and sources of information. In a hospital, for example, UR is rarely done prospectively. Prospective review occurs prior to a patient actually receiving services. The hospital admissions office may prospectively verify a patient's health plan has approved an admission, but this is not prospective UR on the part of the hospital. It is the health plan conducting prospective review. The review done by an insurer usually consists of pre-admission certification (determination of the need for inpatient hospital care) and prior authorization (coverage approval). Without preadmission certification and prior authorization hospitalization costs may not be paid by the patient's insurer. Similar prior authorizations are conducted by health plans for high cost diagnostic tests and outpatient treatments.

The second significant difference between UR activities in provider organizations and health plans is the source of information used to make decisions. The provider (hospital, long-term care facility, physician clinic, etc.) has direct access to patient health records. These records contain information about a patient's history, current illness, diagnostic test results, and other pertinent medical details. Individuals working for a health plan do not have ready access to all of this information. For UR purposes, they often must obtain pertinent information through verbal information exchanges with providers.

Utilization Guidelines

Providers and insurers use decision support tools – utilization guidelines – to assist in making decisions about the most appropriate care for specific conditions and diagnoses, as well as prevent overuse and guard against underuse. Two commercially available assessment tools commonly used by hospitals, health systems, Medicare fiscal intermediaries and other organizations are the Milliman Care Guidelines, now known as MCG guidelines, and InterQual® Criteria. These tools include evidence-based clinical guidelines that cover the entire continuum of care. A high-level overview of some MCG and InterQual Criteria components is found in Exhibit 8.2 below.

Exhibit 8.2. High-Level Overview of Some MCG and InterQual Criteria Components

MCG	InterQual Criteria
- Clinical indications for admission - Goal or reasonable length of stay - Description of optimal care and patient status (e.g. level of care, clinical status, interventions, and medications) - Current best evidence, including evidence summaries, references and footnotes - Description of conditions and clinical situations for which a hospital stay may exceed the goal length of stay (GLOS), including estimates of the duration of those extended stays - Readmission risk factors, risk reduction guidance, and risk screening tools	- Appropriateness of care decision support - Level of care criteria - Planning criteria to identify when services are appropriate (e.g., imaging studies, procedures, medications, and specialty referral) - CMS content to support consistent application of third-party content - Coordinated care content to generate a patient-specific care plan for complex cases and high-risk members with a patented blended assessment

Tools such as MCG and InterQual Criteria are used in assessment of 'appropriate payment,' by documenting 'justification' of medical need for the admission, consistency in coding, facility resource allocation for time and intensity, and length of stay. In addition, these tools predict facility payments for levels of acute care within the interpretations of complex Medicare and commercial insurance payment regulations.

These tools are not intended as rigid standards of care or prescriptions for treatment. They are merely recommendations. Determining appropriate use of healthcare services for a particular patient requires professional assessment of presenting symptoms and circumstances. Guidelines cannot address all situations for all patients and never replace clinical judgment.

Exhibit 8.3 illustrates the MCG guidelines for what constitutes an appropriate inpatient admission for a child or adolescent in need of behavioral health services (Aetna Better Health of Kentucky, 2016). If these criteria are not met, the facility may be denied payment by the patient's insurance company.

Exhibit 8.3. MCG Guidelines for Child or Adolescent Inpatient Admission for Behavioral Health Services

Admission to Inpatient Level of Care for Child or Adolescent is judged appropriate as indicated by 1 or more of the following:
- Inpatient behavioral care is needed as indicated by ALL of the following:
  - Treatment is needed because of patient risk due to 1 or more of the following:
    - Imminent danger to self is present
    - Imminent danger to others is present
    - Behavioral health disorder is present with ALL of the following:
      - Severe psychiatric or behavioral symptoms or conditions are present
      - Severe dysfunction in daily living is present
  - Treatment situation and needs are appropriate for inpatient level (instead of lower level of care)
- Inpatient treatment is needed due to presence of significant delirium.
- Patient has behavioral health disorder and requires somatic treatment for which around the clock medical or nursing care must be used because of severe adverse effect risk or medical comorbidity

InterQual® products, available from Change Healthcare (www.changehealthcare.com) are packaged in electronic criteria sets that are continuously evolving in response to new medical knowledge and treatment options. The InterQual® criteria used in hospitals are set up on the following paradigm:
- Severity of Illness (S.I.) criteria are used to establish whether a patient is sick enough to require hospital care, for purposes of justifying admission
- Intensity of Service (I.S.) criteria are used to establish the daily requirement of services justifying a patient's need for continued hospitalization
- Discharge Screens are criteria used to establish a patient's discharge plan

Both MCG and InterQual Criteria include software and algorithms with a user interface so that clinical and administrative staff can best use the guidelines when updating patient records to indicate health status, assess acuity, initiate a care plan and/or admission, and to support medical need for purposes of payment. Organizations using MCG or InterQual® Criteria must pay a license fee which can be significant depending on the size of the user organization

In addition to MCG and InterQual® Criteria there are utilization criteria sets for specific conditions and health management situations. For instance, the American Society of Addiction Medicine (ASAM) publishes the *ASAM Criteria: Treatment Criteria for Addictive, Substance-Related, and Co-Occurring Conditions* (Mee-Lee, 2013). The ASAM criteria are clinical guides to be used in making placement decisions about the most appropriate level of care for patients with substance abuse problems. The criteria contain descriptions of treatment programs at each level of care, including the setting, staffing, therapies, and treatment plans usually found at each level. These criteria address five levels of care for substance abuse: early intervention; outpatient treatment; intensive outpatient/partial hospitalization treatment; residential/ inpatient treatment;

and medically managed intensive inpatient treatment. Guidelines developed by groups such as ASAM can be purchased with no license fee required.

The CMS has not issued any guidance to facilities on which specific utilization assessment tool may be used and none are considered to be CMS-approved. In all cases, in addition to screening tools, CMS encourages reviewers to apply his/her own clinical judgment to make a medical review determination based on the documentation in the medical record (CMS, 2017).

Acute Care UR Process

Hospitals and other acute care facilities employ people to perform UR activities. These individuals often have clinical backgrounds (nurses, social workers) however some have health information management (HIM) or other allied health credentials. People responsible for UR may have other resource management duties, such as case management (described later in this chapter). When UR is an individual's only responsibility, they often have the title, UR coordinator or UR manager.

Utilization guidelines are used for decision making during prospective, concurrent and retrospective review. In a hospital, the UR process starts with a patient's first contact with hospital providers. In the case of scheduled admissions, this contact may occur during the pre-admission phase. Someone in the physician office, the hospital admissions office or a designated hospital preadmission coordinator gathers clinical and financial information from the patient. The patient's health plan is contacted to verify insurance coverage and obtain prior-authorization for the planned hospital admission. The admitting physician determines the appropriate level of care for the patient (for example, outpatient, observation, or inpatient) based on the patient's condition and utilization guidelines. When patients are admitted directly to the hospital from another facility, from home, or through the emergency department (ED), UR starts at the time of admission.

A UR coordinator becomes involves in the review process either prospectively or when a patient is admitted and continues to evaluate appropriate service utilization until discharge occurs. The activities of a UR coordinator are summarized in the flowchart in Exhibit 8.4.

Exhibit 8.4. Hospital UR Process

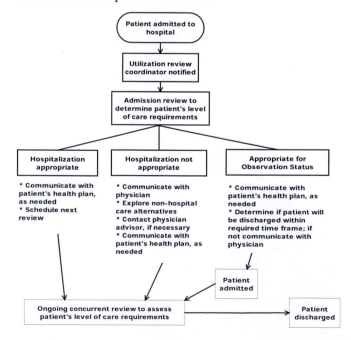

If the patient's first contact with the hospital is in the ED, clinical staff in that department may assist in determining the appropriate level of care for the patient. Some hospitals have UR coordinators assigned to the ED.

The UR coordinator reviews information in the patient's record and utilization guidelines to determine if acute care admission is appropriate, not appropriate, or if the patient is eligible for observation status. If an inpatient admission is medically necessary, the next review is scheduled. The patient's health plan may be contacted and information provided about the admission.

If a patient's condition is appropriate only for observation status, the UR coordinator determines if the hospital stay is likely to last beyond 24-48 hours. The attending physician can always order inpatient admission if the patient's status changes.

When a patient's condition and need for services does not meet level of care criteria for hospital admission, the UR coordinator (or the ED physician) discusses the situation with the admitting physician and helps him or her plan non-hospital alternatives for the patient. Any time level of care criteria are not met (at admission or after admission) it may be necessary for the UR coordinator to request a second level review of the case by a physician advisor.

Physician advisors are members of the hospital UM committee or may be appointed from within each medical staff department. A physician advisor conducts second-level reviews, taking into consideration patient factors that may not be clearly defined by utilization criteria. Physician advisors may need to arbitrate differences of opinion between UR guidelines and attending physicians.

Physician advisors foster cost-effective practices by suggesting treatment alternatives or creative non-hospital patient management solutions. If a physician advisor agrees with the judgment of the patient's physician, acute care services are approved. In some instances, the physician advisor may disagree with the judgment of the patient's physician. In these situations, hospitals have a well-defined appeals process involving a second review by another physician advisor or appeals to medical staff department chairmen or medical staff president. Inpatients are never discharged without the attending physician's consent.

The UR coordinator continues to periodically review care provided to hospitalized patients throughout their stay. As long as patients require acute care services, as evidenced by meeting UR guidelines, hospitalization is considered appropriate. Other types of facilities such as long-term care, home health, rehabilitation, and behavioral health services have similar admission and continued stay review activities.

The UR coordinator documents review findings. Documentation starts with the patient's admission and continues until discharge. Documentation serves as a data source for utilization performance measures and is also important for validating interactions with health plan representatives. In many facilities UR coordinators use an electronic database to record and manage the review information. Some facilities use paper worksheets. An example of a paper UR worksheet used in a hospital is shown in Exhibit 8.5.

Exhibit 8.5. Utilization Review Worksheet

PATIENT NAME: _____ ADMIT DATE: _____ UNIT: _____

FIRST REVIEW DATE: _____ **Description of Patient's Condition and Need for Hospitalization:** _____

_____

_____

—   Admission meets acute care guidelines
—   Admission questioned:
      —   Patient requires no institutional care, but is admitted or retained because:
      —   Patient requires subacute level of care, but is admitted or retained because:
      —   Case referred to physician advisor for review on _____ (date)

Date/time Health Plan UR Coordinator contacted: _____   Name: _____
Number of additional days approved: _____ Expected discharge date: _____   Comments:

SECOND REVIEW DATE: _____
—   Continued stay meets acute care guidelines
—   Case referred to physician advisor for review on _____ (date).

Date/time Health Plan UR Coordinator contacted: _____   Name: _____
Number of additional days approved: _____ Expected discharge date: _____   Comments:

DISCHARGE DATE: _____   Total length of stay: _____ days
Total days guidelines met: _____   Total number of non-acute days: _____

Health Plan UR Process

The UR process in health plans involves prospective, concurrent and retrospective review of healthcare services provided to plan beneficiaries. Health plan UR coordinators review health services using UR guidelines to determine if services are medically necessary and being provided in the least costly setting. Prospective review is conducted for high cost services, such as hospitalizations, outpatient procedures, and high cost treatments or tests. Information used to conduct prospective reviews is obtained from the patient's attending physician or from another provider familiar with the patient's situation. Concurrent reviews are conducted throughout prolonged courses of treatment – during hospital stays, while patients are receiving home health services, while patients are undergoing rehabilitative services. Information used to conduct concurrent reviews is obtained from the patient's attending physician or the provider facility. Some insurers contract with provider organizations to allow health plan UR coordinators to conduct onsite patient assessments and review patient records.

Health plans also use retrospective (pre- or post-payment) reviews to identify utilization concerns. Insurance claims are processed, in part, on the assumption that providers are honest and correct information is being recorded on the billing claim. However, the claims data must be supported by documentation contained in patient files and must be available to insurers upon request. Retrospective review of record documentation may be triggered by insurance claims that exceed established cost norms or exhibit abnormal patterns of practice.

Once a claim has been selected for retrospective review, the provider is notified of the review and patient records requested. The record information is reviewed, using utilization guidelines, to determine whether services were medically necessary and whether documentation supports the level of service being billed. The health plan may deny payment when there is suspected overuse of services, when the level of care (the site where services were provided) doesn't appear justified, or when the frequency of services rendered may not be appropriate for the patient's condition. Providers are referred to the insurer's fraud unit if deceptive billing is suspected. When insurance payments are denied, patients and providers can appeal the decision.

Health plans are required by state and federal regulations to have a fair and consistent process for making utilization decisions (Cornell, 2011). The review process must be under the supervision of a knowledgeable physician and suitable specialists must be used when payment denials are based on issues of clinical appropriateness. The people making first level review decisions are to have sufficient knowledge and skills to evaluate patients' working diagnoses and proposed treatment plans. Payment decisions must be made in a timely manner that reflect the clinical urgency of the situation and minimize disruptions to the provision of services. The health plan must have a fair appeals mechanism in place and ensure practitioners and patients understand their appeal rights.

The frequency and scope of retrospective UR activities for Medicare patients were expanded by The Improvement and Modernization Act of 2003. This act requires CMS use recovery audit contractors (RACs) to identify underpayments and overpayments for services paid by Medicare (Part A and B). "The Medicare Fee for Service Recovery Audit Program's mission is to identify and correct Medicare improper payments through the efficient detection and collection of overpayments made on claims of health care services provided to Medicare beneficiaries, and the identification of underpayments to providers so that the CMS can implement actions that will prevent future improper payments in all 50 states" (CMS, 2018b). The focus of these prospective, post-payment recovery audits and the requirements frequently change. To find the latest details on this UR program go to the Medicare Fee for Service Recovery Audit Program website: www.cms.gov/Research-Statistics-Data-and-Systems/Monitoring-Programs/Medicare-FFS-Compliance-Programs/Recovery-Audit-Program/Index.html.

Improvement of Resource Use

The second UM function involves analysis of aggregate information on resource use. Measures of utilization practices are analyzed, improvement opportunities identified and projects undertaken to achieve desired goals. Utilization performance measures vary among healthcare organizations. It is common to find the following utilization measures within hospitals:
- Average length of stay for different groups of patients
- Average total charges for different groups of patients
- Average profit margin (reimbursement minus charges or cost) for Medicare and Medicaid discharges

- Number of hospital days denied reimbursement by commercial health plans
- Average length of stay in intensive, cardiac and other special care units for different groups of patients

Comparison data are often used to identify improvement opportunities. Shown in Exhibit 8.6 is a tabular report created for UM purposes in a hospital. The report shows the mean length of stay (LOS) for each of the hospital's top five diagnostic groups of Medicare patients (by volume) as compared to the nationwide mean length of stay reported by CMS for Medicare patients in these groups.

Exhibit 8.6. Length-of-Stay Comparison Report for Top Five Medicare Patient Groups

Principal Diagnosis	No. of Cases	Hospital Mean LOS	CMS Mean LOS
Septicemia	197	8.7	8.0
Pneumonia	172	5.6	6.8
Osteoarthritis	134	4.6	4.43
Acute myocardial infarction	94	3.6	4.2
Atrial fibrillation	73	4.5	5.4

Focused measurement activities are also conducted to look at overall resource use and factors affecting the cost of care. Shown in Exhibit 8.7 is a set of utilization-related performance measures for patients undergoing total hip replacements (not due to traumatic injury). The data are presented in the aggregate and also stratified to show results for the three surgeons performing hip replacements.

Exhibit 8.7. Report of Resource Use for Total Hip Replacement Patients

Measures	1st Quarter (37 patients)	2nd Quarter (49 patients)	3rd Quarter (41 patients)
Average length of stay	2.4	3.1	3.4
% admitted day of surgery	85%	87%	88%
% receiving preoperative antibiotics	100%	100%	100%
% patients with intraoperative complications	0%	0%	.5%
Average estimated blood loss during procedure (cc's)	560	524	570
% patients having complications occur in the recovery room	0%	3.2%	4.1%
Average length of time until postop pain medication is administered orally (hrs/min)	8:01	10:42	09:50
Length of time after procedure patient is ambulating any distance (with walker) (hrs/min)	08:30	08:50	09:50
% patients that attended preadmission class	78%	82%	85%

Utilization data by surgeon:

MD#	Total Cases for Three Quarters	Average Length of Stay	Average Charges
01	40	3.3 days	$ 26,635
02	37	3.0 days	$ 25,447
03	50	2.1 days	$ 24,824

Average Charges in Expense Categories ($)

MD#	Pharmacy	Laboratory	Operating Room	Physical Therapy	Radiology	Nuclear Medicine	Supplies
01	2384	634	3308	1110	371	632	6975
02	2175	454	3368	1253	225	302	7101
03	2003	394	2808	1613	236	0	7378

Utilization reports assist hospital leaders evaluate effectiveness of UM activities and find improvement opportunities. Changing practice patterns can be difficult if meaningful data are not provided to the medical staff and administration.

Health plans are also constantly analyzing utilization data in an effort to manage resource use. Common measures used by health plans to evaluate service consumption and financial viability include:

- Total revenue
- Net income
- Medical loss ratio
- Operating profit margin
- Annual costs per covered-life
- Hospitalization rates for various conditions
- Rate of ancillary service use for various conditions
- Average number of primary care physician visits
- Average number of specialty physician visits
- Average number of hospital admissions per hospitalized mental health patient

Making improvements in effective use of healthcare resources also requires commitments from provider organizations to operate as efficiently as possible. It is common to discover system factors are contributing to higher healthcare costs. Sometimes even small changes in the way healthcare is delivered can reduce costs. In Exhibit 8.8 is a summary of a hospital improvement project undertaken to improve efficiency of the patient discharge process.

Exhibit 8.8. Discharge Process Improvement Project

All hospital units were asked to work toward achieving a target of three patient discharges before lunchtime each day. This enables patients to flow from ICU, ED, or other areas more efficiently instead of using observation beds or experiencing extensive waits. Before this initiative was started, it was rare for beds on general units (medical and surgical beds) to be available for new patients much before 2 pm each day.

A discharge lounge was created to accommodate 12 patients. Each morning the nursing staff prepares patients for discharge home. When the physician's discharge order is received patients are then transferred to the discharge lounge to await transport. Pending patient discharges are identified by the unit assistants and bed managers are notified by fax first thing each morning.

Pharmacy staff changed the way their day is organized so patient take-home prescriptions can be processed earlier in the day. Now patients can leave sooner with their discharge medications. Laboratory staff has changed the timing of their equipment quality controls to 7 am instead of later in the morning. This enables blood tests to be processed earlier which results in earlier patient discharges.

The percentage of patients discharged before lunchtime rose to more than 40 percent in the first three months after implementation of these changes. Often general units start the day with free beds and no patients are waiting to be admitted from the ED or transfer to a general unit from ICU.

Large health systems such as the Veterans Health Administration and HCA Healthcare have clinical data warehouses where information from the many patient visits to their facilities is stored. The data in these systems are reviewed by health system data analysts to find ways to improve practices and reduce costs. In one project, HCA studied data about 18,000 births in their hospitals to determine if there was a difference in the rate of newborns going to the neonatal intensive-care unit (NICU) after an early elective delivery. The HCA analysts found that compared to babies delivered at full term (39 weeks) those delivered electively at 37 weeks were four times more likely to have a complication requiring transfer to the NICU and those delivered at 38 weeks were 2 times more likely to require NICU care (Livingston, 2018). This finding led to changes in obstetrical practices. By discouraging early elective deliveries physicians were able to improve newborn outcomes and also reduce costs associated with complications.

Case Management

For many years The Joint Commission, the Commission on Accreditation of Rehabilitation Facilities and other accreditation groups have had standards requiring discharge planning. State and federal regulations governing healthcare facilities and health plans have similar requirements. Discharge planning is a process that involves planning and arranging for the needs of patients as they move from one care setting to another. In the past, the discharge planning process had little influence on effective use of resources. Discharge planning staff simply arranged for whatever patient services were ordered by physicians. As pressures for healthcare cost containment grew, traditionally passive discharge planning activities transitioned to a more prominent case management function. In some organizations, this function is still referred to as discharge planning although the responsibilities of discharge planning staff are similar to those of case managers.

Case management is a method of ensuring coordination and continuity of care during a patient's episode of illness. The goal of case management is to efficiently move patients through the healthcare system by effective use of internal and external resources. Today, case management can be found in a variety of organizations, including

- State and county public health agencies (long term care, community health, residential care)
- Employers (Workers compensation, employee assistance programs)
- Home-based providers (Visiting nurse associations, private home healthcare agencies, hospital-based home healthcare programs, hospice)
- Hospitals (inpatient acute care and program-specific outpatient services such as cardiovascular, oncology, perinatal, postpartum/neonatal, pediatrics)
- Rehabilitation facilities (Bureau of Vocational Rehabilitation, consumer-directed independent living programs, cognitive rehabilitation/head injury programs, physical medicine/physiatry)
- Purchasers (Managed care organizations, private commercial health plans)
- Physician clinics (primary care physicians, group practices)
- Independent, community-based case practices (patients/clients can personally contract for case management services from practitioners)

Most individuals receiving health services need some level of care coordination and discharge planning. However, people with complex or special needs are frequently assigned a case manager. A case manager is an individual specially trained in coordinating care and services for a population of patients. Case managers often have a nursing or social work background. For those patients not assigned to a case manager, care coordination and discharge planning activities are done by the patient's primary care physician, nurses, social workers, or rehabilitation specialists.

Reducing hospital readmissions for patients with complex medical needs is an area of potential resource overuse that can be impacted by more interventional case management. Preventing readmissions is an improvement target for Medicare, Medicaid and private insurance plans. A readmission is defined as a return hospitalization to an acute care hospital that follows a prior acute care admission within a specified time interval, called the readmission time interval. Although policymakers and researchers sometimes use intervals such as 5, 60 or 90 days, the time interval currently used by CMS is 30 days (CMS, 2018c). There are no magic bullets for reducing readmissions, however some studies show a combination of effective care coordination and post-discharge support can reduce some readmissions (Brooks, 2015).

Case Management Process

Each organization defines the group of patients to be assigned a case manager and criteria differ. Facilities admitting many high-risk patients may assign case managers to every patient (for example, children's hospital, cancer hospitals, rehabilitation facilities). Health plans, general hospitals, home health agencies, and nursing facilities may only assign case managers to patients likely to have complex care coordination or discharge planning needs such as those with:

- Age-related discharge planning challenges (e.g., those over age 75 or under the age of 12 months)

- History of recurrent hospitalizations or at risk for future re-hospitalizations
- Psychosocial or medical conditions putting them at high risk for placement problems
- Serious chronic conditions, such as lung/breathing problems, brittle diabetes, symptomatic coronary artery disease, cancer, AIDS/HIV, extensive burns, spinal cord injury, significant mental retardation or inability to function independently due to mental illness

Regardless of the care setting, case managers perform four key activities:
1. Assess and prioritize the individual's healthcare needs.
2. Develop a plan of care addressing the individual's health needs in the most cost-effective manner.
3. Arrange and coordinate the services needed by the individual.
4. Monitor the individual's condition and responses to services so updates to the plan of care can be made if necessary.

The hospital case management process starts with a patient's admission and continues through the hospitalization. Some hospital-based case managers continue to stay in contact with patients after discharge and may periodically make phone calls or home visits to assess a patient's condition. This model of case management is sometimes referred to as care coordination because management of patient care does not end with a patient's discharge (Young, 2018).

Large companies self-insured for worker accidents often hire case managers to coordinate health services received by injured employees. The employer-based case manager reviews and coordinates provision of medical, rehabilitative services and related care from multiple medical care providers. Employer-based case managers are responsible for ensuring medical care received by an injured worker conforms to applicable regulations and guidelines and is consistent with accepted medical practices. A significant aspect of this work involves regular contact with medical professionals and administrative staff, company officials, employees or their representatives.

Case Management Tools

The need for better patient care coordination and more effective use of resources has led to development of several patient care management tools. Case managers and direct caregivers use these tools to promote more effective, high quality patient care: clinical paths, standard order sets, protocols, other point-of-care reminders, and disease management.

Care management tools assist physicians, nurses, and other clinicians in reaching defined patient outcome goals in an efficient and cost-effective manner. These tools are consistent with human factors principles for work system improvements you learned about in chapter 6. Care management tools standardize patient care activities, reduce reliance on memory, and improve information access. These tools serve as reminders of what health services are most likely needed, but not what must be done for every patient. Healthcare providers that have adopted an electronic health record system (EHR) integrate these reminders into the system.

Accreditation standards and government regulations do not mandate any particular care management tools. However, Joint Commission standards do require evidence-based information (for example, clinical practice guidelines) is used in developing care management recommendations. Care management tools are a way of providing evidence-based recommendations to caregivers when it is most needed – at the time patient care decisions are being made.

Clinical Paths

Clinical paths are care management tool used to organize, sequence, and time the major patient care activities and interventions of the entire interdisciplinary team for a particular diagnosis or procedure over a specified time period (hours, days, phases of care). There are many different names given to these tools: caremap, critical path, collaborative care plan, clinical pathway, and managed care. plan.

In Exhibit 8.9 is a clinical path used to guide patient care for children admitted to the hospital for management of non-ruptured appendicitis.

Exhibit 8.9. Inpatient Appendectomy Clinical Path for Children (non-ruptured appendix)

INTERVENTION	Phase I Emergency Department to Immediately Prior to Surgery	Phase II Post-Anesthesia Recovery Unit to Discharge
Consultations	- Anesthesia - Surgical	
Tests	- Complete blood count - Metabolic panel - Urinalysis including pregnancy test per protocol - Abdominal ultrasound as indicated	
Treatments		- Give oxygen per nasal cannula to maintain oxygen saturation $\geq$ 92% - Pulse oximetry if receiving oxygen - Wean to room air as tolerated - Incentive spirometry every 1 hour x 24 hours, while awake, and then every 6 hours while awake - Remove surgical dressing 24 hours after surgery
Medications	- Cefoxitin 40 mg/kg/dose every 6 hours (maximum = 2 mg per dose). For pain: - Morphine sulfate 0.05 mg/kg IV every 2 hours as needed for moderate to severe pain - Morphine sulfate 0.1 mg/kg IV every 2 hours as need for severe pain if pain is unrelieved by lower dose - Acetaminophen 15 mg/kg (maximum = 650 mg/dose) per rectum or orally every 4 hours as needed for mild pain or temperature of > 101.5F° (oral)	- Cefoxitin 40 mg/kg/dose every 6 hours (maximum = 2 mg per dose). Discontinue after 4 doses - Arrangements made for home IV antibiotic therapy if IV antibiotic therapy not completed in hospital For mild pain: - Ketorolac 0.5 mg/kg (maximum = 30 mg per dose) IV times 1 (loading dose) then Ketorolac n0.25 mg/kg (maximum = 30 mg per dose) IV every 6 hours times 7 doses - If patient tolerating oral intake discontinue Ketorolac and give Ibuprophen 10 mg/kg (maximum = 600 mg per dose) orally every 6 hours for the remainder of the 7 doses. Then every 6 hours as needed for pain. For moderate to severe pain: - Morphine sulfate 0.05 mg/kg IV every 2 hours as needed for moderate to severe pain - Morphine sulfate 0.1 mg/kg IV every 2 hours as need for severe pain if pain is unrelieved by lower dose
Activity	- Assist with care - Activity as tolerated	---> - Out of bed to chair in AM - Advance ambulation as tolerated - May resume bathing/showering 48 hours post-op
Nutrition / Intravenous Therapy	- Nothing by mouth - Lactated Ringers 20 ml/kg IV over 30 minutes then: Dextrose 5 Lactated Ringers(D5LR) at twice maintenance rate for weight _____ ml per hour	- Clear liquids if bowel sounds present, no abdominal distention, no nausea/emesis; no carbonated beverages - Advance to regular diet as tolerated - D5LR at 1 ½ maintenance rate for weight _____ ml per hour - IV bag/tubing change every 96 hours - Discontinue IV when oral intake adequate
Assessments	- Routine vital signs and pain assessment - Record intake and output each shift	---> - If patient develops a temperature of > 100° F (oral), notify physician ---> - If no urine output in 8 hours, without bladder distention, give IV bolus of Lactate Ringers 20 mg/kg x1; if patient does not void within 4 hours, notify physician - Check incision - IV site inspection with dressing changes per protocol
Activity	- Assist with care - Activity as tolerated	---> - Out of bed to chair in AM - Advance ambulation as tolerated - May resume bathing/showering 48 hours post-op - Cough & deep breathe with vital signs

Clinical paths can be used in any type of healthcare setting to:
- remind all caregivers of what patients might need and when they might need it
- improve communication among the healthcare team and between different care settings
- decrease under- and overuse of resources
- improve coordination and continuity of care

Protocols

Protocols are instructions for managing patients with specific clinical conditions. Protocols are made available to practitioners at the point-of-care to remind them of the best way to manage patients. Shown in Exhibit 8.10 is a protocol for managing hospitalized patients with hypoglycemia (low blood sugar). The protocol instructs nurses what to do if a patient's blood glucose falls below a defined level. The hospital medical staff has approved the protocol so nurses can take these emergency actions without waiting for a physician order.

Exhibit 8.10. Protocol for Managing Conscious Patients with Hypoglycemia

If the patient has laboratory blood glucose (BG) of between 50 and 69, begin treatment according to the following treatment guidelines:

1. Hold all diabetic medications and notify physician.
2. If the patient is conscious and is able to take food by mouth, give him 15 gms of carbohydrate in any of the following forms: 15 gram tube of glucose gel (preferred); 4 ounces of fruit juice; 8 ounces of skim milk; 4 ounces of regular pop (not diet); 1 tablespoon of sugar or 6 packets of sugar
3. Check the BG again in fifteen minutes and record in Meditech. If still less than 70, repeat above procedure until BG is 70 or more.
4. If BG is 49 or less treat with double the amount of the same items listed above.
5. Do not attempt to give anything by mouth if the patient is semi-conscious or unconscious. Aspiration may occur.

Standard Order Sets

Many physicians, both in their private offices and in institutions, make use of standard order sets to streamline treatment prescribing. Order sets are also a commonly used care management tool intended to decrease under- and overuse of resources. Physicians caring for a group of patients work together to identify what will be listed on an order set for that particular patient population. For example, there may be a set of orders for all patients scheduled to undergo a certain operation. Standard orders are also commonly used for some medications, such as total parenteral nutrition solutions and chemotherapy infusions, where the orders can be complex and confusing.

Evidence-based information found in clinical practices guidelines and current medical literature is considered when creating order sets. The orders reflect what most likely needs to be done for patients as well as the least costly way of achieving the best patient outcomes.

Order sets are usually presented as some sort of paper or electronic form. The form lists physician orders commonly written for patients in certain circumstances. The list can include medications, laboratory tests, x-rays, other diagnostic tests, diet restrictions, preoperative preparation, and many other things. Physicians using the order set can simply indicate which of the items they wish their patients to receive and provide various necessary details, such as dose or duration.

Facilities with computerized order entry systems integrate standard order sets into the system. Physicians can then choose among various alternatives as they input orders into the computer. Standard order sets may be used instead of clinical paths or the orders may be developed in conjunction with the development of clinical paths.

While physicians may be expected to use order sets when managing patients, the treatment recommendations are not mandatory. Physicians are encouraged to revise orders as necessary to meet the clinical needs of individual patients. In Exhibit 8.11 is a standard set of orders used by surgeons when admitting patients for a laparoscopic cholecystectomy.

Exhibit 8.11. Standard Physician Orders for Patients Undergoing Laparoscopic Cholecystectomy

Pre-operative laparoscopic cholecystectomy
Check-off orders that apply to your patient/ Add additional orders as necessary.

1. Pre-op Testing:
   - ☐ Complete blood count
   - ☐ Urinalysis
   - ☐ Liver profile
   - ☐ Amylase
   - ☐ Chest x-ray per anesthesia order
   - ☐ EKG per anesthesia order
   - ☐ Others: _____
2. IV: 1000cc LR on arrival to Same Day Surgery Unit
3. Medications:
   - ☐ Zofran 4mg IV in Same Day Surgery Unit
   - ☐ Ancef 1gm IV as patient goes to operating room. *If allergic to penicillin: Clindamycin 900mg IV x 1, Aztreonam 1.0 gm IV x1*
4. Void prior to transport to operating room

Other Point-of-Care Reminders

Clinical paths, protocols, standard order sets are the most commonly used point-of-care reminders, however there are others. For example, in Exhibit 8.12 is a one-page form placed in the outpatient clinic record of a patient with diabetes. When the patient has a clinic visit the information on the form helps remind the practitioner of interventions that may be necessary. The form is also used to document the care provided. If the clinic is using an EHR, similar reminders can be incorporated into the electronic system as a fill-in-the blank checklist.

Exhibit 8.12. Care Management Reminders in the Clinic Chart of a Patient with Diabetes

Care Functions	Interventions (initial below as each item is done)

Tests and Procedures	Consider:
	    Complete blood count _____ ECG _____
	    Chem 7 _____ Thyroid & lipid profile _____
	24 hour urine @ 3 years for protein _____ Random plasma glucose @ 6 mos _____
	HbAc @ 4 mos _____ PPD yearly (if risk factors present) _____

Consults	Diabetic foot clinic prn _____ Dietary _____ Ophthalmology @ year ___ (last visit) _____ Dental ____
Treatment and Assessments	Height _____ Weight _____ Blood Pressure_____ Pulse _____ Assess skin: ulcers ____ sores ____ breaks ____ Assess feet: color ____ temp ____ circulation ____ sensation ____ Complete H&P (to include visual acuity) _____ Pneumovax (if not previously given) _____ Influenza vaccination (if not previously given) _____
Medications	Assess blood sugar, self-blood glucose monitoring tag, and adjust insulin/oral agents as needed _____
Activity	Assess activity/exercise & revise/encourage patient as tolerated _____

Disease Management

Disease management is a case management approach aimed at controlling quality and costs for patients certain high cost medical conditions. Disease management initiatives focus on the whole person. For example, in treating diabetes, the vast majority of healthcare dollars associated with this chronic disease are spent on people with severe complications. Using disease management techniques clinicians spend time teaching people with diabetics about their disease so they learn to control their symptoms and complications through diet, exercise and drug therapy. Not only does disease management lead to a better quality of life for people with chronic diseases, but it can also reduce healthcare expenditures by preventing costly complications. The goal of disease management is simple: Meet patients' needs earlier – before they need costly healthcare services.

Disease management initiatives usually target conditions in which pharmaceutical and educational interventions can produce clinical and cost improvements with relative speed. This includes high treatment cost conditions such as asthma, chronic pulmonary disease, reflux esophagitis, spinal cord injury, diabetes, AIDS/HIV, and ischemic heart disease.

Disease management involves many of the common resource management tools and techniques. In addition, patient empowerment is an important element of disease management. Studies have shown up to 80% of all healthcare services involve problems that could be treated at home. Effective home management of these problems can prevent the patient's illness or injury from progressing to the point of needing professional intervention. Components of disease management include treatment guidelines, educational programs for practitioners and patients, and outcome assessments. Disease management interventions for patients at high-risk of hospital readmission are particularly important because CMS has linked Medicare reimbursement to reduction of readmissions (CMS, 2018a). Like all resource management initiatives, the elements of a disease management program vary considerably according to the goals of the program and the patient population.

IT and Case Management

Electronic information systems are greatly expanding opportunities for coordinating patient care and incorporating point-of-care reminders into processes of patient care. Automation has long been recognized as an important factor in reducing human errors in work processes, including those involving delivery of healthcare. Clinical decision support systems can be designed to perform many clinical support functions: diagnosis, drug dose determination, preventive care reminders, and active (diagnostic or therapeutic) care advice.

Computer-aided diagnosis systems assist clinicians in determining a patient's exact diagnosis or the condition underlying his or her presenting health problem. The systems take as input a patient's vital signs and symptoms, physical findings, test results, and background information, and then report one or more possible diagnoses matching that combination of characteristics. Rather than attempting to cover all diagnoses, most systems focus on specific health problems.

Drug dose determination systems are designed to assist the clinician calculate the proper dosage of a specific drug for a patient. Data about a patient is entered into the system and algorithms in the knowledge base then ascertain the proper dosage of the drug in question, either as an exact quantity or as a permissible range. Commercial programs have also been developed for dosing of selected drugs based on patient-specific characteristics and measured drug concentrations.

Preventive care notification systems remind clinicians to administer a particular preventive service when patients reach a certain stage in the process of care for a given health problem (e.g., retinal examination for diabetics) or simply a certain stage of life (e.g., childhood immunizations). Unlike computer-aided diagnosis and drug-dose determination, which are usually designed to provide a single report in response to a specific set of data on a given patient, a preventive care reminder system requires repeated input of data on the patient over time. This includes not only the patient's diagnoses and other clinical characteristics, but also treatments and tests administered and when they were administered. To the extent the set of rules for generating reminders represents a model of the disease process for which a preventive service is to be administered, they constitute a type of formal clinical protocol. The protocol specifies exactly what preventive treatments should be performed at each stage in the process of care for the health problem at hand, based either on the amount of time that has elapsed since the previous stage (for example, since a previous treatment or test) or on data values measuring a patient's condition at that point in time.

Active-care advice systems assist clinicians in performing diagnostic or therapeutic procedures (including pharmaceutical treatments) when patients reach certain stages in the process of care for a given health problem, again often modeled in a formal clinical protocol. An active-care advisory system requires repeated input of data on the patient's health problems, tests, and treatments over time. The protocol specifies exactly what diagnostic and therapeutic procedures should be performed at each stage in the process of care for the health problem at hand.

Seamless transitions from one provider to the next require a common understanding of a patient's health status, needs, and treatment plan. Electronic communication between providers helps standardize the format and content of information and ensure patients are receiving cost-efficient services without gaps in care. In 2018 CMS finalized a rule intended to advance health data exchange among providers and patients as part of the MyHealthEData Initiative (Leventhal, 2018). Information technology continues to evolve and practitioners will be increasingly reliant on electronic decision-support, point-of-care reminder tools, data storage and communication.

Outcomes Management

In 1988 Dr. Paul Ellwood, a managed care pioneer, suggest healthcare organizations implement a system of outcomes management. Outcomes management, as proposed by Ellwood, integrates four well-known quality improvement techniques (1988).

- Establish guidelines for physicians to use in collecting clinical and follow-up information on patients
- Routinely and systematically measure the functioning and well-being of patients, as well as disease-specific clinical outcomes, at appropriate time intervals
- Pool clinical and outcome data on a national basis
- Analyze and disseminate results of this data collection to healthcare decision makers

The goal of outcomes management is to identify ideal patient care practices, encourage caregivers to implement those practices, and then measure the results. Since the early 1990s, a number of healthcare organizations have initiated outcomes management projects. In some organizations these projects are part of the resource management program with case managers or UR coordinators involved in the initiatives. Other organizations consider outcomes management an element of the overall quality management program with staff in the quality department supporting the initiatives. In some large organizations outcomes management projects are conducted by researchers within a designated outcomes management (or similarly named) department.

An outcomes management project is similar to the PDSA or PDCA improvement models. In fact, in the mid-1990s some quality departments changed their designation to outcomes management department without significantly altering the work done within the department. The three steps of an outcomes management project are described below.

- *Define the ideal process*. The best way to care for patients is identified through studies conducted within the organization and by reviewing current medical literature, clinical practice guidelines, and other published evidence-based recommendations.
- *Operationalize the ideal process*. The goal is to get everyone to use the ideal process (same treatments, procedures, and materials, equipment) to achieve desired patient outcomes. Protocols, clinical paths,

standard order sets, and reminder tools are common methods for communicating the ideal process to caregivers.

- *Analyze the effect of process on outcome.* Data are gathered to determine if patients treated using the ideal process are more likely to achieve desired outcome goals as compared to patients managed in a traditional manner.

Once a patient population for an outcomes management project is selected a multidisciplinary team of people involved in caring for these patients is formed. The team is given measurable goals for the project. After studying the process as it currently exists, the project team selects actions necessary for achieving the goals. Any number of actions can be taken in an outcomes management project. The project team analyzes practice pattern data to determine the best interventions and then monitors the success of various strategies. A successful outcomes management project requires more than good clinical skills. Each initiative requires timely feedback of process and outcome measures to the involved caregivers.

In Exhibit 8.13 is a tabular data report from an outcomes management project evaluating the difference between two monitoring techniques used while weaning patients from ventilators. The project goal was to reduce the amount of time and resources used to wean patients off ventilators. Physicians were encouraged (but not mandated) to use pulse oximetry saturations rather than arterial blood gases to monitor a patient's condition during ventilator weaning. As the data reveal, use of pulse oximetry saturation tests alone, without a repeat arterial blood gas (ABG) determination, allowed for shorter weaning times (pulse oximetry tests can be done by nursing staff; an ABG is a blood analysis performed by the laboratory). Plus, the additional cost of the second ABG determination did not appear to be necessary. Data such as this helped convince practitioners of the cost efficiency of using only pulse oximetry saturation testing whenever possible.

Exhibit 8.13. Results from Ventilator Weaning Outcomes Management Study

Time period: Jan 1 - Jun 31	Average time from beginning of wean until extubation	Average time from arrival in ICU until weaning began	Time from arrival in ICU until extubation
GROUP 1: Initial ABG's were obtained; then patient weaned by oximetry only N = 27	2:03	9:35	11:38
GROUP 2: Initial ABG's; then patient weaned by oximetry; repeat ABG prior to extubation N = 36	2:45	10:21	13:06
ICU = Intensive Care Unit			

Clinicians are involved in all phases of an outcomes management project. Their advice, support, and expertise are crucial to the success of the project. Outcomes management represents a growing area of research in medicine, with significant opportunities to improve efficiency, lessen waste, and provide a reasonable standard of care satisfying both patients and caregivers. Regardless how a healthcare organization implements outcomes-based practice, there's one certainty – valid, reliable and timely information about the relationship between care management decisions and patient outcomes will always be needed by clinicians.

Value-Based Purchasing

Value-based purchasing (VPB), sometimes called pay-for-performance (P4P), is a reimbursement approach aimed at decreasing under- and overuse of healthcare resources and improving healthcare quality. The contemporary VPB model began in 2001 when an Institute of Medicine (IOM) report suggested performance-based financial arrangements could improve the quality of care by encouraging adoption of ideal patient care practices (IOM, 2001). The Congress demonstrated support for financial incentives by calling on the Department of Health and Human Services (HHS) to develop a plan for hospital VBP by 2009 (CMS, 2005). The initiative began as a pay-for-participation measurement system. Hospitals providing CMS with data for a defined set of performance measures were financially rewarded for participating in the system. In fiscal year 2007, nearly 95 percent of U.S. hospitals participated successfully in the reporting program and received the full market basket (the measure of inflation in costs of goods and services used by hospitals in treating Medicare patients) update for fiscal year 2008. In 2011, the hospital VBP program changed and hospitals began to receive incentive payments based on their actual performance on a number of health care quality measures (CMS, 2018c). You learned about measures of performance required by CMS and other government agencies in chapter 3. Many of these measures are the basis for determining reimbursement in VBP systems.

Similar value-based payment programs have been or will be enacted by Medicare for all healthcare settings. The current hospital and physician practice measurement reporting requirements and payment incentives are available on the CMS website.

Performance-based payment incentives are also routinely used by private payers and many reward providers for attaining specific performance expectations. Targeted performance goals, reimbursement amounts at risk, and payment formulas vary among commercial health plans.

The performance measures used to evaluate and reward physicians and hospitals have changed over time. Although many VBP programs began with a focus on process measures of quality (for example, prescription of appropriate medications), outcomes, cost efficiency, and information technology measures are increasingly common program elements.

Exhibit 8.14. Prescription of Medications for Patients with Asthma

Asthma: Appropriate Medication

□ Clinic A   □ Clinic B   □ Clinic C   □ Clinic D

Illustrated in Exhibit 8.14 is a comparative performance report for four clinics showing appropriate medication prescription for patients with asthma in different age groups. If this were an insurer's year-end report, Clinic D might be eligible for a monetary bonus for doing better than other clinics in providing appropriate care for health plan participants with asthma. The health plan contract with Clinic B might be terminated if inappropriate practices continue.

Another reimbursement model being tested by Medicare to improve quality and reduce health care expenditures is Bundled Payments for Care Improvement (BPCI). This initiative combines reimbursement for inpatient and professional services delivered during an initial hospital stay as well as services that are received 90 days post-discharge (Romley & Ginsburg, 2018). One example is the Comprehensive Care for Joint Replacement (CJR) Model that started in 2016 and focused on the episode of care for a group of patients (MS-DRGs 469 and 470 for major joint replacement of the lower extremity). Providers are paid a fixed amount for all patient services over the episode of care. An evaluation of treatment patterns for hospitals participating in the CJR model found decreased use of institutional post-acute care services (in particular, skilled nursing facilities and inpatient rehabilitation facilities) and an increased use of home health (Romley & Ginsburg, 2018). Patients receiving less costly post-acute services had outcomes similar to patients who were treated at hospitals not participating in the CJR model.

Initially participation in the CJR model was mandatory in select metropolitan areas. Participation was changed to voluntary in January 2018. As of May 2018, 246 hospitals were voluntarily participating in the CJR payment model. Some of the BPCI models within the Medicare program are not based on an acute hospitalization. The Oncology Care Model initiates an episode of care with chemotherapy, which may be administered in a physician's office, or in some cases taken orally (CMS Innovation Center, 2018). The Center for Medicare and Medicaid Innovation (CMMI) Center is tasked with testing new payment and delivery models and has undertaken a number of initiatives that bundle payment for episodes of care. The latest information about these efforts can be found at the CCMI website (https://innovation.cms.gov).

Summary

Managing healthcare resources is subset of quality management. It promotes effective use of resources and encompasses a diverse set of tactics ranging from UR to P4P. Resource management activities are rapidly evolving in the healthcare industry due to demands for containing costs, demonstrating value, and reducing fragmented services.

Utilization management focuses on the costs of services, how people access services, and utilization rates. Case management is a collaborative process that assesses, plans, implements, monitors, and evaluates cases to meet individual patient needs and improve outcomes cost-efficiently. Disease management advocates prevention and self-care management, as well as evidence-based care, to minimize complications in patient groups with chronic diseases or conditions. Utilization management activities primarily involve concurrent and retrospective evaluation of healthcare appropriateness and duration of care and level of services. Case management takes a more proactive approach – patients' needs are anticipated so effective services can be arranged to meet those needs.

Outcomes management is an improvement model designed to identify ideal practices (best outcomes for the least costs) and encourage adoption of these practices. Value-based purchasing is a payment tactic intended to reduce under- and overuse of healthcare resources and improve quality through financial incentives.

Student Activities

1. Familiarize yourself with the utilization information available in the Healthcare Cost and Utilization Project (http://hcupnet.ahrq.gov) database. Describe the data sources used by the project and list the types of reports that can be obtained for providers in your state.
2. Review the benefits material from your health plan (or another health plan). Identify and describe three resource management tactics mentioned in the insurance benefits material that are likely to decrease your under- or overuse of healthcare services.
3. Research the CMS value-based purchasing initiatives being developed by the CMS Center for Innovation. Describe the reimbursement incentives currently being tested by Medicare to decrease under- and overuse of healthcare resources and improve quality.

Website Resources

Case Management Society of America
www.cmsa.org

CMS Chronic Care Management Resources
www.cms.gov/About-CMS/Agency-Information/OMH/equity-initiatives/chronic-care-management.html

CMS Hospital Value-based Purchasing Program
www.cms.hhs.gov/HospitalQualityInits

CMS Innovation Center
https://innovation.cms.gov

Healthcare Financial Management Association payment, reimbursement, and managed care resources
www.hfma.org

Health Care Cost Institute
https://www.healthcostinstitute.org/

Medicare Hospital Payment Monitoring Program
www.pepperresources.org

Partners in Information Access for Public Health Workforce (links to healthcare utilization statistics)
http://phpartners.org

Taking Action on Overuse
https://takingactiononoveruse.org/

References

Aetna Better Health of Kentucky. (2016). *Behavioral Health Medical Necessity Criteria Milliman Care Guidelines, 20th edition*. [Online document; retrieved 10/1/2018).
www.aetnabetterhealth.com/kentucky/assets/pdf/providers/library/Behavioral%20Health%20MCG%20MNC.pdf

Agency for Healthcare Research and Quality (AHRQ). (2018). *2017 National Healthcare Quality and Disparities Report*. AHRQ Pub. No. 18-0033-EF. Rockville, MD: Agency for Healthcare Research and Quality.

Brooks, J.A. (2015). Reducing hospital readmissions. *American Journal of Nursing*, 115(1), 62-65.

Centers for Medicare & Medicaid Services (CMS). (2018a, August 2). The hospital value-based Purchasing (VBP) program. [Online document, accessed 10/22/2018]. www.cms.gov/Medicare/Quality-Initiatives-Patient-Assessment-Instruments/Value-Based-Programs/Value-Based-Programs.html

_____. (2018b, July 30). Medicare fee for service recovery audit program. [Online document; retrieved 10/5/2018.] www.cms.gov/research-statistics-data-and-systems/monitoring-programs/medicare-ffs-compliance-programs/recovery-audit-program/

_____. (2018c, March 26). Hospital readmissions reduction program. [Online document; retrieved 10/5/2018.] www.cms.gov/Medicare/Quality-Initiatives-Patient-Assessment-Instruments/Value-Based-Programs/HRRP/Hospital-Readmission-Reduction-Program.html

_____. (2017, June). Guidance on hospital inpatient admission decisions. [Online information; retrieved 10/4/2018.] https://www.cms.gov/Outreach-and-Education/Medicare-Learning-Network-MLN/MLNMattersArticles/downloads/se1037.pdf

_____. (2011). Part 482. Conditions of Participation for Hospitals. Sec. 482.30. Conditions of participation: Utilization review. [Online information; retrieved 1/23/13.] www.gpo.gov/fdsys/pkg/CFR-2011-title42-vol5/xml/CFR-2011-title42-vol5-sec482-30.xml

_____. (2005). Deficit Reduction Act of 2005. S. 1932 Section 5001 Public Law No. 109-171.

CMS Innovation Center. (2018, October 17).Oncology care model. [Online document, accessed 10/22/2018]. https://innovation.cms.gov/initiatives/oncology-care/

Cornell, L.D. (2011, November). Managed care nuts and bolts. Presentation at the Fundamentals of Health Care meeting of the American Health Lawyers Association, Chicago, IL.

Ellwood, P. (1988). Outcomes management. A technology of patient experience. *New England Journal of Medicine, 318(*23), 1549-1556.

Institute of Medicine (IOM). (2001). *Crossing the Quality Chasm: A New Health System for the 21st Century*. Washington, D.C.: National Academy Press.

Jazrawi, L., Gold, H.T., & Zuckerman, J.D. (2018). Physical therapy or arthroscopic surgery for treatment of meniscal tears. Is noninferiority enough? *JAMA*. 320(13).1326–1327.

Leventhal, R. (2018, April 24). CMS to rebrand meaningful use program with new emphasis on interoperability, burden reduction. *Healthcare Informatics.* [Online document; retrieved 10/5/2018.] www.healthcare-informatics.com/article/payment/breaking-cms-overhaul-meaningful-use-program-new-emphasis-interoperability

Livingston, S. (2018). The HCA playbook. *Modern Healthcare,* 48(41), 24-26.

Mee-Lee, D. (2013). *The ASAM Criteria: Treatment Criteria for Addictive, Substance-Related, and Co-Occurring Conditions.* Chevy Chase, MD: American Society of Addiction Medicine.

Romley, J.A. & Ginsburg, P.A. (2018, May 24). *Improving bundled payments in the Medicare program.* [Online document, accessed 10/22/2018]. www.brookings.edu/research/improving-bundled-payments-in-the-medicare-program/

Young, M. (2018). Case management in hospitals is being transformed to care coordination. *Hospital Case Management,* 26(11), 141-143.

9

ENSURING INDIVIDUAL COMPETENCE

Reader Objectives

After reading this chapter and reflecting on the contents, you will be able to:
1. Describe the governing board and medical staff roles in maintaining a competency evaluation system for physicians and licensed independent practitioners.
2. Demonstrate an understanding of medical staff credentialing, reappointment, and professional practice evaluation processes.
3. Explain the difference between medical staff credentialing and privilege delineation.
4. Recognize how non-physicians support the medical staff competency evaluation system.
5. Identify methods to ensure competence of dependent practitioners and non-clinical employees.

Key Terms

Case review: Care provided to an individual patient is evaluated by peer practitioners to identify improvement opportunities.

Certification: Process whereby a peer group judges the entry-level qualifications of an individual; certification is not necessarily equivalent with competency.

Competence: Ability of an individual to perform acceptably or fulfill job responsibilities.

Competency evaluation system: Systematic process for evaluating individual competence.

Credentialing: Process of collecting and verifying a medical staff applicant's credentials (licensure, education, training, experience, and other qualifications).

Credentials verification organization (CVO): An organization that provides information on an individual's professional credentials.

Dependent practitioners: Individuals allowed by law to provide patient care services only with direction or supervision.

Due process: Formal proceedings conducted in a way that protects the rights of all the people involved.

Job description: Document defining responsibilities and essential functions for a particular job.

Licensed independent practitioners: Individuals allowed by law to provide patient care services without direction or supervision, within the scope of his or her license.

Licensure: Process by which a state grants permission to an individual to engage in an occupation upon finding the applicant has attained the minimal degree of competence necessary to ensure the public health, safety, and welfare will be reasonably well protected.

National Practitioner Data Bank (NPDB): A centralized source of physician practice and quality performance information.

Occurrence screening: System of concurrent or retrospective identification of unusual patient occurrences through review of patient records using objective screening criteria.

Occurrence screens: Criteria used to identify cases for peer review; sometimes called trigger events.

Peer: Person who is of equal standing with another or belongs to the same professional group.

Peer review: Analysis of the performance of colleagues by professionals with similar types of expertise.

Privilege delineation: Process of defining specific patient care tasks a physician or a licensed independent practitioner can carry out within a facility based on the individual's professional license and his or her training, experience, competence, ability, and judgment.

Privileges: Specific tasks of patient care practice.

Professional practice evaluation: Systematic process to evaluate and confirm the current competence of practitioners based on their performance.

Competent Individuals

Much of the work of quality management is directed at improving healthcare processes. In addition, organizations must assure individuals doing the work are sufficiently capable to perform satisfactorily. The organization's governing board (sometimes call the board of trustees) is legally and morally responsible for the quality of services provided by physicians and staff working in the organization. To meet this responsibility, the board makes sure there are systems in place to confirm people have adequate training and skills and are able to carry out duties in a competent manner. This chapter primarily describes the competency evaluation systems for people with patient care responsibilities, although the techniques are applicable to any individual working in a healthcare organization. Individuals providing care for patients fall into two general categories:

- Physicians and other clinicians allowed by law to provide patient care services without direction or supervision, within the scope of their license. The latter, known as licensed independent practitioners (LIP), are physician assistants, advanced practice registered nurses, psychologists, clinical social workers and similarly trained and licensed individuals. Because licensure regulations vary among states, the LIP definition also varies. In addition, healthcare organizations have some flexibility in allowing LIPs to practice independently. For instance, certified nurse anesthetists (CRNAs) can practice independently in some facilities, while others require CRNAs to practice under the supervision of an anesthesiologist. The practice limitations for LIPs are established by the organization's governing board, with input from physicians and LIPs.

- Individuals not allowed by law to provide patient care services without direction or supervision. These individuals are often known as dependent practitioners. This category includes registered and licensed practical nurses, licensed pharmacists, certified nurse assistants, licensed or certified technicians and therapists, and others who have direct or indirect patient care responsibilities.

Within every organization there is some type of human resource (HR) management system that includes mechanisms for hiring employees and periodically evaluating employee performance. These topics are covered in general management courses and will not be addressed in this chapter. Not covered in general management literature is how healthcare organizations carry out these HR activities for physicians and LIPs. This competency evaluation system, unique to healthcare, is described in the next sections.

Medical Staff Competence Evaluation

In the 1960s hospitals became legally liable for patient injuries resulting from the actions of physicians practicing independently in the facility (see chapter 7). This liability has broadened over the years to include anywhere physicians care for patients and to health plans contracting with physicians to provide care for plan beneficiaries. Since the 1960s healthcare organizations have had mechanisms to ensure physicians and other LIPs are competent to provide patient care services. The governing board is ultimately responsible for quality of patient care which includes ensuring there is an adequate competency evaluation system for physicians and LIPs. In a hospital, the board delegates the functioning of this system to the organized medical staff. In non-hospital settings, a medical director is often accountable for implementing a competency evaluation system. In all situations, however, the board (or organized group or individual who assumes full legal authority and responsibility for operations of the organization) retains ultimate responsibility for ensuring physicians and LIPs are competent to care for patients.

The ability to practice medicine in a healthcare institution is not automatically given to every licensed physician and LIP. It is a right extended by the board in accordance with applicable federal and state laws and accreditation standards. The board is responsible for approving who can practice in the facility and what these individuals can do. The Medicare Hospital Conditions of Participation (COPs) reinforce this responsibility by stating the governing board makes it clear the medical staff is accountable to the governing body for the quality of care provided to patients (CMS, 2012; CMS 2014).

The governing board has a duty to patients to exercise care in selecting, retaining, and supervising the performance of physicians and LIPs. In a hospital, the board delegates to the organized medical staff the task of evaluating physician and LIP competence. To fulfill this obligation, the medical staff has mechanisms to:

- Evaluate the professional and personal backgrounds of physicians and LIPs requesting to provide patient care in the facility (credentialing);
- Assign specific patient care rights and responsibilities appropriate to the training and experience of the physician or LIP (privilege delineation); and
- Periodically evaluate the competence of physicians and LIPs (professional practice evaluation).

Delegation of these duties to the hospital medical staff does not relieve the governing board of its responsibilities to oversee the process and ensure quality patient care. An overview of the medical staff competence evaluation system is shown in Exhibit 9.1.

Exhibit 9.1. Competence Evaluation System

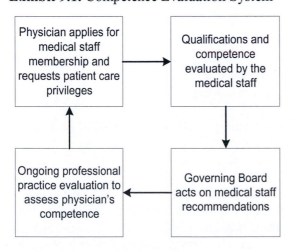

All physicians and LIPs allowed membership in the organized medical staff undergo credentialing and privilege delineation. Some individuals are new applicants to the medical staff and some have been members for a while. Information obtained from an applicant is used to judge the individual's qualifications and competence. This evaluation results in a final recommendation to the governing board concerning the individual's medical staff membership and patient care rights and responsibilities (otherwise known as privileges).

The board acts on the recommendations; often approving them. The board can modify the recommendations prior to approval. The manner of conducting credentialing and privileging is described in the medical staff bylaws and rules and regulations.

Review of physician and LIP competence is ongoing. The medical staff has a process for periodically evaluating the quality of patient care provided by physicians and LIPs. This process, known as professional practice evaluation, helps to ensure continuing competence of individuals providing patient care in the hospital. At regular intervals, physicians and LIPs undergo reappointment and privilege delineation. There is a similar cyclical process for conducting physician and LIP competency evaluations in non-hospital settings.

The following sections describe the hospital medical staff competency evaluation system illustrated in Exhibit 9.1. From this point forward the term *physician* will be used to denote both licensed physicians (M.D., D.O.) and LIPs. Only where there are significant differences in the evaluation process are the two groups recognized separately.

New Medical Staff Applicants

To provide patient care services within a hospital, all physicians – both independent and hospital-employed physicians – must be members of the organized medical staff. The organized medical staff is composed of physicians who are doctors of medicine or doctors of osteopathy. In addition, the medical staff may include doctors of podiatric medicine, doctors of optometry, and chiropractors.

Membership involves a formal application process. A new applicant for medical staff membership is asked for extensive information on his or her training and experience. The application requirements vary among hospitals; however, the following information is commonly requested:

- Evidence of current licensure along with information of any loss of previous or current state licensure, including denials, probations, involuntary removal for disciplinary reasons, or the voluntary relinquishment of such licensure
- Drug Enforcement Administration (DEA) certificate and number along with information regarding any previous denials, revocations, changes, or voluntary relinquishment
- Statement of health status
- Evidence of professional liability insurance (if required for medical staff membership)
- Details of professional education, training, and experience in a chronological format
- Evidence of board certification/recertification
- All professional experience including sabbaticals, leaves of absence, missionary work, and military assignments
- Medical society memberships, including denials, revocations, terminations, or disciplinary actions
- Letters of recommendations from peers familiar with the applicant's work
- Filed, pending, or settled medical litigation involving the applicant, with confirming information provided by the practitioner's attorney or from court records
- Unfavorable peer reviews at previous or other currently used facilities
- Felony convictions
- Voluntary or involuntary reduction of clinical privileges elsewhere
- Voluntary or involuntary medical staff resignations, suspensions, denials, or changes

For purposes of verifying information, an applicant signs a statement releasing the institution and references or sources from liability, assuming investigation of applicant's background is done in good faith.

Patient Care Privilege Requests

In addition to supplying the aforementioned information, applicants request a particular medical staff membership category (for example: active, affiliate, courtesy, consulting, resident and/or fellow, allied health) and they request the right to provide certain types of patient care services. These services are called privileges because the physician is granted the 'privilege' of providing these services by the hospital's governing board (Pickard, 2016). Specialty-specific lists of services are used by applicants to identify the types of patient care they want to provide. For instance, a general surgeon applying for privileges chooses from a list of all surgical procedures any general surgeon might perform and all patient conditions any general surgeon might treat. The privilege lists are developed by each medical staff service and are specific to the patient populations served by the hospital. For example, if the hospital does not have facilities for open-heart surgery, this procedure is not included on the surgical privilege list.

Hospitals often have a set of specialty-specific 'core privileges' covering the usual practices of a physician in that specialty. Shown in Exhibit 9.2 are core privileges for hospitalists (hospital-based physicians). If the applicant is a hospitalist and does not wish to practice beyond what is covered by the core privileges, he or she merely requests core privileges. If the applicant wishes to provide patient care services not covered by the core privileges, he or she identifies the additional privileges being requested.

Exhibit 9.2. Core Privileges for Hospitalists

Admit, evaluate, diagnose and treat individuals with complex or severe illnesses or problems and those with immediate or serious threats to life requiring skills achieved during training sufficient to attain eligibility for board certification in Medicine. Physicians in this category may act as consultants to others and, in turn, should request consultation when diagnosis or management is in doubt, when unexpected complications arise or when hazardous procedures or treatment are contemplated. Core privileges:

□ Endotracheal intubation □ EKG interpretation □ Ventilator management
□ BiPap management □ Total parenteral nutrition □ Cardiopulmonary resuscitation

An alternative to core privileges is a privilege categorization system. This type of privilege list classifies patient care services either by the degree of complexity of the procedures or illnesses treated, or the level of a physician's training and experience. Categorized services for physicians applying for clinical nuclear medicine privileges are shown in Exhibit 9.3. The approach used by the medical staff to define privileges is found in the medical staff rules and regulations and credentialing procedures.

Exhibit 9.3. Categorized Privileges for Clinical Nuclear Medicine Privileges

Select the procedure class that best describes procedures you want to perform independently within the hospital and for which you are qualified based on training and experience. Applicants must be able to demonstrate competency and adequate training and experience before privileges will be granted.

❑ Consultation, performance, and interpretation of all routine and non-routine nuclear medicine procedures to make diagnostic evaluations, by both in vivo and in vitro techniques, of the anatomic and/or physiologic conditions of the body and to provide therapy with unsealed radioactive sources.

❑ Consultation, performance, and interpretation of all routine and non-routine nuclear medicine procedures to make diagnostic evaluations, by in vivo techniques only, of the anatomic and/or physiologic conditions of the body and to provide therapy with unsealed radioactive sources.

❑ Consultation, performance, and interpretation of all routine and non-routine nuclear medicine procedures to make diagnostic evaluations, by in vitro (non-imaging) techniques only, of the anatomic and/or physiologic conditions of the body and to provide therapy with unsealed radioactive sources.

❑ Consultation, performance, and interpretation of either individual procedures or categories of nuclear medicine procedures as specified below. List specific procedure(s) you are requesting privileges to perform:

There may be times when a physician only requests medical staff membership and does not seek privileges to care for patients in the facility. This situation is becoming more commonplace with the growth in the use of hospitalists to manage the care of hospitalized patients. Primary care physicians may request membership on a hospital medical staff to enjoy various benefits, e.g. continuing education opportunities, professional networking. However, all in-hospital care for patients of these physicians is provided by hospitalists. Thus, there is no need for the primary care physician to request patient care privileges.

In addition to information submitted by the applicant, healthcare facilities are required by federal law to obtain a report concerning each applicant from the National Practitioner Data Bank (NPDB). The Healthcare Quality Improvement Act of 1986 established this centralized source of physician practice and quality performance information (NPDB, 2017). The purpose of the data bank is to prevent physicians who have had their privileges restricted or terminated at one hospital from simply obtaining practice privileges at another hospital without disclosure of the previous adverse actions. Healthcare facilities are required to report actions affecting the clinical privileges of their medical staff. Reportable actions include:

- Reduction, restriction, suspension or revocation of clinical privileges for at least 31 days;
- Voluntary resignation of clinical privileges either while peer review of a potential quality concern is taking place or in lieu of the peer review process; and
- Denial of clinical privileges to a new or existing medical staff member when peer review judgment is involved.

The NPDB also contains practitioner-specific information on adverse actions taken by state licensure boards and medical societies, significant malpractice awards made on behalf of the practitioner, adverse actions and decisions made by federal agencies and health plans, and health-care related civil judgments and criminal convictions. In 2010 NPDB expanded to include licensure actions taken against all health care practitioners, not just physicians and dentists, as well as health care entities.

Qualifications Verified

All information submitted by applicants is verified for accuracy by the hospital on behalf of the medical staff. The medical staff coordinator or another qualified individual within the facility performs this step. Verification must come from primary sources, whenever feasible. If the hospital contracts with an independent agency (known as a credentials verification organization) to collect information from the primary source(s) about an applicant, the agency must give the facility all the information provided by the primary source. The hospital itself then uses this information to verify the information from the applicant.

In a growing number of locations, the credentialing process for medical staffs at several hospitals in one area has been consolidated and standardized. This is done through one centralized data collection and storage agency such as the state medical society or other appropriate organization. This arrangement has some obvious advantages. For physicians on staff at multiple hospitals, only one membership application is completed for all participating hospitals. At the same time, the hospitals are relieved of application review and data verification tasks. However, information gathering and verification are only the first steps in the credentialing process. The medical staff in each facility must still critically assess an applicant's information and independently determine the individual's qualifications for membership and privileges.

During the verification process an applicant is asked to explain any gaps in clinical experience. The hospital may request additional information regarding prior professional activities to ensure an applicant is capable of providing quality patient care. Findings that may prompt further investigation include frequent geographic moves by the applicant, graduation from a medical school of uncertain reputation, medical litigation, and professional disciplinary actions. In some instances, extensive written documentation and verification by telephone or other means may be requested. If there is any indication of previous substance or alcohol abuse the applicant is asked to submit documentation of successful completion of an impaired physician or substance abuse treatment program.

Competence and Requested Privileges Evaluated

Information submitted by an applicant and additional information gathered by the medical staff coordinator is reviewed by medical staff members. To ensure each applicant is evaluated fairly and granted appropriate privileges, multiple levels of review are included in the credentialing process. Professional peers with similar training and background provide input at several levels. Generally, the credentialing process includes review of an applicant's file by at least three of the following individuals or groups: chair of the medical staff department, department credentials committee, medical staff credentials committee, medical director, and the medical staff executive committee.

Individuals and groups reviewing an applicant's information are charged with determining whether the individual has the credentials necessary to care for patients at the facility. Appointment to the medical staff and delineation of privileges are based on at least the following criteria:

- Licensure. The applicant should have a current license allowing them to practice independently and perform the privileges they have requested.
- Education and training. The applicant should have the education and training necessary to perform the privileges they have requested.
- Current competence. The applicant should have demonstrated competence in performing the privileges they have requested.
- Health status. The applicant should be free of or have under adequate control any significant physical or behavioral impairment that could interfere with providing optimal medical care.
- Attitude. The applicant should exhibit a willingness to work with and positively relate to members of the medical staff and all other members of the healthcare team including nurses, therapists, administrators, and support personnel.

Joint Commission standards require the medical staff use an objective, evidence-based process when granting patient care privileges to individuals. One way for the medical staff to meet this requirement is by defining the minimum level of education, training, and demonstrated competence necessary to provide quality patient care. In Exhibit 9.4 are competency criteria developed by the medical staff at one hospital to judge the qualifications of an applicant requesting robotic surgery privileges.

Exhibit 9.4. Criteria to Evaluate Physician Qualifications for Robotic Surgery Privileges

To be eligible for clinical privileges in Robotic Surgery, the applicant must meet the following qualifications:
- Hold clinical privileges at the hospital
- Complete Robotic Surgery training course, which includes didactic and laboratory training as evidenced by a certificate of completion
- Document completion of five successful cases under supervision of an approved proctor, and provide an evaluation from the proctor confirming the supervision and an evaluation of the applicant's skills.

Robotic Surgery Clinical Privileges: Privileges granted allow this technique to be utilized on any procedure for which the practitioner has been granted open or laparoscopic privileges.

Methods of granting or restricting medical staff privileges must be reasonable and not rely on subjective impressions. Criteria based on sex, race, creed, or national origin, membership in certain professional societies, or membership in the provider panel of a certain health plan must be avoided. Physicians from different specialties can rightfully be allowed to care for patients with the same conditions and perform the same procedures if they meet qualification criteria.

Credentialing Recommendation

Information received from applicants and from the NPDB is used by the medical staff for two purposes. The medical staff determines if a physician meets eligibility requirements for the requested membership category. The medical staff also judges whether a physician is competent to perform the patient care services he or she wants to provide. These decisions are made independent of one another. For instance, an applicant can be eligible for active staff membership but not deemed competent to perform all requested privileges.

The medical staff has several choices of what can be recommended to the governing board concerning an applicant's request for medical staff membership and privileges. For example:
- Deferral: Action on the application can be deferred pending receipt of additional information. Generally, deferrals must be followed up within a specified time frame (for example, 45 days) with subsequent recommendation of appointment with specified privileges or rejection of membership or privileges.
- Favorable Recommendation: When the recommendation of the medical staff is favorable to an applicant, the recommendation, together with the application summary and its accompanying information, is forwarded to the board.

- Adverse Recommendation: When the recommendation of the medical staff is adverse to an applicant (denial of membership, denial of specific privileges) the recommendation, together with the application summary and its accompanying information, is forwarded to the board. If an adverse recommendation is made at the medical staff executive committee or board level the applicant is entitled to reconsideration and due process. The reconsideration process is described in medical staff bylaws and rules and regulations.

Medical Staff Reappointment

At least every two years, each member of the hospital medical staff undergoes reappointment. This process involves updating of a physician's credentials and evaluation of continued competence. In many ways, the reappointment process resembles an initial appointment. To be reappointed to the medical staff, physicians complete an application containing the same information provided by an initial applicant. Physicians also reapply for specific patient care privileges. Information on a physician's application is verified with the state licensure board, medical disciplinary board, and any other agency required by the medical staff bylaws. The NPDB is queried to determine if it contains any new adverse decisions involving the practitioner.

Also evaluated by the medical staff are the physician's activities within the hospital since the last appointment. Quality management staff, the HIM department, and other groups assist in gathering this information, which is compiled into a physician practice profile. The practice profile is used to evaluate an applicant's current competence at the time of reappointment. Common data elements included on physician practice profiles are listed in Exhibit 9.5.

Exhibit 9.5. Physician Reappointment Practice Profile Data Elements

Activity	Clinical
- # Admissions	- Patient mortality rates compared to peers
- # Surgical/invasive procedures	- Patient complication rates compared to peers
- # Consultations	- Hospital acquired infection rates compared to peers
- Committee attendance	- # Suspensions due to incomplete patient records
- Continuing medical education	- Patient length of stay compared to hospital average length of stay
	- # Quality concerns identified in focused professional practice evaluations
Risk management	
- # Claims pending	- # Adverse patient incidents specifically attributed to practitioner
- # Claims settled	- Patient satisfaction survey results compared to hospital average
- # Actions by regulatory agencies	- # Patient/family complaints concerning practitioner

In the same manner as initial credentialing and privilege delineation, a physician's qualifications and competence are judged by the medical staff. Recommendations are made to the governing board which in turn acts on the recommendations. Only in rare circumstances will the board reject, in whole or in part, the advice of the medical staff. In these situations, the physician or LIP affected by the decision has a right to formally appeal the decision. The individual's right to due process is outline in the medical staff bylaws. Two types of due process exist: substantive and procedural.

Substantive due process relates to whether the rules and criteria stipulated in the bylaws are reasonable, fair, and not arbitrary, and whether decisions made by the medical staff are based on relevant and reliable evidence. Procedural due process is concerned with whether the credentialing and privileges rules of the medical staff are administered properly and applied equally to all members. In view of increasing litigation in this area, institutions usually consult with an attorney to help guarantee compliance with all relevant appeal and due process requirements.

Professional Practice Evaluation

The first *Manual of Hospital Standards* published in 1918 by the American College of Surgeons included a standard requiring physician practices be evaluated to determine whether patient care is in accordance with present day scientific medicine (Gorgas, 1945). This standard evolved into the physician peer review requirements found today in government regulations as well as accreditation standards.

Peer review occurs when physicians evaluate and critique the medical decision-making and quality of care provided by other physicians. Peer review is performed by physicians who possess appropriate clinical judgment based on their training, education and experience. Physicians are also responsible for reviewing the care provided by LIPs. The Medicare regulations for hospitals are clear on this requirement. For instance, the COPs for critical access hospitals (small rural hospitals) state:

> The quality and appropriateness of the diagnosis and treatment furnished by nurse practitioners, clinical nurse specialists, and physician assistants at the critical access hospital (CAH) are evaluated by a member of the CAH staff who is a doctor of medicine or osteopathy or by another doctor of medicine or osteopathy under contract with the CAH (CMS, 2011).

For many years hospital peer review occurred in one of two scenarios. In the first scenario, a physician applied or reapplied for appointment to a hospital's medical staff and requested specific privileges. This application triggered the peer review process where the doctor's credentials and competence are evaluated by multiple individuals and committees within the hospital. In the second scenario, concerns about the quality of care provided by a physician triggered some form of peer review

In 2007, The Joint Commission published new standards that transformed episodic peer review into an ongoing process. Hospitals are now expected to continually look at physician practices. This ongoing evaluation is in addition to reviews occurring during initial and reappointment processes described earlier. The 2007 standards replaced the traditional phrase, *peer review*, with the phrase, *professional practice evaluation* (Joint Commission, 2007). This change in terminology is being adopted in Joint Commission accredited hospitals; however the phrase *peer review* continues to be commonly used in many healthcare settings. The two phrases have essentially the same meaning and are therefore used interchangeably throughout this section.

The purpose of peer review or professional practice evaluation (PPE) is to improve professional competence and practices. Physician performance is reviewed to identify improvement opportunities for individuals and systems of care. One aspect of PPE involves looking at the practice of physicians on an ongoing basis. Performance is evaluated by analyzing aggregate practice pattern data and reviewing care provided to individual patients. The second aspect of PPE is focused PPE, which is a more intense evaluation of one aspect of a physician's practice. If ongoing monitoring demonstrates an opportunity for improvement, the involved physician undergoes focused review. Specific areas of practice are looked at in much greater detail to determine whether a competence problem exists. Ongoing PPE and focused review are described in the next sections.

Ongoing Review

Ongoing PPE allows the medical staff to identify undesirable practice trends that could impact the quality of care and patient safety. Multiple measures of physician performance are regularly evaluated by various committees of the medical staff. This includes peer review of individual cases and analysis of physician-specific performance rates for select measures. The medical staff has some latitude when determining which cases will undergo peer review and what performance measures will be used. In Joint Commission accredited hospitals, the medical staff is expected to monitor clinical practice patterns of physicians using parameters chosen by each department or the medical staff as a whole. The organization may use various methodologies for collecting information for ongoing PPE including: periodic chart reviews, direct observations, monitoring of diagnostic and treatment techniques, and discussion with other individuals involved in the care of patients.

The frequency of such evaluations can be defined by the organized medical staff, but Joint Commission standards require the evaluations occur more frequently than every 12 months, e.g. every three months, six months, nine months, etc. Many organizations conduct evaluations every eight months so they will have three complete sets of data at the time of a physician's two-year re-credentialing cycle.

In addition, the Joint Commission requires active medical staff involvement in the measurement, assessment, and improvement of several different aspects of patient care (see Exhibit 9.6). Physician practice information derived from these activities is another component of ongoing PPE.

Exhibit 9.6. Medical Staff Measurement, Assessment, and Improvement Activities

Aspect of Patient Care	Description of Activities
Use of medications	Frequently used, high-risk, high cost or problem-prone medications are evaluated to determine whether medications are appropriately prescribed and monitored by physicians.
Use of blood and blood components	Transfusions of blood and blood components are evaluated to determine the acceptability of the transfusion decision based on the patient's diagnosis.
Operative and other procedures	High-risk, high-volume, high cost and problem-prone procedures are evaluated to determine the acceptability of procedures undertaken and patient preparation. This determination is based on the patient's preoperative, postoperative, and pathological diagnoses.
Patient records	Patient records are evaluated to determine accurate, timely, and legible completion by physicians.
Patient safety	Cases involving a sentinel event are evaluated to identify opportunities for improving physician performance and aggregate patient safety data are reviewed to identify opportunities for improving physician performance.

Two primary strategies are used to evaluate physician practices and comply with topic-specific review requirements. The first involves the use of performance measurement data. Reports of measurement results are evaluated at the medical staff service level and within various multidisciplinary committees. The purpose of this assessment is to identify physician practice patterns differing significantly from performance expectations. In Exhibit 9.7 is a report showing compliance with aspects of care considered appropriate for hospitalized patients with congestive heart failure. The performance target is shown along with the actual six-month compliance rate for each physician managing patients with congestive heart failure. Reports such as this are regularly reviewed by physicians in the hospital's medicine service to identify variant clinical practice patterns or problematic trends.

Exhibit 9.7. Congestive Heart Failure Performance Report

Congestive Heart Failure Performance Report - Jan thru Jun							
	Target	MD#102	MD#104	MD#106	MD#108	MD#110	MD#112
Number of patients		32	23	15	41	62	42
Left ventricular failure (LVF) assessment documented	100%	93.8%	87.0%	100%	100%	95.2%	75.0%
ACE inhibitor for left ventricular systolic dysfunction (LVSD) prescribed at discharge	100%	100%	95.7%	53.3%	98.0%	88.7%	93.0%
Smoking cessation advice documented	100%	0.0%	65.2%	88.9%	100.0%	0.0%	52.4%
Influenza vaccination status assessed	100%	87.5%	100%	73.3%	100%	100%	92.9%
Pneumococcal vaccination status assessed	100%	87.5%	100%	87.5%	100%	98.4%	88.9%
Influenza vaccination given if appropriate	100%	90.0%	100%	44.4%	100%	66.7%	100%
Pneumococcal vaccination given if appropriate	100%	75.0%	100%	66.7%	100%	50.0%	100%

The second PPE strategy used to monitor clinical practices is case review. The care provided to an individual patient is evaluated by peer physicians to identify improvement opportunities. Cases selected for peer review are often identified through retrospective record review. This review process usually involves the following steps:

1. The medical staff defines patient care events or situations (sometimes called occurrences or trigger events) signaling a need for closer examination of the case.
2. Staff in the quality and/or HIM department review records of discharged patients to identify cases in which one or more of these events or situations occurred (this review is often called occurrence screening).
3. Cases identified through the retrospective review process undergo a first level analysis by a nurse, HIM professional, or physician to determine if more in-depth peer review is warranted.
4. Cases selected for more in-depth review are evaluated by one or more peer physicians who were not professionally involved in the care of the patient whose case is being reviewed.
5. The peer review process results in a final decision about the quality of care provided and recommendations for improvement.

Cases for peer review may also be identified concurrently by case managers or utilization review staff. Other sources of information include patient incident reports, sentinel event investigations, risk management liability claims review, family or patient complaints, and staff complaints.

The presence of an event or situation suggesting the need for peer review is not an indication substandard care was provided to the patient. The existence of an occurrence merely sets in motion the peer review process. A peer review committee will examine records associated with the case and ask physicians involved in the case for additional input as needed. The final decision resulting from the peer review process determines whether physician practices were appropriate or suboptimal. A list of occurrences (sometimes called trigger events) the medical staff could use to identify surgery cases needing closer examination by surgery department peers is found in Exhibit 9.8.

Exhibit 9.8. Occurrences Triggering Surgery Department Peer Review

- Unplanned return to surgery
- Unexpected change in procedure
- Unplanned intensive care unit admission postoperatively
- Intubation or reintubation in post-anesthesia recovery unit (PACU)
- Unplanned x-ray intraoperatively or in PACU
- Overnight stay of day surgery patient
- Cardiac/pulmonary arrest
- Intraoperative or postoperative death
- Mechanical ventilation lasting longer than 24 hours postoperatively
- Intraoperative use of Epinephrine or Norepinephrine
- Deep vein thrombosis/pulmonary embolism
- Consultation requested in surgical suite or in PACU
- Pathology report normal or unrelated to diagnosis
- Operative time greater than 6 hours
- Unplanned organ removal, injury, repair
- Postoperative Troponin level greater than 1.5
- Postoperative abrupt drop of greater than 25% in hematocrit or hemoglobin

Criteria used to identify cases for peer review can also be condition-specific. These criteria are often derived from evidence-based clinical practice guidelines (see chapter 2). Condition-specific screening criteria frequently include exclusions and explanatory notes to improve reliability of data collection. A condition-specific criterion related to appropriateness of C-section births is shown in Exhibit 9.9.

Exhibit 9.9. Condition-Specific Occurrence Triggering OB-GYN Service Peer Review

Criterion: Caesarean section performed without evidence of appropriate indications.
Exclusion: Woman has had previous caesarean section birth.
Explanatory Notes: The case is selected for further review if one or more of the following indications for a primary caesarean section are <u>not</u> documented in the patient's record:
1.   Third-trimester bleeding;
2.   Prolapsed umbilical cord;
3.   Failure of induction or augmentation of labor for obstetrical or medical indications;
4.   Fetal distress as indicated by fetal heart rate of less than 60 beats per minute or persistent severe variable or late decelerations; or
5.   Active lower genital tract herpes simplex virus Type II.

If a case is identified as needing peer review, it may undergo a preliminary first level analysis by staff in the quality or HIM department or by physician representatives of the medical staff. The purpose of first level reviews is to eliminate cases not requiring in-depth peer review. For instance, some ambulatory surgery patients need to stay overnight due to uncontrollable pain. The first level case analysis would identify those patients who, despite caregivers doing all the right things, could not safely be discharged any sooner. Peer review of individual cases is time-consuming for physicians. First level reviews can reduce the number of cases needing in-depth peer examination.

A case may undergo peer review in several committees. Below is a description of a surgical case selected for peer review by more than one group.

> A 35-year-old female patient presented to the hospital to undergo routine hysteroscopic removal of a uterine fibroid. The machine to be used in the procedure was new to the hospital and being tried out for the first time with this procedure. The nurses in the operating room that day had not been trained to use the equipment. The doctor told them the sales representative for the equipment company would be manning the machine. In fact, the surgeon himself did not have privileges to perform the procedure. A nurse responsible for monitoring the patient's inflow and outflow of fluid during the procedure alerted the surgeon the outflow had stopped. She raised this concern several times, but the surgeon informed the nurse it was not a problem. Over the course of the procedure the patient had nine liters of saline pumped into her body and a few hours after the procedure she died from the excessive fluid infusion.

For the case described above, peer surgeons will evaluate whether the surgeon's actions were acceptable. Peer anesthesiologists will evaluate whether the anesthesiologist's actions were acceptable. Specifically, why didn't he or she speak up when it was apparent the surgeon was not listening to the nurse? In addition to conducting peer review, medical staff leaders will work with hospital administration to resolve some of the system problems evident in the incident. For instance, the surgery scheduling process needs strengthening to prevent surgeons from scheduling procedures for which they do not have privileges. Situations in which equipment sales representatives are allowed in the operating room should be clarified. Better teamwork among caregivers in the operating room is needed.

Peer review decisions regarding individual cases are documented, often using some type of secure and confidential electronic reporting system. Final judgments about the quality of care provided to the patient are made in consultation with other physicians in the department. See Exhibit 9.10 for an example of the range of final determinations that might be made about a case selected for peer review.

Exhibit 9.10. Final Determinations Following a Case Review

Final Determination (Select one):
☐   No substantial physician practice improvement opportunities are identified.
☐   Systems improvement issues identified. Not attributable to physician omission or commission
☐   Care could have been better (select one of the following subcategories)
    ☐   Care was grossly and flagrantly unacceptable
    ☐   Care failed generally accepted guidelines or usual practice
    ☐   Care could reasonably have been expected to be better

If a quality of care concern is identified during case review, remedial action may be required. Such remedial action can involve:

- Face-to-face peer discussion with involved physician
- Reporting of concern to physician's department chairperson
- Initiation of a focused PPE
- Formal disciplinary action such as reducing, suspending or terminating physician's privileges

The risk management department is often notified of cases identified for peer review and adverse peer review decisions. This department is not involved in the peer review process itself but does need to be alerted to situations representing potentially compensable events (see chapter 7). It is important the risk manager is aware of any occurrences that may lead to lawsuits.

Focused Review

The purpose of focused PPE is to look more closely at the practices of an individual physician or LIP. There are several situations which cause a focused review to be initiated. Physicians granted medical staff membership and privileges for the first time often undergo a defined period of practice evaluation. This focused PPE may be conducted in several ways:

- Prospective evaluation: Cases are reviewed prior to the physician providing treatment to ensure planned treatment is appropriate.
- Concurrent evaluation: Real time review of patient care provided by the physician; for example: observation of physician's surgical technique, evaluation of the physician's treatment decisions
- Retrospective evaluation: Review of cases after patient care has been provided; may also involve interviews with caregivers familiar with the physician's work.

In addition to new medical staff members, physician members given privileges they have never had before can undergo focused PPE related to the new privileges. For instance, an internal medicine physician who has practiced at the hospital for several years asks for and is granted privileges to do gastrointestinal endoscopy procedures. Peer physicians review the internist's ability to perform a few of these procedures to be certain she is capable. The physician's other existing privileges are not affected by the focused PPE.

For initial appointment and reappointment, the scope and time period for a physician's focused PPE can vary. The parameters are set by the medical staff during credentialing. Throughout the time of evaluation, the physician's membership and privileges are considered to be provisional. If no problems are found during the focused PPE, provisional status is removed. Medical staff policies governing extensions of provisional status, including length of time and number of extensions allowed are described in medical staff bylaws.

A focused review may be conducted at any time – it is not just done for new medical staff applicants and physicians undergoing reappointment. If individual case reviews or performance measures reveal a competence question, a focused review may be initiated. For example, if an obstetrician has a Caesarean section rate more than 10 percent higher than his or her colleagues, the OB-GYN department might conduct a focused PPE on the delivery practices of this physician. At one hospital, the medical staff established the following thresholds for focused PPEs:

- When a physician has a growing number of longer lengths of stay compared to peer practitioners.
- Frequent or repeat readmission suggesting possibly poor or inadequate initial management/treatment.
- Patterns of unnecessary diagnostic testing/treatments.
- Any single egregious case or sentinel event involving a physician or LIP, as judged by the chief of staff or the medical director of quality management.
- When performance measurement targets are not met twice within any 12 month period of time.
- When the number of case review final determinations rated as 'care could have been better' exceed the threshold set by the medical staff department or committee.

Like focused PPEs done for medical staff appointments and reappointments, the reviews can be done prospectively, concurrently or retrospectively. Physicians undergoing a focused review are not placed on provisional membership status (unlike the appointment/reappointment process) and are not in any way restricted in caring for patients. If a physician is considered an imminent threat to patients, a focused review would not be done. The medical staff would recommend to the governing board the physician be immediately suspended from patient care responsibilities.

Focused reviews are to be conducted in a timely manner. The policy of one hospital medical staff is to complete focused PPEs of routine cases within 90 days from the date review is initiated. Complex cases, those requiring input from multiple services or practitioners, may require additional time. In some situations, the medical staff may seek external review by someone who does not practice at the hospital.

External review is the process of having an unprejudiced peer who is an appropriately licensed, board certified, and actively practicing physician or LIP in the same medical specialty evaluate another individual practitioner's performance. The external peer reviewer evaluates the practitioner and judges the competence of the practitioner based on medical evidence. Conducting a focused PPE using a practicing physician or LIP who is outside the influence of the hospital yet who has the specific subject matter expertise to evaluate the practitioner results in an unbiased review. There are several situations that might prompt a medical staff to obtain external review during a focused PPE, including:

- Potential conflict of interest between internal peer reviewers and the practitioner under review.
- Potential conflict of interest or dissension between the practitioner under review and the peer review committee.
- A substantial internal difference of opinion regarding the professional conduct of the practitioner under review.
- Practitioner under review has potentially violated a state or federal law and has retained an attorney.
- Practitioner under review is likely to initiate litigation to prevent an adverse peer review decision.
- Other reasons dictated by the circumstances such as legal violations, sexual harassment, and inappropriate disruptive behavior.

Exhibit 9.11. Physician Use of Corticosteroids

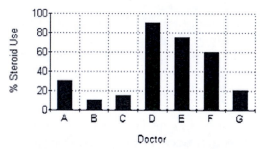

The outcome of a focused review is dependent on the review findings. For example, four obstetricians at one hospital underwent focused PPE to evaluate why their use of corticosteroids is significantly different from other physicians.

Administration of corticosteroids to mothers presenting in premature labor is often used to help the fetus' lungs mature quicker. As shown in Exhibit 9.11, four physicians used this medication in far fewer cases as compared to their peers. This practice difference triggered focused reviews of physicians with low rates of steroid use.

After reviewing records of patients not receiving steroids, the physician chair of the OB/GYN department met individually with each 'low-use' physician to discuss their rationale for not prescribing steroids. The department chair discovered the physicians had no medically appropriate reason for not ordering the medication. The physicians were educated on the indications and contraindications of prenatal steroids.

In addition, a standard physician order set for mothers admitted in preterm labor was developed and integrated into the hospital's computerized order entry system. The order set included 'pop-up' reminders of steroid indications and contraindications. No disciplinary or punitive actions were taken against the four physicians with low rates of steroid use. When the effectiveness of the focused review and the system change were measured, the OB/GYN department discovered the performance of all physicians had improved.

If formal disciplinary action is taken against a physician, an explicit process documented in the medical staff bylaws is followed. The involved physician has due process with full hearing and appeal rights as set forth in the bylaws.

Competence Evaluation System Support Structure

The medical staff competence evaluation system (Exhibit 9.1) is supported by various individuals and committees. Accomplishing these tasks requires involvement by medical staff members as well as individuals employed by the facility. Below are common medical staff committees involved in competence evaluations.

- Credentials Committee: This group is responsible for reviewing completed applications for initial appointment and reappointment, including membership and clinical privileges. This is a multi-specialty committee of medical staff members with an experienced physician leader as chairperson.
- Peer Review Committee: This group is responsible for ongoing and focused PPE activities. Each medical staff department may form a peer review committee or PPE may be done by the department as a whole. In small hospitals, the medical staff often has only one peer review committee and it is responsible for ongoing and focused PPE for all physicians. This committee may also serve as the medical executive committee and the credentials committee.
- Multidisciplinary Committees: These groups are responsible for ongoing PPE activities in specified topic areas. For example, the hospital may have pharmacy and therapeutics committee comprised of physicians and non-physicians. One responsibility of this committee is assessment of performance measurement data on appropriate prescription of medications. When variant physician practice patterns are identified, the issue is referred to a medical staff peer review committee for further investigation.

Individuals and departments within a hospital provide significant support for the medical staff competency evaluation system. Below are the common support functions.

- Medical staff services department: This department coordinates activities of medical staff committees, records meeting minutes which summarize peer review results and performance evaluation discussions, etc. The department is involved in all aspects of the credentialing and privileging function. In small hospitals one person may serve as the quality director and the medical staff coordinator. It is common for HIM professionals to work in this department.
- Quality department: This department is often delegated primary data collection and reporting responsibilities for all ongoing and focused PPE reviews, as well as collection of data for physician practice profiles. Nurses and other clinical staff often work alongside HIM professionals in this department to support peer review and data analysis activities.
- Concurrent reviewers: Case managers, UR coordinators, or other individuals (such as those from the HIM department doing concurrent coding) gather information on physician performance while patients are hospitalized. Staff from other departments may be involved in some aspect of data gathering. For example, pharmacists often collect information on physicians' medication ordering practices.
- HIM department: After patients are discharged, HIM employees (coders, information analysts) gather data needed for physician practice profiles and for ongoing and focused PPE.

Credentialing in Managed Care Organizations

Managed care organizations (MCOs) such as health maintenance organizations (HMOs), preferred provider organizations (PPOs) and accountable care organizations (ACOs) are integral components of healthcare delivery. These organizations have the legal responsibility to select and contract with practitioners who will provide quality services to health plan and network participants. Like healthcare facilities, MCOs use a credentialing process when contracting with practitioners to participate in the health plan. The credentialing process applies to all physicians and LIPs providing care to MCO plan members. This includes practitioners who are employed by the health plan (such as in a staff-based HMO) and those people who independently contract with health plans to provide services to network patients.

MCOs have a structured credentialing process. This is required by accreditation standards of the National Committee on Quality Assurance (NCQA) and by federal and state regulations. The process of practitioner credentialing in an MCO is similar to credentialing done by healthcare institutions except for privilege delineation. An MCO does not define specific patient care tasks to be carried out by individual physicians, LIPs, or dependent practitioners. Privilege delineation is done only by facilities in which practitioners are taking care of patients. Outlined in the next section are the steps involved in the MCO credentialing process.

Accountable care organizations (ACOs) are another type of healthcare delivery model. An ACO is a group of doctors, hospitals, and other health care providers, who come together voluntarily to give coordinated high-quality care to the patients they serve (CMS, 2019). The ACO will have a structured credentialing process if it is organized like an MCO. In some instances, physician credentialing done at the provider level (such as the hospital process described earlier) is sufficient for providers in an ACO.

New Applicants

Practitioners seeking MCO participation complete an application that includes much of the same information found on applications for hospital medical staff membership. An example of a health plan network application can be found on the Council for Affordable Quality Health Care website (see end of chapter).

The application is accompanied by a copy of the practitioner's current professional license, current DEA registration (if applicable), and confirmation of liability insurance coverage. Applicants also provide information about his or her ability to perform patient care functions, history of illegal drug use and loss of license or felony convictions, and loss or limitations of privileges or disciplinary actions.

Applications are reviewed by the MCO credentialing coordinator and the medical director to determine completeness and if applicants meet basic qualification requirements the MCO has defined for participating practitioners. The credentialing coordinator also verifies accuracy of information submitted by applicants. The NCQA standards stipulate five elements must be verified from the primary source (2017):

- Valid license to practice
- Valid Drug Enforcement Agency (DEA) or Controlled Dangerous Substance (CDS) certificate
- Education and training of practitioner
- Board certification (if practitioner states he/she is board certified on application)
- History of professional liability claims resulting in settlements or judgments paid by or on behalf of the practitioner

NCQA standards also require verification of the applicant's work history; however primary source verification is not required. Other items the MCO may choose to verify include:

- Current malpractice coverage in accordance with the MCO policies.
- Status of applicant's clinical privileges at institutions where the practitioner admits patients.

It is permissible for the MCO to use external agencies (for example, county medical society, hospital association, credentials verification organization) to conduct primary source verifications. Many health plans use provider data management services offered by the Council for Affordable Quality Healthcare (CAQH). The CAQH ProView electronic database contains provider data that can be used by health plans for credentialing, claims processing, quality assurance, emergency response, and member services (CAQH, 2018). Hospitals and other healthcare organizations can also use the CAQH services for physician credentialing and other purposes.

Like hospitals, the MCO can discover if an applicant has had their license or clinical privileges restricted or terminated or any significant malpractice claims by querying the NPDB. In addition, the MCO may conduct a site visit for new applicants. The quality of a practitioner's facility and patient records are evaluated during this visit. This task may be delegated to an external agency such as a medical society although the MCO maintains oversight responsibilities and sets the level of acceptable performance. Examples of criteria that might be used to evaluate the quality of a practitioner's patient records and patient management practices are listed in Exhibit 9.12.

Exhibit 9.12. Examples of Criteria Used for Provider Site Evaluation by MCO

Is patient management appropriate, as evidenced by:
- Lab and other studies ordered appropriately
- Working diagnoses consistent with findings
- Plans of action/treatment consistent with patient's diagnosis
- Unresolved problems from previous visits are addressed
- Consultants used appropriately
- Effective coordination of care between primary and specialty practitioners
- Explicit follow-up notation for consultations and abnormal lab and imaging studies
- Medically appropriate patient care
- Initiation of immunization record for children
- Appropriate use of preventive services
- Appropriate patient education

Information obtained during a practitioner's initial application is reviewed by the MCO credentials committee which is comprised of a range of participating practitioners. The decision to accept or reject an individual's application is made by the committee and acted on by the MCO's governing board. Like healthcare facilities, the MCO has a well-defined procedure for individuals to appeal adverse decisions and obtain due process.

Reappointment

To meet NCQA standards practitioners must be re-credentialed within two years of their last credentialing date. The re-credentialing process is similar to the initial application with the addition of practitioner-specific utilization and performance data that were gathered by the MCO during the interval between appointments. The MCO credentials committee considers information on the practitioner's application and utilization and performance measurement results at the time of re-credentialing.

Professional Practice Evaluation

Practitioners are subject to ongoing performance monitoring by the MCO. NCQA standards require MCOs to implement monitoring and take appropriate interventions by collecting and reviewing practitioner-specific data such as:
- Medicare and Medicaid sanctions
- Sanctions or limitations on licensure
- Beneficiary complaints
- Information from identified adverse events

The MCO implements interventions when it identifies instances of poor quality. Interventions range from subjecting the practitioner to closer scrutiny (focused review) to removal of the practitioner from the MCO panel of providers. The range of actions available to the MCO and the practitioner's appeal process are described in MCO credentialing policies.

Staff Competence Evaluation

Healthcare organizations have the legal responsibility to ensure the competence of all licensed and non-licensed full-time and part-time workers and volunteers. To fulfill this responsibility employers evaluate individual qualifications before hiring people and periodically re-evaluate everyone's ability to satisfactorily perform their job. The competence of all employees, whether or not they provide direct patient care, must be assessed

- At pre-employment (validation of licensure, reference checks, portfolio screening)
- At the end of orientation through completion of a competency checklist
- On a periodic basis through a formal performance appraisal process

Medicare-certified healthcare providers are expected to comply with the personnel credentialing requirements found in the COPs. For instance, home health agencies must have appropriate written personnel policies and personnel records which include current qualifications and licenses (CMS, 2000).

Facilities accredited by the Joint Commission and other accrediting groups must comply with specific standards related to management of human resources. However, these standards do not add burdens beyond what would otherwise be done to meet legal requirements. Courts and juries are increasingly holding companies liable in negligent hiring cases for what the company knew about an employee when they hired the person and also for what they should have known. Companies are also being held responsible for negligent retention of employees who are known to be unfit or who the employer should have known to be unfit.

Pre-Employment Assessment

Position job descriptions define the essential functions of the job and the minimum qualifications. Only candidates meeting minimum qualifications and able to perform essential functions of the position should be considered for the job. Minimum qualifications can include:

- Specific training and experience
- Required knowledge, abilities and skills
- Required licenses, registrations, and certificates

Applicants for a position are screened to determine if they meet minimum qualifications. All information supplied by job applicants must be verified. For some healthcare positions, criminal background checks are required by state and federal regulations. For example, federal regulations require criminal background checks of all employees prior to being hired at Medicare/Medicaid participating nursing homes and similar background checks of home health aides working for home care agencies (AHFSA, 2017). Most states have comparable requirements.

Joint Commission standards require department managers in accredited facilities participate in defining the staff qualifications and competencies necessary to meet the objectives of their department or service (Joint Commission, 2017). Managers must identify responsibilities and competencies that individuals must demonstrate prior to being hired or assigned to a particular job. These responsibilities and competencies are written into the job description for the position. Job descriptions should also include measurable standards of performance or expectations. The table in Exhibit 9.13 illustrates the relationship between a job requirement, a competency statement and performance expectations.

Exhibit 9.13. Job Responsibility, Competency Statement and Performance Expectations

Job Responsibility	Competency	Performance Expectations
Decision-making	Able to make information-based decisions	1. Uses relevant sources of data to make informed decisions. 2. Responds decisively. 3. Makes decisions quickly when situation requires immediate action.

For patient care positions, Joint Commission standards (2017) require managers define the essential functions that must be performed to meet the specific needs of patient populations served by the facility. For instance, if the facility provides care for children, dependent practitioners (nurses, technicians, therapists, etc.) must be able to assess, treat, and provide care for children. This includes:
- Ability to obtain and interpret information regarding children
- Understanding of the range of treatments for children
- Ability to recognize growth and development issues for children

Orientation

Newly hired individuals undergo an orientation process. This includes some type of general organization-wide orientation and a department-specific orientation. Facilities establish a time frame for completion of the orientation. In some situations, employees may not start their new position until they have completed the required orientation sessions and have demonstrated their ability to competently perform their job duties. Documenting completion of required orientation and training activities is an important component of the hiring process.

Joint Commission standards require all employees be provided general and specific training on patient safety hazards in the workplace and how to reduce risks of patient harm. This training is to be provided when employees are first hired, when a new hazard is introduced into the workplace, and when there are changes to employee's job assignment.

Performance Appraisal

Employee performance is periodically evaluated to determine if individuals are:
- Working with current licenses, registration, and/or certifications when required by the job position
- Compliant in attending education activities required by the facility or by regulatory agencies or accreditation groups
- Meeting the performance expectations for their position
- Competent to provide care appropriate to the patient population served

According to Joint Commission standards (2017), formal employee performance appraisals should be done at least every three years. Many facilities require more frequent appraisals. Joint Commission standards do not mandate a specific method for assessing staff performance. Any number of evaluation activities can be done:
- Observation of daily work (in the absence of staff error, competence can be assumed)
- Objective performance appraisal (e.g. tests)
- Demonstration feedback

Every department should have a mechanism for taking appropriate action when performance information suggests an employee is unfit for his or her position. This mechanism is triggered any time the employer has reason to believe a staff member has a problem that potentially interferes with performing the job or threatens the welfare of fellow employees, patients, clients, visitors, and others. Healthcare organizations have the legal responsibility to investigate instances suggestive of an employee's unfitness and respond reasonably to whatever is learned. For example, if a department manager knows (or should know) about allegations, rumors, or clear evidence of patient abuse by an employee, the manager has a duty to investigate the allegation and respond to the findings. Reasonable interventions should be taken to prevent recurrence if the allegations are found to be true.

Summary

Ensuring competence of individuals providing healthcare services is a vital element in strengthening patient care quality and safety. In hospitals, the organized medical staff is delegated by the board the task of maintaining a competency evaluation system for physicians and LIPs. Delegation of these duties to the hospital medical staff does not relieve the governing board of its ultimate accountability for the quality of patient care. The board is responsible for final approval of an individual's medical staff membership and privileges.

The purpose of the physician/LIP competency evaluation system is to confirm practitioners meet – at all times – basic competence requirements set by the medical staff and the hospital for performing specific tasks. The system also identifies potentially suboptimal practitioners who require support to improve their performance or whose performance is at such variance with accepted practice that their privileges must be restricted. On rare occasions, a practitioner's performance is found to fundamentally threaten patient safety. In that circumstance, the governing board has the authority to deny privileges and remove the individual from the medical staff.

In non-hospital provider settings and managed care organizations, the physician/LIP competency evaluation system is overseen by the governing board with functional aspects of the process delegated to a medical director. In both hospital and non-hospital settings considerable support is provided by employees who assist with appointments, reappointments and professional practice evaluations.

The process for ensuring competence of dependent practitioners and other employees is documented in the organization's human resource policies and procedures. This competency evaluation system includes pre-employment assessment, re-assessment at the end of an orientation period, and periodic appraisals to ensuring continuing competence.

Student Activities

1. Contact three healthcare facilities to find out the academic background of the medical staff services coordinator and other individuals working in the medical staff services department.
2. Obtain a copy of one hospital's medical staff bylaws. An Internet search should yield some online examples or contact a local hospital to obtain a copy. Summarize the competency evaluation system activities (appointment, reappointment, and professional practice evaluation) described in the bylaws.
3. Familiarize yourself with the practitioner-specific information found in the National Practitioner Data Bank (www.npdb.hrsa.gov). Describe the entities responsible for reporting information to this data bank and types of actions that must be reported.

Website Resources

American Academy of Physician Assistants, links to state Medical licensing boards
www.aapa.org/advocacy-central/state-advocacy/state-licensing/list-of-licensing-boards/

American Health Information Management certifications
www.ahima.org/certification

American Medical Association, free educational Webinars on credentialing
http://info.commerce.ama-assn.org/ama-free-webinars

American Nurses Credentialing Center
http://www.nursecredentialing.org/

Council for Affordable Quality Healthcare (CAQH), Universal Provider Data source
www.caqh.org

CAQH application used by doctors when applying for participation in some health plan networks.
www.caqh.org/sites/default/files/solutions/proview/paper-application.pdf

Joint Commission, credentialing and privileging tips for ambulatory health care
www.jointcommission.org/ahc_credentialing_privileging_tips/

National Association Medical Staff Services
www.namss.org

National Board of Medical Examiners
www.nbme.org

National Practitioner Data Bank
www.npdb.hrsa.gov

NCQA Credentials Verification Organization (CVO) Certification
www.ncqa.org/Programs/Certification/CredentialsVerificationOrganizationCVO.aspx

Physician Assistant Credentialing and Privileging
www.aapa.org

References

Association of Health Facility Survey Agencies (AHFSA). (2017). *Federal Certification Requirements for Back-ground Checks in Nursing Home, Home Health and Hospice Agency Employment.* [Online information; retrieved 3/2/19]
www.ahfsa.org/resources/Documents/Forum_Federal_Certification_Requirements_for_BG_Checks_in_LTC_employment.pdf

Centers for Medicare and Medicaid Services (CMS). (2019). Accountable care organizations: General information. [Online document; retrieved 1/14/19.] https://innovation.cms.gov/initiatives/aco/

_____. (2014). § 482.22 Condition of participation: Medical staff. [Online document; retrieved 10/2/18.]
www.govinfo.gov/content/pkg/FR-2014-05-12/pdf/2014-10687.pdf

_____. (2012). Conditions of Participation: Hospitals. § 482.12 Condition of participation: Governing body. [Online document; retrieved 1/15/19.] www.govinfo.gov/app/details/CFR-2011-title42-vol5/CFR-2011-title42-vol5-sec482-12

_____. (2011). Conditions of Participation: Specialized Providers, Subpart F Conditions of Participation: Critical Access Hospitals. § 485.641 Condition of participation: Periodic evaluation and quality assurance review. [Online document; accessed 11/20/19.]
www.gpo.gov/fdsys/pkg/CFR-2011-title42-vol5/pdf/CFR-2011-title42-vol5-sec485-641.pdf

_____. (2000). CFR 484.14(e). Condition of participation: Personnel policies. [Online document; retrieved 1/15/19.]
www.gpo.gov/fdsys/pkg/CFR-2000-title42-vol3/xml/CFR-2000-title42-vol3-sec484-14.xml

Council for Affordable Quality Healthcare (CAQH). (2018). CAQH ProView [Online information; retrieved 11/2/18.] www.caqh.org/solutions/caqh-proview

Gorgas, N. (1945). Assessing the medical record's value today. In: *Medical Record Administration: A Collection of Readings Selected from the Literature in the Field* (pp. 17-23). Chicago, IL: The American Hospital Association.

Joint Commission, The. (2017). Human resources. In *Comprehensive Accreditation Manual for Hospitals, 2018.* Oakbrook Terrace, IL: The Joint Commission.

_____. (2007, April 30). Credentialing and privileging conference call [transcript]. Oakbrook Terrace, IL: The Joint Commission.

National Committee for Quality Assurance (NCQA). (2017). *2018 Standards and Guidelines for Managed Care Organizations*. Washington, DC: NCQA.

National Practitioner Data Bank (NPDB). 2017. NPDB history. [Online information; retrieved 11/14/18.] www.npdb.hrsa.gov/topNavigation/timeline.jsp

Pickard, T. (2016). The administrative process: Credentialing, privileges, and maintenance of certification. In: Taylor D., Sherry S., Sing R. (eds). *Interventional Critical Care*. Springer, Cham.